What People Are S

Chicken Soup for the Canadian Soul . . .

"This book is full of heart-opening stories that truly capture the essence of what being Canadian is all about. They brought me to tears time and time again, providing me with new insights as to what it means to be Canadian. Definitely a book I want to share with my children. I loved these stories!"

Barbara Underhill
world champion figure skater, Canadian Olympian, TV
Colour commentator, motivational speaker, mom

"The soul is forever seeking expansion, fuller expression and positive reinforcement. This book delivers. You will enjoy every page. Pick any story and you'll see. . . . It will make you feel better. I loved reading it."

Bob Proctor
speaker, trainer and author of bestselling book,
You Were Born Rich

"How wonderful to have a book of stories like this to share with our young people as an inspiration to achieve their dreams—and live their lives as loving, compassionate beings. As you read these stories, share them with your kids, share them with your students, share them with your friends."

Donna Leonard
chief commissioner,
Girl Guides of Canada

"The answer to 'What makes a Canadian a Canadian?' is finally clear. It's in our stories. We now have something to pass on to our children and our children's children and they to theirs. We can stand up and be proud of our accomplishments as Canadians. *Chicken Soup for the Canadian Soul* gives us a legacy."

Deane Parkes
writer, motivational trainer, speaker, mentor, businessman,
and creator, National Post's HealthVenture

"*Chicken Soup for the Canadian Soul* brings to life the work of Canadians in shaping our nation into one of community heroes. From East Coast to West Coast, to the Northwest Territories and Nunavut, their inspiring stories capture our unique culture, historical heritage and our love of the land. This is a must-read for every Canadian."

Ruth Ramsden-Wood
president, United Way of Calgary and Area

"My heart was touched and my soul was moved as I read the stories of some of our greatest Canadian heroes in their own words. But it's the soulful and compassionate stories of the ordinary Canadians that weave the tapestry into a whole, providing a picture to the world of who we really are as a people. Read this book an celebrate what it is to be Canadian."

Kathy Ryndak
psychotherapist and
cofounder, Transformational Arts College

"I've always suspected it, but never knew how much talent, courage and greatness we have in Canada until I read the wonderful stories in *Chicken Soup for the Canadian Soul*. To finally have all these wonderful stories in one place will make this book one of our greatest literary legacies."

Lynrod Douglas
publisher, *Black Pages Canada*

"Thank you for putting all these amazing stories together so that others can be inspired by these remarkable Canadians! All of us will be encouraged by the talent, courage and genius we have in this great land and the stories in *Chicken Soup for the Canadian Soul* are a perfect source! This book is destined to become a beacon in our magnificent heritage."

Frances Wright
president and CEO, Famous 5 Foundation
author, speaker, entrepreneur, proud Canadian

"What makes a Canadian, Canadian? It's our love of the land, our courtesy and kindness, our saying 'I'm sorry' even when it's not our fault. It's our love of the CBC and it's our steadfast loyalty. It's our stories and it's our story. Read this book. It'll nourish your Canadian soul."

Martin Rutte
speaker, trainer, president, Livelihood Inc.

"As a geologist, I've had the opportunity of knowing Canada and Canadians from Newfoundland to BC, and from Southern Ontario to the High Arctic. I read with great pride these wonderful stories that paint a remarkably accurate picture of our great nation, and offer the reader a rare glimpse into the very heart of Canada and its people."

Dr. Donald H. Gorman
professor emeritus of geology,
University of Toronto

"Not everyone has a talent for music or art, but we each have the gift for story. And, as the words in this book so beautifully illustrate, our stories matter. They remind us of the many ways that the beauty of this land and the diversity of its people bring us home to ourselves and help us find our own place of the heart."

Michael Jones
pianist, composer, recording artist, speaker and
author, *Creating an Imaginative Life*

"I enjoyed reading the diverse stories about my homeland, and this outpouring of simple humanity reminds me why I remain a Canadian citizen after many years of living away from home."

Wayne Patterson
senior fellow, Howard University
vice president, Liberal Party of Canada, 1980–1984

"*Chicken Soup for the Canadian Soul* is an enormously inspirational book that will remind Canadians everywhere of the very best within us."

Robin Sharma, LL.B., LL.M.
author of the worldwide
bestseller, *The Monk Who Sold His Ferrari,*
CEO, Sharma Leadership International

CHICKEN SOUP
FOR THE
CANADIAN SOUL

Stories to Inspire and Uplift the Hearts of Canadians

Jack Canfield
Mark Victor Hansen
Janet Matthews
Raymond Aaron

Health Communications, Inc.
Deerfield Beach, Florida

www.hci-online.com
www.chickensoup.com

We would like to acknowledge the following publishers and individuals for permission to reprint the following material. (Note: The stories that were penned anonymously, that are public domain, or that were written by Jack Canfield, Mark Victor Hansen, Janet Matthews or Raymond Aaron are not included in this listing.)

A Canadian's Story. Reprinted by permission of Pat Fowler. ©1995 Pat Fowler.

We Stand on Guard for Thee. Reprinted by permission of Penny Fedorczenko. ©2000 Penny Fedorczenko.

The Loonie That Turned to Gold. Reprinted by permission of Peter Jordan. ©2002 Peter Jordan.

The Unity Rally—Canada's Woodstock. Reprinted by permission of Mark Leiren-Young. ©2002 Mark Leiren-Young.

The Goal of the Century. Reprinted by permission of Paul Henderson. ©2001 Paul Henderson.

(Continued on page 379)

Library of Congress Cataloging-in-Publication Data

Chicken soup for the Canadian soul : stories to inspire and uplift the hearts of Canadians / Janet Matthews . . . [et al.].

    p.   cm.

    ISBN 0-7573-0028-6 (trade paper)

    1. National characteristics, Canadian—Anecdotes. 2. Canada—Social life and customs—Anecdotes. 3. Social values—Canada—Anecdotes. 4. Conduct of life—Anecdotes. 5. Canada—History—Anecdotes. 6. Canada—Biography—Anecdotes. 7. National characteristics, Canadian—Literary collections. 8. Canada—Literary collections. I. Matthews, Janet, 1951–

F1021.C47 2002

971—dc21   2002068561

© 2002 Jack Canfield and Mark Victor Hansen

ISBN 0-7573-0028-6 (trade paper) — ISBN 0-7573-0029-4 (hardcover)

Publisher: Health Communications, Inc.
          3201 S.W. 15th Street
          Deerfield Beach, FL 33442-8190

Cover design by Lisa Camp
Inside formatting by Lawna Patterson Oldfield

From our hearts to yours,
we dedicate this book to all those Canadians
who walked the endless forests and paddled the majestic
rivers before the Europeans came; to those Canadians,
our parents, grandparents and great-grandparents,
who braved the storms and crossed the seas
to find a better life in a free land;
to those Canadians who chose this country,
bringing cultures from other nations, helping
to weave our ever-evolving cultural mosaic;
to all those Canadians, then and now,
who by their choice to serve, in office or in uniform,
protect and keep this land glorious and free.
And for all those who love Canada,
because in so doing they have built a nation
that is more than worthy of the love
that is in our hearts, and yours.

Contents

2. LIVING YOUR DREAM

3. OVERCOMING OBSTACLES

4. ON LOVE

5. ON KINDNESS

6. ON FAMILY

7. SURVIVING LOSS

8. A MATTER OF PERSPECTIVE

Acknowledgments

Chicken Soup for the Canadian Soul has taken over three years to write, compile and edit. The project began as a challenge that soon grew into an all-consuming passion. Special acknowledgments are due for certain people whose contributions were central to the success of this book.

Our families and friends, who shared with us the exciting times—and supported, inspired and encouraged us through the tough times. Without you, this book would simply not have been finished.

Leslie Riskin, in Jack Canfield's office, for her tremendous work in handling all the permissions. We appreciate all your hard work and expertise, as well as your friendly voice and your huge heart.

Heather McNamara, for her meticulous and insightful editing and her amazing ability to always produce the final manuscript with perfection. You are awesome!

D'ette Corona, for her dedicated help with assembling the manuscript, and for encouraging and guiding us through the last stages of the book. You are one awesome lady.

Patty Aubery, for always being there in the crucial stages. We can't say enough good things about you.

Deborah Hatchell, who was so helpful in the early

stages of this book, and Maria Nickless for her always creative marketing ideas and cheerful voice.

Nancy Autio, Veronica Romero, Robin Yerian, Teresa Esparza, Vince Wong, Cindy Holland, Stephanie Thatcher, Amber Setrakian, Kathy Brennan-Thompson and Dana Drobny for your commitment, dedication and professionalism—and for making sure Jack's office runs so smoothly.

Patty Hansen and Dawn Henschall, for making sure all the legal *t*'s and *i*'s were crossed and dotted. We can't thank you enough.

Darlene Montgomery, our publicist, dear friend and all-around great assistant. In addition to soliciting stories and getting us radio and TV interviews, her persistent efforts in finding and writing special stories was invaluable; we could not have completed this project without her. Thanks Dar!

Raymond's amazing staff for their tireless help and support of this project in so many ways: Liz Ventrella, Geoff Taylor, Wendy Kuchar, Sue Lacher, Sue Higgins, Patty Sibolibane, Chris Johnson, Donna Sylvestre and Jared Westover. From our hearts, we thank you.

Peter du Chemin, who created our wonderful Web site, *www.canadiansoul.com,* and keeps it up to date. Thank you Peter—we love our flying maple leaves!

Wanda James, whose research and writing was invaluable and Debbie Taylor, for her helpful research and energetic marketing efforts.

Brad Gauvreau, for the beautiful photos.

Darlene Herbert at the CBC, Trudy Van Buskirk, Dave Mitchell, Louise Larouche, Martin Herzog, Janine Violini, Lorraine Quartaro, Louise Gravelle, Mary Linstead and Hunter Fulghum for their contributions along the way.

Barry Spilchuk, for your support in gathering stories in the early stages of the project, and Rebecca Kubica for sending us a story that became one of our favourites.

Those dedicated souls who read and reread our proposed stories and made so many valuable contributions and suggestions: Jim Allen, Fred Angelis, Angela and Terry Belford, Sue Bond, Judith Bridgehall, Judy Carter, Clare Corrigan, Russ Coultrup, Nancy Lee and Dale Doige, Trish French, Evi Glassman, Sue Higgins, Wanda James, Sylvia Jong, Beth Kalisz, Barb Kerr, Iris Koshman, Sue Lacher, Sharon Leach, Darlene, Michelle and Mary Montgomery, Diane Nicholson, Janet McOrmond, Diane Parent, David Platt, Bob Quinn, Shirley Rainer, John Seagrave, Sam Seupersad, Janine Smith, Noah St. John, Keeth Stone, Edna Sutherland, Debbie Taylor, Marla Taylor, Bridget Ubochi, Liz Ventrella, Harish Vaishnav and Jamie Yeo.

Peter Vegso, Terry Burke, Kelly Maragni, Elizabeth Rinaldi, Lori Golden and Irena Xanthos at Health Communications, Inc., for their wonderful sales and marketing efforts.

Christine Belleris, Lisa Drucker, Allison Janse, Susan Tobias and Kathy Grant, our editors at Health Communications, Inc., for their combined hard work editing and designing this book with such expertise and dedication.

Kim Weiss, Paola Fernandez and Maria Dinoia, Health Communications' brilliant publicity team, whose efforts continue to keep our books on the bestseller lists.

Randee Feldman, *Chicken Soup for the Soul* product manager at Health Communications, Inc., for her masterful coordination and support of all the *Chicken Soup* projects.

Lisa Camp and Larissa Hise at Health Communications, Inc., for their inspiring and cooperative efforts to complete the cover design of this book.

In Toronto, Dan Sullivan, teacher and mentor, whose wisdom has brought greater clarity, ease and abundance to so many.

The special members of the Monthly Mentor and The Wealth Creator Source across Canada, who make

Raymond's work the greatest joy a person could experience.

Raymond's dear friends Lon Rosen, Tim Johnson, Our Wayne Patterson, Stephen Bezruchka, and Martin Rutte. How empty Raymond's life would be without having you guys to love in this lifetime.

Janet's dear friends Alex McLeish, Ramona Machado, Darlene Montgomery, Shirley Rainer, Barb Allport, Marilyn Lake-Lee, Sheila Jeffrey, James Corby, Jamie Yeo and Frannie Kalusa. When the going got tough, you guys showed up.

Peter and Maureen Kolossa, Helen Valleau, Dale De Nunzio and Dawn Johnson of the Hoffman Quadrinity Process (*www.quadrinity.com*). The wonderful work you do in helping others (like us) find their way back to themselves is instrumental in creating world peace, one person at a time. Thank you for your dedication and your love.

Barbara Underhill, Paul Martini, Kurt Browning, Rick Hansen, Paul Henderson, Natalie MacMaster, Jann Arden, Pamela Wallin, Faye Dance, Ted Mahovlich, Lynn Johnston, Leslie Scrivener and Sally Armstrong for opening their hearts and sharing, in their own words, their special stories with all Canadians. We can't thank you enough.

And last, but not least, Marilyn Bell Di Lascio. The image she shared in her own words of swimming, so many years ago, through the night—exhausted, frightened of the lake, petrified of the dark and yet filled with such dogged determination to reach her goal—will stay with us forever. She inspired and moved us in ways that cannot be put into words. Thank you Marilyn—we will be forever grateful.

Because of the immensity of this project, it is possible we may have left out the names of some people who helped us along the way. If so, please accept our apologies and know that you are appreciated. We are so very grateful for the many hands and hearts that helped make this book possible. We love you all!

Introduction

   During the nearly four years it took to compile this book, we were asked several questions repeatedly: "What will make this *Chicken Soup* book different from all the other *Chicken Soup* titles? How will you make this book a true reflection of our diverse and historic Canadian heritage?" "What exactly is *Chicken Soup for the Canadian Soul* anyway?"

   When we first began collecting stories, the answers to these questions were not clear. After all, the Canadian identity is multidimensional as well as multicultural. As Canadians, we find our roots in so many different places around the world. How could we create a collection of stories that represented them all? In addition, *Chicken Soup for the Soul* stories are traditionally nonpolitical and noncontroversial. Yet Canada, by its very existence, is a political entity, and its historic origins are steeped in controversy. Many of those controversies are part of the Canadian fabric of life to this day; they continuously challenge us to stretch and grow and to be the best people and country we can be.

   How could we assemble a collection of stories that would truly represent everything Canada is—and everyone who lives here? At some point it became apparent we simply could not. But we knew we *could* put together a book of wonderful, inspirational, heart-opening stories, which people would love to read and which would make us feel proud to be Canadians.

We decided we needed stories from people living in as many different places in Canada as possible. We searched from Cape Breton Island to Vancouver Island, and in every province and territory in between. We looked for stories in big cities, small towns, villages and rural communities all across this beautiful country. We sought stories from teachers and students, professional writers and professional homemakers, athletes and musicians, journalists and entertainers, First Nations Communities, historians and war veterans, the Royal Canadian Mounted Police and the Canadian Coast Guard—just about anybody we could think of. We did our best to tell our storytellers just what we were after. And then the stories started to arrive.

When we had a group of stories we liked, we ran them past a panel of Canadian readers and asked the panel for comments. They told us what they liked and what they didn't. Eventually, a pattern began to emerge—and our spines started to tingle. We realized that what we were doing had never been done before in this country, and we were honoured to the tips of our toes to be doing it! Our love and commitment to this unique and special project grew into a passion.

What we present to you now is the result of reading over 6,000 stories during the past four years. In addition to the rich treasure of ordinary Canadians telling us their personal and heretofore unknown stories, we tried our best to include the stories of many well-known and beloved Canadians as well. Barbara Underhill and Paul Martini were delighted to share with us the story of their memorable gold medal skate at the 1984 World Championships in Ottawa. "For Better or For Worse" cartoonist Lynn Johnston submitted a wonderful story about an encounter with Wayne Gretzky. Cape Breton fiddler Natalie MacMaster shared a very touching story with us, proving she is as delightful offstage as she is on. Kurt Browning sent us a story sharing his unique perspective on skating in the Olympics. Pamela Wallin gave her insight into how patriotic Canadians really are. *Toronto Star* writer Leslie Scrivener tells us again the story we all carry in our hearts—the legacy of Terry Fox. We are honoured to present you with these and all the other wonderful stories we found. We hope you are as touched and proud reading these stories as we have been compiling and editing them.

There are many stories we have not told in this book. We may not have included a story on a particular theme, person, group of people or Canadian region because we either couldn't find a story appropriate for a *Chicken Soup for the Soul* collection, or we couldn't find the writer of a story we did have.

If you have or know of a story that you feel should have been in the book but wasn't, we invite you to submit it to us for consideration for a second edition.

That being said, we feel we have assembled a wonderful collection of stories that all Canadians can truly be proud of. And while there are many diverse stories from ordinary people exploring universal themes of love, compassion, forgiveness, family, acceptance and courage, there is one golden thread that weaves its way through this book—sometimes subtly, sometimes dramatically. That thread is the passionate love all Canadians have for this land that offers them so much, this land they call home. In the end, these stories are not about language, culture, politics, or where one's parents or grandparents came from. These stories are about the love, pride and gratitude we all share in being Canadian. We hope these tales will in turn inspire you, touch your heart and make you smile.

From our hearts to yours, we are thrilled and proud to offer you *Chicken Soup for the Canadian Soul.*

Share with Us

We would love to hear your reactions to the stories in this book. Please let us know what your favourite stories were and how they affected you.

We also invite you to send us stories you would like to see published in future editions of *Chicken Soup for the Canadian Soul*. You can send us either stories you have written or stories written by others. Please send submissions to:

Chicken Soup for the Canadian Soul
2-9225 Leslie Street
Richmond Hill
ON Canada L4B 3H6
Fax: 905-881-8996
Phone: 905-881-8995 x28
stories@canadiansoul.com

You can also access e-mail or find a current list of planned books at the *Chicken Soup for the Soul* Web site at *www.chickensoup.com*. Find out about our Internet service at *www.clubchickensoup.com*.

We hope you enjoy reading this book as much as we enjoyed compiling, editing and writing it.

I Am a Canadian

I am a Canadian,
free to speak without fear,
free to worship in my own way,
free to stand for what I think right,
free to oppose what I believe wrong,
or free to choose those
who shall govern my country.
This heritage of freedom
I pledge to uphold
for myself and all mankind.

Former Prime Minister John G. Diefenbaker

1

ON BEING CANADIAN

*One thing you know about Canadian
people is they're proud to be Canadian.
My kids were born in the United States.
They should be proud of their country
and they are, but I'm a Canadian.
I was born in Canada and I'm proud
of my country. That never leaves you.*

Wayne Gretzky

A Canadian's Story

I liken Canada to a garden . . . a garden into which have been transplanted the hardiest and brightest flowers from many lands, each retaining in its new environment the best of the qualities for which it was loved and prized in its native land.

Former Prime Minister John G. Diefenbaker

One day when I was seventeen my best friend, Shelley, invited me to her home after school to meet her grandmother. When we arrived, a slim, fragile-looking, elderly lady with white hair and many wrinkles greeted us warmly. In a thick accent she invited us to help ourselves to freshly baked chocolate chip cookies. While we ate she asked many questions about our personal lives and listened intently to our answers. We both felt her genuine interest, and in spite of her accent, we understood her clearly. Her piercing, deep-blue eyes sparkled as we talked, and her smile radiated a lifetime of inner strength and integrity. She captivated me.

She noted how fortunate we were to have such beautiful

clothes, nice furniture and time to spend with our friends. When she excused herself for a moment, Shelley and I stared at each other in astonishment at her grandmother's appreciation of all the little things that we took for granted. In a whisper, Shelley explained that her grandmother had grown up in the Ukraine, where life had been very difficult. When she returned to the room, Grandma expressed her great pleasure in seeing all her children and grandchildren able to go to school and learn. When the conversation turned to my approaching eighteenth birthday, Grandma was thrilled and exclaimed how excited I must be at the thought of voting for the first time. Frankly, I had thought of all sorts of good things I would be able to do when I was eighteen, but voting wasn't one of them. I told her so.

A little saddened by my cynicism, Shelley's grandmother asked in her broken English if I would like to hear the story of her journey to Canada. She said she had not shared the details with many people, including Shelley. When I agreed, she began to tell her tale.

"Grandpa, myself and our six children lived in extremely modest conditions in the Ukraine. Everyone in the family who was old enough had to work. Our two eldest children were eight and ten. They did odd jobs for people who paid them with food rather than money.

"The other four children were too young to work, so they helped me with the household chores. The government did not want the people to be independent and think for themselves, and to ensure this, they prevented us from attending any religious services and forced us to worship the government. They also banned reading and writing, closed all the schools and destroyed all the books that disagreed with their oppressive philosophy. Anyone caught not complying with the new, closed-minded edict was put in prison. In spite of these severe consequences, those who knew how to read and write secretly taught those who did not. Many people managed to hide some of their beloved classic books before they could be destroyed.

"Many villagers dreamed of immigrating to Canada where they believed people were allowed to make choices and work hard to make a life for themselves. Although we were prevented from leaving with threats of imprisonment, many people attempted to flee because we were starving in the homeland. Grandpa and I and our six children were among those who made plans to escape.

"Our village was twenty miles from the border. We would have to walk and sneak past the border guards. On the other side of the border, we would be met by people to whom we paid our life's savings to help us travel across the land to the ocean, and across the ocean to Canada.

"Crossing the border was extremely dangerous—the guards were ordered to shoot anyone caught trying to pass illegally. For this part of the journey, we were on our own.

"Late at night, taking only what we could carry, we left our home and quietly stole out of the village. Because three of our children were still quite small, it took us five days to reach the border. When we arrived, we hid in the trees on the edge of a mile-wide open area that ran along it. We planned to wait until dark before trying to cross.

"As the sun began to set, my husband and I carried the three smallest children while our other three joined hands. We could see the border and began to run across that mile-wide open area towards freedom. Just as we reached the borderline a bright spotlight flashed on and caught in its glare the two older boys running with their younger brother, who was literally suspended in midair between them. A loud voice boomed over a bullhorn— 'Halt! Immediately!'—but my sons paid no attention and continued to run.

"Gunshots rang out and continued even after we had crossed into the neutral country on the other side. The light still followed us and suddenly found me as I ran carrying the baby. When our eldest son, John, saw this, he let go of his two brothers and yelled for them to run. Then John began to draw the guards' attention by jumping, yelling and waving his hands. The bright light settled on him as the rest of us finally reached the protective barrier of the trees on the other side of the border. As we turned back to look, several shots rang out. John, my ten-year-old son, fell to the ground and lay still.

"Thankfully, the guards left my son there, because he lay outside their jurisdiction. Your grandpa crawled out and dragged John back to where we were huddled in the trees. My child had been hit by one of the bullets, and he died there in my arms. We wept in agony, but our hearts were filled with pride for his heroism. If not for John's selfless actions, the baby and I would have certainly been shot. He gave his life that night so the rest of us might live.

"After we buried John, with heavy hearts we continued on and eventually found our way to Canada, and so to freedom."

When Shelley's grandmother finished her story, I had tears in my eyes.

"Since arriving in Canada I have enjoyed my freedom immensely," she continued. "I take great pleasure in every single choice I have made—including the time I took an evening job scrubbing floors so that Shelley's father could go to university."

As she clutched at her heart, the dear lady then expressed great pride in her second oldest son, who was eight during the family's flight to freedom. Out of gratitude for their new life in Canada, and because of the horror of seeing his brother shot down so long ago, he had enlisted in the Canadian army to defend his new country with his life.

Grandma confided that she valued her right to vote as very dear to her heart and had never missed her chance to have "her say." She told me then that she viewed voting as not only a right and a privilege, but also a responsibility. By voting, she believed she could ensure that Canada would be run by good people and never by the kind of people who would shoot and kill someone making a choice.

My life changed profoundly that day, as I looked through the window that this special woman had opened into a different world. I made my own commitment on the spot to seize every opportunity I was ever given to vote. And I began to understand, in some small way, the passion that motivates our Canadian soldiers, who volunteer to defend our country.

When Grandma finished her story, Shelley, who had become very quiet, softly asked, "Who was the baby you were carrying when you ran across the border, Grandma?"

As Grandma caressed her cheek, she replied, "The baby was your father, my dear."

Pat Fowler
Sherwood Park, Alberta

We Stand on Guard for Thee

Pollsters say Canadians are depressed right now. They say we're discouraged. Don't be. Think of all the good things we have. Think of how lucky we are. To be Canadian.

Gary Lautens, November 1990

Some time ago during my vacation, I had the pleasure of travelling to Europe to tour the various regions of France. Our tour group was comprised of forty-five travellers from a variety of countries. My three friends and myself made up the Canadian contingent on the bus.

As the days and weeks passed, we had the chance to get to know each other better. In some ways, the new friendships that grew became as valuable and as memorable as the trip itself.

On the second to last day of the tour, we were making our way to Calais and the ferryboat that would take us back across the English Channel, on to London and finally to the airport. Throughout the trip, as we rode along in the coach, our wonderful French guide provided a colourful and interesting commentary to give us a better understanding of what we were seeing out the window.

About two hours out of Paris, driving through the peaceful French countryside, our guide came on the microphone. His richly accented voice was serious and sombre.

"We are presently passing through the World War I battlefields just south of Vimy Ridge. If you look to your right, just across the field there, you will see the war memorial that the people of France erected to the Canadian soldiers who fought so bravely here. Even today, some of the residents from the surrounding towns place flowers on the memorial regularly. Some lived through the fighting and have never forgotten the soldiers who took up their cause. And so, my dear Canadian friends at the back of the bus, I would like to say thank you from the people here in Vimy for the unselfish acts of your Canadian soldiers."

Across the grassy field, the stone monument stood erect and proud against the French sky. A Canadian flag rippled softly in the calm breeze. The passengers, each deep in their own thoughts, stared silently out the windows. Lost in the moment, I could visualize the sights and sounds of war. Suddenly, an unexpected wave of emotion swept over me. I felt immense sadness for those men who never returned home to Canadian soil, but at the same time, my heart swelled with an enormous sense of pride. Tears filled my eyes. I was embarrassed by my uncontrolled reaction. As I turned around, I realized that each of my friends had experienced the same feelings—their eyes were also wet with tears. We smiled knowingly at each other, not speaking a word.

I had travelled all this way to appreciate what it means to be Canadian.

Penny Fedorczenko
Oshawa, Ontario

The Loonie That Turned to Gold

"Should we tell him about the Loonie?" Trent Evans asked Dan Craig. Dan was head of the Green Team, the icemakers responsible for all the hockey rinks at the Salt Lake City Winter Olympics.

"You know I can't officially know anything about that Loonie," replied Dan. He turned to me with a huge smile and unzipped his green Salt Lake parka to proudly display his Roots Team Canada T-shirt. As he turned and left, the twinkle in his eye was unmistakable. "I have to check on the temperature of the ice," he announced, evading my questioning eyes. Now I'm no investigative reporter, but something was clearly up.

I was working at the 2002 Winter Olympics in Salt Lake City, as a TV features reporter for CBC Sports. My assignment was to profile Olympians by actually trying their sport for a day—the kind of opportunity television people dream of. It allowed me to spend time with Canada's best and brightest as they prepared for their events. From skating with Catriona Le May Doan to playing goal with the women's hockey team, from rocketing headfirst downhill at breakneck speed (hopefully not literally) with the Skeleton Team to being a brakeman with the bobsled team, I was amazed as I played with Canada's best. But there's more to an Olympic performance than the athletes. There are so many exceptional people who make things work behind the scenes, and I got to meet a few of them as well.

Back when Wayne Gretzky and the Edmonton Oilers were winning all those Stanley Cups, they were known as the fastest team with the fastest ice. The crew making that ice was run by Dan Craig. Dan rose up the ranks to eventually oversee ice-making operations for the entire NHL. Taking over for him in Edmonton was the rising star of ice-makers, Trent Evans. Just like the athletes who work and train for years hoping to qualify for the Olympics, Dan, Trent and their team had become the icemakers to call if you needed the best. Here in Salt Lake, because of their green jackets, they were known as the "Green Team," and this would be *their* Olympics.

It was my day with the Green Team. We had started our "typical day in the life of an ice-maker" early that morning. With fifty-five games and even more practices in four different arenas, all needing perfect ice, the Green Team regularly put in sixteen-hour days during these games. It was hard work, but they had a lot of fun, too. While they were teaching me to drive a Zamboni, I was so busy watching all the dials and levers and gauges I forgot about the driving. Fortunately, one of them was holding a sign at the end boards that read "TURN." After I parked the Zamboni, the guys gathered around to demonstrate how to tell if we'd done a good job. "Eat some of the snow out of the Zamboni," they told me. "It should taste clean and melt in your mouth." I dutifully obeyed, searching for the right taste and texture. When I saw them all laughing so hard they had to hold each other up, I realized I'd been had.

After a busy morning, we had to put the finishing touches on the E Centre, the gold medal hockey arena.

We arrived at the rink just as rehearsals for the gold medal presentation ceremony were finishing. To our chagrin, the organizers were practicing as if the USA had won the gold. Maybe that's what prompted Trent to tell me about the Loonie. We were standing behind the Zamboni, as the strains of the "Star-Spangled Banner" died out, when he began.

The first thing ice-makers do before making any ice, Trent told me, is to mark out the surface of the rink, starting at the centre. That marker becomes the face-off circle, and everything else is measured from there. Usually they just painted a dot, but there was no paint handy, so Trent reached into his pocket, came up with a dime, and put it down to mark the exact centre. Then they began the flood. But it was actually the next day when Trent had his real flash of inspiration.

It was a slightly beat-up 1987 Loonie, but it was all Trent had left in his pocket. He put it down on top of the dime and finished flooding the ice. As he drove the Zamboni late into the night, putting layer upon layer of ice over it, he hoped the Loonie would bring good luck to the Canadian hockey teams. He also knew that if anyone were to find out, he would not only have to remove it, he would probably be on thin ice with the Olympic organizing committee.

A couple of days later the rink was nearly done when Trent's worst fears were realized. The Loonie had been spotted by one of the Americans on the crew, who promptly reported it. Trent was ordered to change the marker. His good-luck talisman was finished.

As Trent began to dig out the coin, he was upset, knowing the Canadian hockey teams could use all the good luck they could get. The women's team had lost eight games in a row to the powerhouse Americans in pre-Olympic tournaments. The men's team hadn't won the gold medal since 1952. In that moment, Trent made a decision that seemed small at the time, but would change his life forever. He left the coin where it was and covered it up with a splotch of yellow paint.

"Now," explained Trent, "came the really hard part, keeping it a secret." All the Green Team knew because, well, they were in on it. The two Canadian hockey teams knew as well. "And now," he said looking at me intently, "so do you."

The games were about to start, and the Green Team agreed to let the CBC tell Canada about the Loonie under the ice, as long as we waited until just before the final game. So, as the games got rolling, as Jamie Salé and David Pelletier skated a gold medal performance and were awarded silver, then later gold, as Catriona dominated on the longtrack in speed skating, the Loonie story sat locked in a producer's desk at the CBC. But every day was agonizing for Canada's icemakers as more and more attention was directed towards centre ice at the hockey arena.

The women's hockey tournament really got going with country after country being eliminated until the final confrontation—Canada versus the United States. The Loonie remained buried under the ice, but the secret was slowly beginning to surface. After playing shorthanded for most of the game, the Canadian underdogs won 3–2. In the exuberance of the moment, members of the Canadian Women's Gold Medal team fell to their knees and kissed centre ice to thank the lucky Loonie.

Trent panicked, thinking for sure the jig was up. There were still three days to go before the men's final. But somehow, the secret held. The entire country watched as the Canadian Men's Team faltered, recovered, then won a place in the finals. Once again, it would be Team Canada against the undefeated Americans.

Was the Loonie really a good luck charm? One thing was clear, the miracles never ceased. The gold medal game was incredible! Wave after wave of the world's best hockey players skated over centre ice in end-to-end, fast-paced hockey, just as it should be. While the world watched, Team Canada skated to a decisive 5–2 victory in front of a screaming crowd and a jubilant Wayne Gretzky. Later, captain Mario Lemieux, wrapped in a Canadian flag, called the triumphant team to centre ice for a picture that would go down in history.

While the team was celebrating in the locker room, Trent Evans ran onto the ice and dug out his coins. The dime he slipped into his pocket. The lucky Loonie he presented to the members of Team Canada 2002. Later that day, Gretzky held it up at a post-win news conference, proclaiming it to the world as a symbol of Canadian victory.

The last time I saw Trent was on the front page of the newspaper. He was touching that 1987 Loonie one more time. But this time it was in its new home at the Hockey Hall of Fame in Toronto. The Loonie rests in a case and is prominently displayed between pictures of the two gold medal teams. There is a hole in the glass so visitors who are touched by the Loonie can reach through and touch it themselves. Trent looked so proud and more than a little surprised. I'm sure he had no idea his good luck charm would end up in the Hall of Fame. I also remember thinking how amazing it was that one person's inspired moment could become a national symbol signifying the Olympic spirit.

It became the Loonie that turned to gold!

Peter Jordan
CBC, Winnipeg, Manitoba

Reprinted by permission of Lo Linkert.

The Unity Rally—
Canada's Woodstock

*All those Canadians [who went to the rallies]
can look at their children and say to them the
next time the Canadian flag flies, they own a
piece of it. They made a difference.*

Jean Charest

It was October 1995, right before the Quebec Referendum, and the future of our country hung in the balance. Like millions of Canadians, I sat at home watching TV to see what would happen. The news had more suspense than the 1972 Canada–Russia hockey series. We're up, we're down, were up, we're down—we're a country, we're not. Québecers had been invited to vote either *"Oui"* to separate from Canada, or *"Non."* Then, as the *"Non"* side began to lead, I began to cheer—just as if Canada had scored. Like many Canadians when the polls started showing Québec might actually go this time, I found myself scared that my country was about to disappear and frustrated because there was absolutely nothing I could do to stop it.

Then my friend Donna called to tell me that a big Unity Rally would be held on Friday, October 27, in Montreal, and Canada's airlines were offering a seat sale so anyone could go. Five minutes later, without any sort of plan, I dropped everything and booked a flight to Montreal. Thousands of other Canadians spontaneously did the same. Like them, I suspect, I had a million good reasons not to fly to Montreal that day. But I also suspected that all of those reasons would have sounded pretty hollow the following Tuesday if the people of Québec had voted "*Oui*" and I had stayed home.

When I told people I was going on the "save the country express," I expected to be teased. After all, it's pretty hokey to fly 3,000 miles just to wave a flag and sing the national anthem. But to my surprise, even my most cynical friends thanked me and said they wished they were going. My dad asked me to hug a Québecer for him.

In the departure lounge at the Vancouver Airport, I wondered how many of us were heading to Montreal in a heartfelt attempt to show the people of *la belle province*, that despite what they may have heard, we really did care about what they decided.

Standing in line, I found a man I knew from work right behind me. "Why are you going to Montreal?" I asked.

"To say no," said Chris, who was bringing his son and daughter along to do the same.

Once onboard, the woman next to me told me she and her husband had been watching TV wishing they could go, but couldn't afford the airfare. Then some politician came on and said the rally was a stupid idea, and who cares what English Canadians have to say. A minute later she was on the phone to a travel agent. The woman explained she was a Franco-Ontarian, and even though she and her husband were broke, they agreed that when they were ninety, she'd be able to tell her grandchildren that she did her best to help keep Canada together.

Then there was the schoolteacher from Bonneville, a small town in Alberta. He was carrying a big flag signed by every single kid in Bonneville.

A flight attendant told me about half the 170 passengers on this regular business flight to Toronto were headed to the Unity Rally. This was not one of the special Unity charters; there were no organized groups on board. No one I met had spoken to anyone except maybe their significant other before deciding to do their bit to help save their country.

Once in Montreal I spotted Much Music vee-jay Terry David Mulligan, who was covering the event for Much Music. At that moment, I realized this was Canada's Woodstock. I half expected the organizers to broadcast warnings that "there's some bad maple syrup out there!"

The Woodstock image was confirmed when I saw a vendor selling souvenir T-shirts depicting a happy face with long hair, dark glasses, a bandanna covered with peace symbols, and the slogan: "Keep Canada Together."

The next morning, Donna and I headed out early to Place du Canada to beat the crowds. The rally was to start at noon, but when we arrived at 10:30 the streets were already packed. Still, we managed to get a great spot right next to the speaker's platform. At 11:05 I heard the first of the numerous spontaneous renditions of "O Canada" that would sweep the crowd that day. Each was endowed with the same depth of feeling as when we sang it back in the original '72 Canada Cup series against the Russians.

At about 11:15, a tiny old woman started forcing her way to the front of the crowd. She quickly attached herself to my left arm to keep from falling over, and held on tightly for most of the next two hours. She was from Richelieu, a half-hour outside Montreal, and I later learned her name was Marie-Josephte. She tugged on my arm occasionally to point out local celebrities like Jean

Charest's kids, and a local Montreal M.P.

As she filled me in on local colour, a man on the other side of the railing began tossing flags to the crowd- real, full-sized flags. The next thing I knew I had this Québec flag in my hands. Not sure what to do with it, I slung it over my shoulder and suddenly there I was, wearing a Vancouver Canucks jersey (which I'd worn to show where I was from) with a fleur de lis cape. My transformation to Captain Canuck was complete when Donna stuck a paper Canadian flag in my ponytail holder. Then Marie-Josephte pulled on my arm and handed me a small Québec flag, indicating I should put it in my hair too.

Under normal circumstance I would have felt ridiculous— but there was nothing about this event even remotely related to "normal." I was surrounded by people of all ages who had drawn maple leafs and fleurs de lis on their faces, plastered their skin with "Non" stickers and dressed themselves in various combinations of Canadian flags. Meanwhile, the biggest flag I had ever seen was moving through the Rally like a living creature. In this crowd—I was positively inconspicuous.

When Jean Charest began speaking, Marie-Josephte started tugging frantically on my arm again. When I turned, she pushed my other arm toward a man in a snazzy business suit. As I said, "Hi, I'm from Vancouver," I realized I was shaking hands with Frank McKenna.

"I'm out from New Brunswick," he said. "Glad to have you here." Marie-Josephte tugged again, then beamed and shouted: "You came all the way from Vancouver. Now you will be on TV with the premier of New Brunswick!"

I tried to be cynical and witty or at least hip and ironic about my feelings as I looked out at the mass of people, but the truth is, like Woodstock, it really was a love-in. We came for the people of Québec to tell them we care, but we also came for ourselves, because for one brief moment it felt like we might be able to make a difference.

As the crowd began dispersing, Marie-Josephte pushed a slip of paper into my hand. It had her address on it. She thanked me for coming and told me to write her. Then she grasped my hand and we hugged each other.

After she left, Donna and I walked away in our Canucks jerseys—or at least tried to. Every few minutes we were stopped by someone asking if we were really from Vancouver, and then after a moment in which they appeared to get lumps in their throats, they'd thank us for making the effort, thank us for helping. Then we'd wish them well on Monday—Referendum Day. "You came from Vancouver," they'd say—some with English accents, some with French, "Thank you so much."

I was told later that the TV newscasts focused on the speeches—but the truth is—no one cared about the speeches. As powerful as their words may have been, they weren't as poignant as the man holding the municipal flag of the city of Yellowknife, the woman with the cardboard sign that read "Edmonton, Alberta loves Québec," or all the people from across the country who, like myself, had never waved a flag in their lives and were now proudly holding a fleur de lis and a maple leaf to show their support for a united Canada.

The only statement that really mattered was that people had come from all over Canada to participate in something no one could have imagined, a powerful and spontaneous outpouring of genuine Canadian patriotism. No one who was there will ever forget it. The biggest cheer came when a speaker announced the crowd was estimated at 150,000. I strongly suspect if the politicians hadn't interrupted, we would have just sung "O Canada" all afternoon.

Mark Leiren-Young
Vancouver, British Columbia

The Goal of the Century

"Avant tout je suis Canadien."— *"Before all I am a Canadian."*

> Sir Georges-Etienne Cartier
> A Québec Father of Confederation

Time was running out! It was September 28, 1972. The place—Luzhniki Arena, Moscow. It was the eighth and final game between the Russian National Team and Canada's best NHL players. The score was tied with less than one minute remaining—and no overtime allowed! With the series tied three games apiece, a tie was no good—we needed a goal and a win!

I had always dreamed of playing in the NHL. Spurred on by my father, a rabid hockey fan, we never missed our weekly ritual of "Hockey Night in Canada" on the radio, with Foster Hewitt doing the play-by-play. Woe betide anyone in our home who talked when Foster Hewitt spoke.

According to my dad, when I first donned skates at the age of eight I was a natural. One day in grade five, with my eyes firmly fixed on the NHL, I landed in the principal's office for practising my autograph in class.

"Don't worry about my schoolwork," I told him confidently, "It won't matter. I'm going to play in the NHL!" He laughed, pointing out that the six-team league used only 108 players and I didn't have much of a chance. But his words only strengthened my resolve.

Growing up in rural Ontario meant old, secondhand hockey equipment. Even so, my speed and strength developed, and I frequently scored goals. After a local play-off game I earned a write-up in the *London Free Press* that attracted NHL scouts, and in 1959 I ended up in Hamilton with the Detroit Red Wings Junior A farm team. By 1962, I had married Eleanor, my childhood sweetheart, and won the Memorial Cup and an invitation to try out with the Detroit Red Wings. It was a banner year, but also a crossroads decision for me at the young age of nineteen.

In those days, the NHL "owned" their players. There was no free agency and only a very modest "take-it-or-leave-it" pay. With serious concerns about the uncertainty of professional hockey, despite my dreams I began leaning towards education and a "normal" career. Once again, my Dad spurred me on: "Paul, if you don't give this a try, for the rest of your life every time you watch, hear or read about the NHL, you'll ask yourself, 'I wonder if I could have made it?' It will drive you crazy."

That did it! I would give hockey two years, and if I hadn't made it by then, I'd hang up the blades, go back to school and get on with life.

I made the Red Wings that year, and I played with them until 1968, when I was traded to the Toronto Maple Leafs. Sadly, Dad died that same year, seven years after suffering a stroke.

In 1972, the thrill of a lifetime came when an eight-game series was announced between the Russian National Hockey Team and a Canadian team of hand-picked NHL stars. Over the years, the Russians had become a hockey powerhouse and regularly beat our best amateur teams at the Olympics. The years of Canadian hockey domination were gone.

The plan, in 1972, was to change all that, put the upstart Russians in their place and show the world hockey was still our national sport.

The whole nation was excited. The first four games would be in Montreal, Toronto, Winnipeg and Vancouver. The remaining four would be in Moscow. The Cold War, today a distant memory, was at its height. This was not just a series between two hockey teams. This was war between their way of life and ours.

Back then, NHL teams carried only twenty players, and there seemed little chance I would be included. But with an expanded roster of thirty-five for this series, I was invited to try out by coach Harry Sinden. Put on a line with Ron Ellis and a brash young kid named Bobby Clark, we had our work cut out for us. But with dogged determination and hard work we made the team!

Overly confident, Team Canada entered the first game of the series in Montreal. To our shock we discovered the Russians to be a superbly disciplined and talented hockey team. After a 7–3, blowout loss, we came crashing to earth. Far from the runaway cakewalk we'd expected, this would be a long, tough series.

With another loss in Vancouver, the country was shocked, the press hostile—and the Vancouver fans actually booed us as we left the ice. We were down two games to one, with one tie and four games left to play in Moscow.

With the sweat pouring off his face, our captain, Phil Esposito, voiced the frustration we all felt in an on-ice, postgame interview:

"Listen!" he cried. "We're doing the best we can! We need your support!"

That message was a wake-up call to which the whole nation responded. Three thousand Canadian fans followed us to Moscow for the final four games, and thousands of others sent telegrams. Now we knew the whole country was behind us, urging us on. In fact, the Canadian fans in Moscow were outnumbered five to one by the Russians, but managed to totally out-cheer them! Even when we narrowly lost a bitterly fought fifth game by one goal, the Canadian fans all rose to their feet at the end and cheered us off the ice. When we returned to the hotel later, there were a thousand Canadian fans there waiting to cheer us on some more.

We needed to win all three remaining games in a hostile land, with the European referees calling a different game than those at home. We knew Canada was behind us, we'd played five games and started to gel as a team, but mostly we simply refused to entertain the thought we could lose.

That was the turning point. We won the sixth and seventh games, and I had the good fortune to score the winning goal in each. In the eighth and final game, however, the Russians led 5–3 after two periods. We needed three goals against a tireless Russian team that always seemed as fresh and strong at the end as at the opening face-off.

On the first shift Esposito scored; halfway through the period, Yvan Cournoyer tied it up 5–5. When we got to the final minute of the game, I was sitting on the bench—and the tension became unbearable. Finally, with the seconds ticking by, I did something I've never done before or since. I stood and yelled at Pete Mahovlich: "Pete! Pete!" He came off the ice, and I leaped over the boards, streaking toward the Russian net. Any hockey fan will tell you that the coach is the only one to make player changes—and looking back it's hard to explain—but in some strange way I felt I could score the winning goal.

Closing in on goal, I reached to catch Cournoyer's pass and the Russian defenseman tripped me, sending me heavily into the boards. *Get up,* I thought. *Get back in the game.* The Russians failed to clear the puck. Esposito took a whack at it right on goal, Tretiak gave up the rebound and the puck came to me. On the second shot I took, I scored—stopping the clock at thirty-four seconds left—the winning goal! With the final play-by-play of that last dramatic minute, here's Foster Hewitt:

"Here's a shot! Henderson made a wild stab. Here's another shot right by and scores! Henderson has scored for Canada! Henderson's right in front of the net and the fans and the team are going wild!"

Between the red light and the ensuing bedlam, I distinctly remember thinking my dad sure would have loved to have seen this one. Then the roof seemed to come off Luzhniki Arena. I jumped into Cournoyer's arms, my teammates swarmed around me, and the three thousand delirious Canadian fans went crazy in the stands. The impossible had happened—we'd won the series!

When we landed in Montreal, Dorval Airport was a madhouse, and Prime Minister Trudeau was there to personally greet us!

On October 1, a reception was held at Nathan Philips Square in Toronto. The rain poured down relentlessly, but the 80,000 Canadian fans seemed oblivious. Their eyes were full of such happiness and excitement, and I could feel the waves of emotion pouring over me. Tony Esposito and Alan Eagleson lifted me onto their shoulders and introduced me to the crowd.

I waved and thought, *Don't these people realize it's pouring out there?* Then together, triumphant and proud, all 80,000 of us sang "O Canada!"

It's a moment in Canadian history I will never forget. The moment the final goal was scored is forever etched in the mind of every Canadian who watched that last game in Moscow.

Recently, of all the Canadian teams that ever played a game of any sport, we were voted "Team of the Century" by the Canadian press. And that momentous final goal was voted the "Sports Moment of the Century."

In the more than twenty-eight years since then, I've crisscrossed this country often, speaking in large cities and rural hamlets. To this day, people still come up to me, shake my hand and tell me about that moment in their lives when Paul Henderson scored the winning goal for Canada, the one that beat the Russians.

What a thrill!

Paul Henderson
Mississauga, Ontario

To Russia with Love

Canadians are very proud of their country. I know I am. . . . One thing we have is the game of hockey. That's ours. And I always try to remember that.

Wayne Gretzky

As Canadians entered the new millennium, many discussions pointed to the 1972 Canada–Russia series as being a defining moment in our recent history. For those who love the game of hockey and believe it to be a key component of our cultural identity, that historic series represents our nation's finest hour. Over the past thirty years, there have been several reunions to celebrate the accomplishments of Team Canada '72. On each of these occasions the team and everyone else involved have been reminded just how much that series means to all Canadians.

In December 1999, at the precise time when Canadians were reflecting on the highlights of the passing century, members of Team Canada received an invitation from their Russian counterparts to compete in a reunion series hosted by Team Russia. And they agreed!

Returning to Russia from the 1972 team would be Yvan Cournoyer, Brad Park, Marcel Dionne, Gilbert Perreault and my father, Frank Mahovlich. Joining this group were other Hall of Famers who played on later editions of Canada's best, such as Bobby Hull, Guy Lafleur and Steve Shutt. The Canadian side was also instructed to bring three sons of players who could play for their team—and Team Russia would do the same.

Over the course of my life, I have frequently been asked what it is like to be the son of a well-known Canadian hockey player. Ordinarily, aside from having to answer just that question, I believe my life has differed little from the lives of my peers. However, the day I received the invitation to play for Team Canada in a Summit Series Reunion was a definite exception. Like Guy Lafleur's son Martin and Gilbert Perreault's son Marc, I was absolutely thrilled and jumped at the chance! From this wonderful experience I offer a couple of reflections from a time when I was keenly aware of my surroundings and enormously proud to be Canadian.

During the eight days we spent in Russia, we were scheduled to play four hockey games. But in addition to that, our Russian hosts made sure we had a full itinerary of functions that exposed us to a diverse sampling of Russian history and culture. Whether we were walking through the Pushkin Museum or one of Moscow's cemeteries that honours their heroes, it was apparent how proud the Russians were to be sharing their history and their lives with us. Amazingly, they were doing so with a group of people who had once been their bitter rivals.

What made this all so relevant from the Canadian perspective is that two vastly different cultures were celebrating a friendship that was born from a game—Canada's game. Although many of the players from both sides had lost more than a stride or two, in each of the four matches the crowd showed their appreciation for both teams with applause for every play. And while Russia in December is a cold place to be, the people were warm and generous. We all found ourselves grateful to be on the receiving end of such kindness.

The actual series became surprisingly competitive as it progressed. Game One in Elektrostal was an 11–6 blowout in our favour. This inspired the Russians to come out flying with a revised lineup for Game Two in a town called Voskresensk. At the end of the third period the score was tied 3–3. With the best players we could throw on the ice, Marcel Dionne and Guy Lafleur were all over the Russian goal. Then, in the dying seconds, the puck came to my dad. Every player on our bench was on his feet screaming, trying to will the puck into the net. The tension was unbearable. I must have jumped five feet in the air when Dad let go of a wrist shot and scored the winning goal!

We had quite the celebration that night; both sides relished the fact that it was a hard fought, close game.

For Game Three the two teams travelled overnight in a charming, old-fashioned train to St. Petersburg. At the conclusion of what we thought would remain a 3–3 tie, securing a series victory for Team Canada, one of the Russian veterans, Vladimir Petrov, skated to our bench. With a friendly smile he suggested, "Why don't we have a shoot-out, but just for fun?" Put on the spot, yet happy to oblige the fans and our gracious hosts, our coaches Bobby Hull and Yvan Cournoyer complied with the request and selected our shooters. To the frenzied delight of the boisterous crowd, the home team scored twice to our nil. The cheering fans poured over the boards to hug and congratulate their team.

In the following day's newspaper the sports page headline read, "Russia Beats Canada in Summit Series Rematch." At breakfast, several jokes flew around about how our coaching staff was duped into letting the Russians back into the series. With a Game Four victory, Russia could conceivably declare the series a draw! While it was nice to witness the joy of the Russian people in St. Petersburg, losing the fourth and final game in Moscow was unthinkable.

That's when I got to see what put these guys at the top of their profession so many years before. The get-down-to-business attitude of Team Canada heading into that final game was a real eye-opener. After spending what had been an emotional week in Russia with their old friends, the Canadians put all pleasantries aside. Neither age nor retirement had diminished the competitive fire of these men. Very little conversation went around the room, save for a few to-the-point words of encouragement.

Indeed, each and every player brought his A game to the rink. When the third-period buzzer sounded in Moscow's historic Luzhniki Ice Palace, this time there was no need for a shoot-out. Team Canada had skated to a decisive 5–2 victory over Team Russia. Throughout the series I played on a line with the other two Canadian sons, Martin Lafleur and Marc Perreault. Never wanting to let the team down, our line contributed two of the five goals in the final game. We were all proud to earn our keep—and the other players let us know that we had. That was an amazing feeling! And although it's not exactly Paul Henderson's story, it was a bright day in Moscow that I'll never forget!

Canada and hockey, we love them both—and we always will.

Ted Mahovlich
Toronto, Ontario

Waiting in Line

God bless you all. This is your victory! It is the
victory of the cause of freedom in every land.

Winston S. Churchill

As I approached the Peace Tower at the Parliament
Buildings in Ottawa, I saw it: a line of orderly, polite,
patient Canadians—waiting. Without a word, I joined the
line and many more followed me. The young man in front
of me carried a backpack large enough to carry four weeks'
worth of food and clothes. He looked like a student, and I
imagined he had come a long way to stand in this line. An
old soldier, wearing a uniform covered in medals,
bypassed the long line. With the assistance of a family
member, he went straight to the front without incident. As
he passed I could only smile at him.

The woman behind me, who had just arrived from
work, approached the RCMP officer on duty. She
returned to tell the rest of us, "It will be about twenty
minutes. I suppose I can wait twenty minutes for him,"
she said with a smile. "He did give his life for us." Several
of us murmured in agreement.

The Ottawa papers had been full of the story. A Canadian soldier—who had left Canada on a World War I troop ship—had died in France in 1917, and his name had been lost forever. Four years ago the Royal Canadian Legion embarked on a mission to bring him home, and a few days ago, his remains had been exhumed and then carried to the Vimy War Memorial in France by a French honour guard. In the emotional ceremony that followed he was turned over to a Canadian honour guard. Then this soldier with no name was flown home to Canada in a maple casket covered in a Canadian flag.

The next day his remains were to be laid to rest at the Canadian War Memorial. But today he lay in state in his flag-draped casket on Parliament Hill, to be honoured by all Canadians as a hero. The 27,500 Canadian mothers who lost their sons to war during the twentieth century, and never knew where their bodies lay, would now have a place to come.

As we waited in line, the flag on Parliament Hill flew at haft-mast and the Peace Tower bells tolled the quarter hour—a dirge for Canada's war dead that sent chills up and down my spine.

I was so proud to be a Canadian that day as I paid my respects. The number of people there astonished me. For me it was a very personal pilgrimage, but it was personal for thousands of others as well. As I stood in line I wondered, *Could this passionate display of quiet respect happen anywhere else?*

When I reached the doors of the building, I climbed the steps. The last time I had climbed those steps I was a wide-eyed child taking my first tour of the Parliament Buildings. But all tours were cancelled on this special day. Instead, I was greeted by a very young cadet who gave me a pamphlet that told the story of the Unknown Soldier and his long journey back home. As we entered the Hall of Honour and drew close, suddenly all conversation in the line stopped. We stood in silent awe and reverence.

Six soldiers in full-dress uniform from all the divisions of the Canadian military protected his remains. Keeping a twenty-four-hour-a-day vigil, these soldiers—men and women, young and old—stood surrounding the coffin with heads bowed in respect for their fallen comrade. Clergy members from all religions, including the First Nations communities, participated in the vigil. Flowers and wreaths from Prime Minister Chrétien and Governor General Adrienne Clarkson, along with many others, cascaded over the casket. Other visitors had left poppies behind. The image was overwhelming.

A veteran signalled the student in front of me to proceed to pay his respects to the Unknown Soldier. As he walked forward, I suddenly realized that I was at a funeral and unprepared. I didn't have a poppy or even some tissue! As I waited, my anxiety built and I wondered, *What do I do? What do I say? How long should I stand there?* These questions rushed through my head. The nod came from the veteran and I moved forward unsteadily.

My anxieties disappeared as I moved close to the casket. What I did was unimportant; my presence was paramount. Suddenly I became aware of all the energy in the room. It wasn't just sorrow or remorse, it was pride! The energy washed over me like a wave. In that moment, I knew I was not alone paying my respects, my whole family was there behind me. My great-grandfather, who fought in both World Wars, stood beside me and saluted. My grandfather, who was killed in World War II, held my hand. Although I probably only spent a moment there in front of that coffin, in many ways it was a lifetime. As I left, I signed the registry for all of us. Over the three days he lay in state, 10,000 Canadians waited in line to pay their respects to the Unknown Soldier.

The next day, during an emotional, hour-long ceremony, the Unknown Soldier was lowered into his final resting place at the Canadian War Memorial. An honour guard of the Royal Canadian Regiment fired three volleys as the coffin disappeared into the new Tomb for the Unknown Soldier. In silence, the audience watched as a silver cup containing soil from the Unknown Soldier's former grave site in France was emptied over the coffin. A parade of veterans representing Royal Canadian Legions across the country followed, scattering soil from every province and territory onto the coffin. Nine buglers played the "Last Post" and Ottawa held two minutes of silence. Then, four CF-18 fighters thundered past overhead, and by the time "O Canada" was sung, most of the audience was in tears.

When I got home, I called my grandma in Uxbridge and recounted every little detail of my time waiting in line for the Unknown Soldier. I needed a hug from her. And even though we were far apart we shared a virtual hug over the telephone lines.

On that day, I learned how very proud I am to be a Canadian.

Katherine Cornell
Markham, Ontario

Meeting the Prime Minister

*In all his legendary freedom of style and
thought, in the midst of storms and upheavals,
he remained faithful to what he held most dear;
his family, his friends, his country, and his faith.*

The Reverend Jean-Guy Duboc
At the State Funeral of Pierre Elliot Trudeau

It was May 1975. I had spent the year travelling through
Central and South America. It was now the last leg of my
trip, and I was in Georgetown, Guyana. I was almost
broke, somewhat battle-scarred by an exciting but turbu-
lent journey, and weakened by the ravages of a tropical
disease I'd picked up in Ecuador six months before.
Wanting to check for mail from home, I went to the
Canadian High Commission in Georgetown.

It was a typically hot, humid day in the tropics. The
High Commissioner, walking around the office in shirt-
sleeves, mentioned that Prime Minister Trudeau was com-
ing to Guyana on a short visit and invited my friend
Cheryl and me to attend a reception for Prime Minister
Trudeau the following week. We were scheduled to leave

Guyana before that, but after the invitation, we decided to stay to attend his reception.

It was too great an opportunity to miss. I had seen Mr. Trudeau before, in the "Trudeaumania" summer of 1968. He had been absolutely mobbed by an adoring public while campaigning at a wild rally in Toronto. I had been an avid fan.

A few weeks after the election, elated that Mr. Trudeau was now the leader of Canada, I left for Spain to pursue my graduate studies at the University of Madrid. Everywhere I went the first word out of people's mouths after I said I was Canadian was "Trudeau." Prime Minister Trudeau had put Canada on the map and made me proud to be a Canadian. Single-handedly, he had given Canada international status and stature. Now, seven years later, in the former British colony of Guyana, I was about to cross paths with my hero again.

On the day of Trudeau's arrival, the streets were lined with schoolchildren waving placards bearing his picture. He was driven to a park in the centre of the city. When Cheryl and I arrived, there he was, looking as dapper and handsome as ever, in a tan safari jacket—the official dress of the Guyanese politicos. Tanned and healthy, Trudeau seemed out of place in the company of the dour Guyanese prime minister. After the speeches, the park was quickly cleared by the military police, who waved us all away with guns in hand. I wondered if we would be able to get through the security later that night for the reception at the Canadian High Commissioner's private residence.

We were driven to the fete by Bill, the owner of Bill's Guesthouse, where we'd been staying. Bill was so thrilled for us that he'd polished his car and sported a chauffeur's cap so we would feel special. However, we were under no illusions as to why we'd been invited. Other than a couple of bankers, geologists and bauxite miners, there were so few Canadians in Guyana that we were there to fill the ranks.

Despite our worries, we made it through the security at the gates and, clutching our invitations, we breezed through the reception line shaking hands with the High Commissioner and a few other officials. Inside, the guests were dressed to the nines. Cheryl and I had managed to pull together a somewhat respectable look, but we were not what one would call "dressed up." After all, we'd been on the road for almost a year—and our clothes showed it.

Suddenly, he was there, sweeping into the room through the reception line. The room went quiet and all eyes focused on Prime Minister Trudeau. He looked so relaxed and casual in his white safari jacket and wide smile.

He was chatting with some people on the other side of the room when he caught sight of us staring at him. Before we knew it, he looked us square in the eyes, strode across the room directly to us and said, "You're a long way from home. How long have you been in Guyana?"

As we talked, he listened so intently to our stories about our travels that we felt as if we were the only people in the room. At one point he peppered us with questions about where we'd been in Canada and seemed pleased that we'd been "from sea to sea," as Cheryl so aptly put it.

Behind him, I noticed a number of officials looking at their watches, pursing their lips and shooting us dirty looks. Anxiously, I pointed them out to the prime minister. He just smiled and said that he was enjoying his chat with us and that was all that mattered.

Five minutes later someone tugged gently at his sleeve. Again, he just smiled and shrugged the man away. It was then I realized that Trudeau was truly the people's prime minister. It was more important to him at that moment, to talk to us—a couple of young, wandering Canadians—

than it was to be rushed off to do something else.

He chatted with us about his own travels as a young man and, before bidding us farewell, he issued us an invitation to visit him and Margaret at 24 Sussex Drive in Ottawa, after we returned to Canada. Cheryl chuckled as if to hint that she didn't really think it was a sincere gesture.

"I'm serious, come and see us when you get home," Trudeau said. And as he turned back to look at us, he added, "I want to know how the adventure ends."

Our greatest regret is that we never took him up on it. Twenty-five years later, overwhelmed with grief, I found myself sitting at my computer at 2:30 A.M., listening to stories about people who had travelled to Parliament Hill from all parts of Canada to pass his flag-draped coffin. I'm still haunted by the fact that none of us, especially those of us who loved and respected him, will ever have the chance to experience his greatness again.

Goodbye, sweet prince. You were a statesman, a father and a true patriot who gave us a reason to believe that it is still a beautiful and magical world.

Elisabeth Munsterhjelm
Windsor, Ontario

The Autograph

It was 1963 in the Toronto suburb of Willowdale. I was eight years old and hockey-crazy. My next-to-nil skills had not stunted my passion for the game. Earning himself a reservation for a warm seat in heaven, my dad would stand shivering beside the boards of the outdoor public rink, watching me ride the bench in the Catholic Minor Hockey League. The Toronto Maple Leafs were, of course, my heroes, and their Bee Hive Corn Syrup photos plastered my bedroom walls in black and white. I had no idea that one of my most revered icons lived a mere three blocks away.

Back then, walk-a-thons and bike-a-thons had not yet been invented, so we raised funds the good old-fashioned way, selling something the public could actually sink its teeth into. In my school's case, it was the annual doughnut drive—Margaret's Doughnuts, big and doughy, choice of honey-glazed or chocolate-glazed, cheaper if you bought two dozen or more.

Door-to-door I went, clipboard in hand. Although it was long ago, I can still smell the Gestetner fluid on the freshly minted order form. I sold dozens of dozens; hardly a soul turned me down. Was the irresistibility in my product or my sales pitch? "After all, mister, EVERYBODY loves doughnuts." My sheet was almost full, and my stomach almost empty, when I reached Wedgewood Drive with its two modest rows of look-alike sidesplits. I went up the south side—no one home, no one home. The next house would be my last; I had already stretched my parents' limit of a two-block radius, and dinner would be on the table in ten minutes.

I rang the doorbell and rehearsed my spiel while staring at the flamingo on the screen door. The bird swung toward me, and my next and indelible memory is looking up from a large pair of fuzzy slippers, way up, to the face peering down. Once it registered, I stood there speechless for what seemed an eternity, opening and closing my mouth like a fish out of water. Collecting my composure, but still unable to go into doughnut-talk overdrive, I told him something he already knew. "Yup, that's me," he replied with a nod and a smile.

Having successfully established a rapport, I followed with new information—that we shared our given name. I have a vague recollection of stammering through my "Please-buy-some-doughnuts-to-help-my-school" speech, and then a vivid one of him taking the clipboard from my hand. Of course, I had no way of comprehending the historical irony of the document he handed back to me. Flushed with pride from our first-name-basis farewells, I flew home clutching the clipboard to my chest. Nobody got a word in edgewise at dinner.

The next morning before the bell, I guardedly showed off the precious paper. In the classroom, my teacher grumbled good-naturedly as she copied out my orders on another sheet—no way would I let go of the form, no way was I giving up that autograph. Doughnut delivery day could not come fast enough, but my return to Wedgewood Drive was anticlimactic—his wife answered the door. There I stood, red-faced in my Maple Leafs sweater, as four school chums who had doubted my story taunted me from the street.

Fast-forward several years and several hundred franchises later: I wonder if the runt at the door was his inspiration. ("After all, EVERYBODY loves doughnuts.") In futile search, I've torn my folks' basement apart, but it seems I've lost that purple-lined piece of Canadiana, the testimony to a feat that is surely mine alone to claim: I sold Tim Horton a dozen doughnuts.

Tim O'Driscoll
Burlington, Ontario

Reprinted by permission of Allan M. Hirsh.

Hey, It's Our National Anthem!

The moments are few and often fleeting—those moments when Canadians wear their patriotism on their sleeves. It seems it's just not *us* to wave the flag too enthusiastically or belt out "O Canada," hand on heart, at a baseball game. But sometimes we strut our patriotic stuff when no one expects it.

It all started with this little British TV show called *Who Wants to Be a Millionaire?* The Americans, recognizing a ratings' golden goose, snapped up the North American broadcast rights. Now that meant that we here, north of the 49th, could watch the show—we just couldn't participate, and so we were feeling a little left out of what was fast becoming an international phenomenon. Then some smart folks at CTV got on the line to their American cousins and all agreed it would be a swell idea to do a special all-Canadian show—on the set in New York City. Of course, everyone knew that an American host would have a difficult time pronouncing "Saskatchewan," never mind "Trois Rivières". And so the phone call came. Would I host this special event? I couldn't say yes fast enough.

Over the next few months, the country was in a tizzy, speed dialing the special hotlines—dozens, even hundreds, of times a day—for a chance at a million dollars, a trip to

New York City and a place in TV history. The first programme (actually, we did two in the end) would be the highest-rated TV show in this country! There were even contests to select the audience members who would be flown to the Big Apple for the necessary cheering and moral support that have helped make the programme such a success.

As the hour approached, the excitement was palpable. The contestants, representing the width and breadth of this country, had been briefed, put through the paces and had tested all the actual high-tech toys that adorned the *Millionaire* set. Were the buzzers and buttons working? Did they understand the rules? Who would have the fastest finger? Would they freeze in the glare of the million-watt lights? Would the folks at home be proud or unforgiving if the answers were wrong? Could these chosen few show up at the office or even at home if they missed what seems so darn obvious when you're sitting smugly in the comfort of your own home?

I was as ready as possible. There had not been a lot of time to rehearse, and the few precious hours squeezed in during Regis's downtime were done at a frantic pace. Then, of course, there was the chair crisis. Regis is no taller than I am, but he does wear pants making his leap into the seat doable. This pedestal was a precarious perch not designed for tight skirts, high heels or a graceful mount.

Details. A discreet little box magically appeared that allowed me to step up to the host hot seat with a little dignity. As I talked with the contestants—trying to calmly reassure them this would be fun, regardless of the outcome—I soon knew I was in a crowd of Canadians. They didn't care about the money, they said, they were just glad for the whole amazing experience. And so was I. This really was going to be a lot of fun.

The countdown to show time was about to begin when

we heard the faint echoes of our national anthem. Backstage of the elaborate set, I peaked around the darkened corner to see what was going on. There was the audience—all those gentle Canadians—rising, some leaping to their feet, in song. This was not part of the plan. There had been no suggestion that we would sing.

It seemed that the poor, misguided, stand-up comic who had been warming up the crowd had offered a free T-shirt to the person who could name—and I quote—"that song of yours." One woman had queried with a look of genuine puzzlement: "Do you mean our national anthem?" "Ya, whatever," he shrugged in reply.

Then, without missing a beat, one lone Canadian man in the back row stood up—stood up tall—and bravely began his solo rendition. Before he even reached "Our home and native land," the whole noisy crowd was on its feet belting out—yes, belting out—our national anthem. As the chorus rose, the tears began to flow. *My make-up!* I thought. *I won't have time to fix the tear streaks carving their way through the powder that coated my face.* I turned to find that the contestants were also crying little rivers. But everyone had a smile on their faces.

As the proud and familiar sound rang through the studio, I could see the tears glistening in the eyes of those who were singing their hearts out. Everyone seized the moment, cheering, leaping about in their seats and hugging the strangers next to them.

Yes, we can do TV every bit as well as our friends south of the border, and yes, when someone appears disrespectful of those symbols we have come to cherish, that represent our Canadian separateness, we react—with our hearts.

Yes, we are Canadians, and we are proud. That night, we were wearing that patriotism on our sleeves, and using them to wipe away the tears of joy.

Pamela Wallin
Toronto, Ontario

I Am Canadian!

All my intensities are defined by my roots, and my roots are entirely Canadian. I'm as Canadian as you'll ever find.

Donald Sutherland, actor

Hey!
I am not a lumberjack, or a fur trader.
I don't live in an igloo,
Or eat blubber, or own a dogsled,
And I don't know Jimmy, Suzy or Sally from Canada,
Although I am certain they are really, really nice.

I have a prime minister, not a president.
I speak English and French, not American.
I pronounce it "about" not "a boot."
I can proudly sew my country's flag on my backpack.
I believe in peacekeeping, not policing,
Diversity, not assimilation,
And that the beaver is a truly proud and noble animal.

The toque is a hat,
A Chesterfield is a couch,
And "z" is pronounced "zed," not "zee," "*zed!*"
Canada is the second largest land mass,
The first nation of hockey and
THE BEST PART OF NORTH AMERICA!!
My name is "Joe," and
"I AM CANADIAN!!!"
Thank you.

Glen Hunt
Toronto, Ontario
Bensimon, Byrne, D'Arcy

Canada Loves New York

Geography has made us neighbours, history has made us friends.

John F. Kennedy

After the terrorist attacks of September 11, 2001, Canadians shared the tragedy and loss with our American neighbours. From the very first, I felt it was an event that required more than tea and sympathy. Canadians were directly involved. Somehow we needed to demonstrate solidarity for all citizens, including Canadians, who were the victims of this horrific event. For me, as for most Canadians, it was up close and personal.

As cochair of the Canada–U.S. Inter-Parliamentary Group, I called my friends and colleagues in the U.S. Congress, both in Washington and New York. Everyone was depressed and overwhelmed. As Canadians, we felt their sorrows deeply and poignantly.

A few days later, with less than twenty-four hours notice, our prime minister had held an open-air service. Over 100,000 people gathered on Parliament Hill. It was clear Canadians wanted to do something. My first thought was a mass benefit concert at Toronto's Skydome to raise money for families of the victims, but that was abandoned when it was quickly overtaken by other concerts.

A friend, producer Gabor Apor, said, "Jerry, your efforts are misplaced. You should organize something in New York." I realized he was right. The more we thought about it, the more we felt a message needed to be made in New York City. We all knew we had to get things back to normal and quickly, or both our economies would slide into recession. The fear of terrorism was affecting consumer confidence on both sides of the border. We were in this together.

Then Mayor Giuliani made a magnificent speech to the United Nations, inviting people who wished to help America to come and enjoy New York. My wife Carole said to me, "Jerry, stop moping about this. Let's organize some volunteers and do something."

A few days later, we called together a handful of outstanding community volunteer leaders. They enthusiastically endorsed the idea, organized a committee and set up an office. The weekend of November 30 to December 2, 2001, was dubbed the "Canada Loves New York" weekend. We had barely one month! A frantic search discovered the historic Roseland Ballroom was available, and the owner was persuaded to accept a nominal fee.

A Web site was created, and an 800 number donated. Leading Canadian newspapers, TV and radio donated full-page ads and media time. Canadian celebrities volunteered their talent and showed up in Canada, New York and Los Angeles to tape commercial spots. Prime Minister Chrétien joined in without hesitation. Special air, bus and train fares, as well as hotel rates, were negotiated for the weekend. Everyone contacted to participate said, "Yes!"

Vigorous volunteer groups quickly formed in Montreal and Ottawa. When other groups across Canada and the United States heard about the rally, they joined in as well. Because so many fire vehicles were destroyed on September 11, a volunteer persuaded the CIDC to donate a new, specially equipped twenty-four-passenger van to the New York Fire Department (NYFD). We wanted to present it directly to Mayor Giuliani and the chief of the NYFD, so the mayor was formally invited to attend the rally on December 1.

A dynamic volunteer committee of young Canadian professionals working in New York was quickly formed. These people's lives had been directly impacted, so they enthusiastically worked nonstop from the very start. Soon, between Canada and New York, upwards of a thousand Canadian volunteers were working eighteen-hour days to bring this idea alive.

Hundreds of thousands of Canadians live within Greater New York, and to reach them we needed something big—and we needed it fast. So we contacted the owner of one of the large screens in Times Square. He offered to not only donate time on his screen, but got all the other big-screen operators in Times Square to participate as well. Now, our message could reach Canadians living in New York! The Jumbotron at Madison Square Garden came onboard. Then we managed to persuade the Empire State Building to be lit up in the Canadian colours of red and white for the weekend!

To our elation, Mayor Giuliani issued a proclamation officially declaring December 1 as "Canada Loves New York Day" in New York City. Then President Bush generously issued a Presidential Message in which he said:

"The United States and Canada are strongly linked by ties of family, friendship, trade, and shared values. Our countries have stood shoulder to shoulder in war, peace, trial, and triumph, and we again stand together today to defeat terrorism. I applaud the 'Canada Loves New York' Committee and the Canadian people for making this event possible in celebration of our solidarity. By responding to Mayor Giuliani's invitation to come to New York, you demonstrate your love for this remarkable city, and build on the special heritage our countries share as lands of freedom and opportunity."

A show was planned, and Canadian entertainers generously donated their time and talent.

At the last moment, a group of rank-and-file Toronto police officers approached us. They had raised over $100,000 selling T-shirts door to door. To ensure the money reached the right source, they wanted to hand the cheque directly to the New York Police Department's (NYPD's) Benevolent Fund. And so we invited the chiefs of both the police and fire departments in Toronto and New York as well.

Charles Pachter, one of Canada's leading artists created an emotional painting called *The Painted Flags*. His generous gift was transformed into a commemorative poster. Don Green of Roots produced a special "Canada Loves New York" cap. We hoped to draw three to four thousand people, but as December 1 approached, we really had no idea how to estimate how many might come. On Thursday, November 29, we left for New York—ready for anything.

The doors to the historic Roseland Ballroom were to open at 1:30 P.M. on Saturday for the rally. To everyone's astonishment, Canadians started lining up at 9 A.M.—in droves. I started walking up and down the line with other volunteers, trying to explain to people they were not likely to get in. But they responded, "We understand, but we're still going to try." As I walked along the thousands of Canadians, I didn't hear one negative comment. The queue started on 52nd street, and then streamed along 53rd Street to 60th Street and beyond! They had lined up along 8th Avenue and Broadway. As I turned and started walking back, I was astounded! The people were lined up on both sides of the streets. With me were some really hardened cops, and I asked one, "How are we doing officer?" And he said, "I've never seen anything like this! Most of these people aren't going to get in. And they're not even angry!"

As the morning wore on, I kept checking the crowds to say, "I'm sorry," and the people said, "Don't worry about it! We're having a good time!" Charmed and disarmed, the tough New York cops repeated to me, "We've never seen anything like this! This is just absolutely amazing."

We'll never know the exact number, but it was estimated that up to 26,000 Canadians converged around the Roseland Ballroom that day. Indeed, 53rd Street was blocked off and a Jumbotron hastily brought in. Those who were unable to enter the ballroom or 53rd Street lingered and then moved happily on to enjoy the sights and sounds of New York. Not one complaint was heard. Two red-coated Mounties in full dress uniform became instant celebrities as they strolled along Broadway.

I met a man near the front of the line who had brought his family all the way from Whitehorse. Others had come all the way from Newfoundland. Like other Montreal corporate leaders, volunteer Laurent Beaudoin, CEO of Bombardier, chartered a plane and flew many of his employees down.

A group of young disabled Canadians from Toronto's Variety Village wanted to attend the rally. With bus and train transportation donated, these young people then travelled for fifteen hours to attend. Given a prominent place, they joyously wrapped themselves in Canadian flags, and were painted in the Canadian colours.

Prime Minister Chrétien, on his way home from Los Angeles, detoured to New York and joined the festivities. As he strolled the crowded streets, he was cheered and welcomed by his fellow Canadians.

The rally was a success beyond our imaginations! During the emotional finale, three Canadian opera singers sang a haunting rendition of "God Bless America." There wasn't a dry eye left inside or outside of the room. With tears in his eyes, New York's Fire Chief thanked us for such an inspiring and emotional event. The chief of the NYPD was obviously and equally overwhelmed.

The highlight of the weekend for me was when Mayor Giuliani came up to me at the end. With a tear in his eye, he put his hand on my shoulder, and whispered that this was one of the most inspirational moments he had experienced since September 11.

At the end of the presentation, we invited him, all New Yorkers, indeed all Americans, to come and visit us in Canada, when things were once again running smoothly in New York. And he enthusiastically accepted.

As Canadians left the Roseland Ballroom and drifted away from the surrounding area, the Mayor thanked me for everything. And I said, "Look, you shouldn't thank me, or the volunteers. All we really did was facilitate something Canadians wanted to do. and they've suprirsed us in overwhelming numbers. Yes, all the volunteers worked nonstop to respond to your compelling invitation. But most of all, we discovered that all you have to do is ask Canadians to do the right thing, and then move out of the way. They will do it, and in overwhelming numbers, in a warm, wonderful and generous spirit."

Just trust the Canadian people. They will surprise you every time!

Senator Jerry S. Grafstein, Q.C.
Toronto and Ottawa, Ontario

A Country Called Canada

I dream of a great statue below Québec City on the Ile d'Orleans, with its arms outstretched in welcome to immigrants as they first see the Canadian heartland. On that statue I would inscribe these words: Leave all your hates behind. Bring us only your love.

                                    Gregory Clark

I have an idea.

Let's start a country. This country would have bright leaders in politics, labour, business, education and other fields. These leaders wouldn't squabble or call each other names. They would try to get along.

In this country, people would work hard—and they would be allowed to keep a lot of their money. They'd help out the handicapped, the old, the sick and those who had been thrown out of work for no fault of their own. But no freeloading would be allowed. You wouldn't be able to sit around twiddling your thumbs, abusing your body, making trouble or just being a nuisance. You would have to do your share and not expect somebody to look after you. You would be responsible for your life—and no running away. You would have to be useful.

In this country, you would be expected to respect other people, and they'd be expected to respect you. You would not be allowed to sit around griping all the time or making a lot of demands. And if you made a mess of things, you would be told to look for the culprit in your own mirror first, before you started pointing a finger at someone else.

You'd have to follow some rules because this country would work best that way. For example, you'd have to keep your mitts off other people, unless you were showing affection. No abusing animals either, or property, or people's dreams. And you'd be asked to understand things, like feelings and hopes.

What about kids? In this country, kids would be special and receive a lot of love and peanut butter sandwiches and talks. In return, they'd be expected to go to school, learn something useful and not be smart alecks. They could keep pets provided they looked after them.

Everyone would be expected to cherish this country and treat it kindly, understand its riches, and make sure something was left for the next generation.

Putting this country in second place to any other country simply wouldn't be allowed. You could wax sentimental about some holiday spot, or a country in your past or some place you saw in *National Geographic*. And, of course, you would be allowed to get dreamy about Paris. Everyone does. But this country would be your number one, top priority—your very own place, your home.

You would feel good about other people from your country, even if they were a little different. You wouldn't act like a goof and insult them or treat them in a way you wouldn't want to be treated.

This country would have a nice touch of pride—but pride in important things, like integrity, intelligence, cleanliness, decency and fairness.

What else?

I think I've left out fun. This country would have lots of fun because life isn't worth much without fun. You wouldn't want a country where everyone has a long face and snaps about the littlest thing, would you? You'd want to hear laughter. It's as important as sunshine.

So. No idlers. No bullies. No grouches. No ingrates. No shouters. No sourpusses. No crybabies. No parasites. No hotheads.

Yes, let's start a country.

We could call it Canada.

Gary Lautens
Toronto, Ontario

2

LIVING YOUR DREAM

Canada is a country built on dreams, dreams of men and women who come here from many of the countries I have travelled through. If you combine the richness of the country with the spirit of the people, our potential as a nation is unlimited.

Rick Hansen

Ryan's Well of Life

Feel the flame forever burn, Teaching lessons we must learn, To bring us closer to the power of the dream.

David Foster

When my son Ryan was six years old and in first grade, his teacher, Nancy, talked to his class about developing countries and how they could help people, particularly children, in other parts of the world. She explained that besides not having toys or enough food, some of them didn't even have clean water. For these children sitting in their comfortable classroom in Kemptville, Ontario, the idea of children not having any toys, or enough food or water, had an enormous impact.

The principal had distributed a list that showed the costs of buying supplies in developing countries. A penny would buy a pencil, a dollar a hot meal, two dollars a blanket. Seventy dollars would buy a well. When Ryan heard people died because they didn't have clean water, he was deeply affected. He came home that day and insisted he needed seventy dollars for class the next morning.

We thought it was very nice that he wanted to do something important, but we didn't take it seriously. My husband Mark and I both do volunteer work, but Ryan was only six years old—and we just brushed it off.

The next day, Ryan came home very upset because he hadn't been able to take the seventy dollars to school. People were dying, and he insisted he needed that money.

Mark and I discussed it, then explained to Ryan that seventy dollars was a lot of money. If he was really interested in doing something, however, he could earn it.

I drew a little thermometer on a sheet of paper and said, "This is how many dollars it takes to get to seventy, and if you're prepared to earn it, we'll give you extra chores." He happily agreed, so we put an old cookie tin on top of the refrigerator and started giving him chores.

Well, Ryan worked and worked and worked. With every two dollars he earned, he got to fill in another line on the thermometer, then throw his money into the cookie tin. He never stopped working. Ryan vacuumed, washed windows and much more.

He did chores for the neighbours and his grandparents, picked up brush after an ice storm—and it all went right into the cookie tin! When we realized he was really serious, we thought, *Okay, what will we do with the money once he's raised it?* We had no clue. After four months, Ryan was nearing his goal.

I called a girlfriend at CUSO (a Canadian International Development Agency) and asked her for suggestions.

"We can take it here at CUSO," she replied. "But let me look around for a more appropriate organization that might specifically build wells."

Brenda contacted WaterCan in Ottawa and set up a meeting for us. WaterCan is a Canadian nonprofit organization providing clean water and sanitation to people in developing countries.

In April 1998 we went for our meeting, and Ryan brought his cookie tin full of money. Nicole, the executive director, and Helen, her assistant, were very gracious, thanked him and told him how important his donation was. Then they told us it would cost a lot more than $70 to build a well—in fact, it would cost $2,000.

Ryan wasn't concerned and replied simply, "That's okay. I'll just do more chores!"

News about what Ryan was doing got out, and soon we were getting calls from the media. When the *Ottawa Citizen* did a story on Ryan's well, we began to receive donations at least once a week. People from all over were catching Ryan's dream and were inspired to give.

A high school in Cornwall, Ontario, sold bottled water and presented WaterCan with a cheque for Ryan's well for $228. Central Children's Choir from Ottawa donated $1,000 for a Singing Well. The Ground Water Association of Eastern Ontario donated $2,700. And for every dollar Ryan raised, the Canadian International Development Agency (CIDA) matched it two for one. It wasn't long before Ryan had raised more than enough money for his well.

Ryan was invited to a board meeting to discuss details of the well. Gizaw, the engineer from Uganda who would design and build the well, was visiting from Africa. Ryan asked him: How long would it take to build the well? Where would it be built? And would he get a picture? When Gizaw asked Ryan where he would like the well to be built, Ryan decided that it would be best near a school.

Ryan's well was built beside Angolo Primary School in Uganda, Africa, and was dedicated in April of 1999!

But Ryan's efforts had only begun. Ryan's entire school embraced his dream. First, a fund-raising project raised about $1,400. Then the school organized a pen pal letter-writing campaign between Ryan's class and the students at Angolo Primary School.

CTV and several big newspapers did lead stories on the project and interviewed Ryan. I was concerned about all the attention going to his head. When I asked Ryan's teacher, Lynn, about it she said, "I don't think so. Ryan never talks about it unless someone asks." She then told me the class had been raising funds throughout the year, and a water can had been placed on her desk. One day she'd walked into her classroom and found Ryan was at the water can, picking his picture off the side. "I already have enough money for my well," he explained. "This well will be for my class."

One day Ryan said, "I'm going to keep working until everyone in Africa has clean water." I thought, *Oh, boy! I'd heard about encouraging your children to be confident and dream big dreams.* I didn't want to say, like I almost had when he asked for the seventy dollars, that he couldn't make a difference. The truth was, he already had!

One night Ryan shared with us that one day, he would love to actually see his well. I replied, "Ryan, you will see your well. You might be twelve by the time we save enough money to visit Africa, but I promise you, will see your well."

One day, when Ryan was over visiting our neighbours, he announced, "When I'm twelve, I'm going to go over to Uganda and see my well." He wrote his pen pal Jimmy Akana in Uganda saying, "When I'm twelve, I'm coming to see you." This news spread like wildfire through the school in Uganda, and all the children wrote back to their pen pals in Ryan's class asking, "Are you coming with Ryan? Did you know Ryan is coming when he's twelve?"

When Jimmy wrote back, he said, "I always drink from your well, and I thank you for the well. We will be so happy to see you in Uganda when you're twelve."

At New Years, our neighbours, the Paynters, presented Ryan with a very special gift—enough air miles to fly three people halfway to Uganda to visit Jimmy and his well! The *Ottawa Citizen* then posted a request for more air miles. As a result of those donations, and some help from WaterCan, my husband and I were able to join Ryan. Together, we would all see the amazing well that has allowed Ryan's friends in Uganda to have fresh, clean water everyday.

On July 27, 2000, we arrived by truck in Angolo, Uganda. As we got close, a small group of children saw us and began calling out, "Ryan! Ryan!"

Ryan was astonished that they knew his name.

"Everybody for a hundred kilometres knows your name, Ryan," our companion Gizaw Shibru announced.

As we rounded a bend, we were stunned to see a crowd of about 5,000 children from nearby schools lining the roadside, waiting for us. As our truck approached, they excitedly began clapping rhythmically in welcome!

Ryan managed to wave a shy hello. A welcoming committee then led us all to Angolo Primary School. Ryan's pen pal, Jimmy, was waiting for him, and after they said hello, Jimmy took Ryan's hand and led him to the well for the ribbon-cutting ceremony. As we approached Ryan's well, we were overcome with joy. It was adorned with flowers, and on the concrete was inscribed: "Ryan's Well: Formed by Ryan H for Comm. of Angolo."

A village elder spoke words of appreciation: "Look around at our children. You can see they're healthy. This is because of Ryan and our friends in Canada. For us, water is life."

Ryan has also raised money for drilling equipment so that all districts can experience having clean, life-giving water. To date, Ryan has raised over $100,000, which, when matched with CIDA funding, totals over $300,000!

Ryan is now eleven years old and still going strong. There is a Ryan's Well Foundation. His dream has changed the lives of so many people, most of whom we will never meet. That special day in Uganda was one of the happiest days of my life, and it will live in my heart forever. Ryan ended that special day the same as usual, with his nightly prayer: "I wish for everyone in Africa to have clean water." Ryan has shown me what the power of dreams can do.

Susan Hreljac
Kemptville, Ontario
As told to Darlene Montgomery

Look at Me Now, Dad

You tend to hit where you aim, so aim high!

Bob Templeton

It started when I was in high school. Growing up in the small town of Palmerston, Ontario, I had a dream: to work in television.

My parents had a little Stedman's store, so we were definitely not fancy people. When I was in grade twelve, I went to a guidance counsellor who told me I could be a nurse, a teacher or a hairdresser. I thought they were all great careers, but I knew I really I wanted to work in television. I was too embarrassed to tell my counsellor, however, or anyone for that matter—except my parents. To me, it sounded like a dream that could never come true.

Thankfully, my parents had raised me and my siblings to have a lot of confidence. Both my parents, but especially my dad, often said, "You can do anything you want to do." My dad believed in total equality, and he was particularly supportive of the girls in the family. He was my steady rock—always there for me. With his help and encouragement, I applied to the radio and television arts program at Ryerson in Toronto. I was ecstatic when I was accepted. I really loved the program and worked hard—and I was named the most outstanding graduate of 1969.

Just by getting into Ryerson and graduating at the top of the class I was already living my dream. I began to think that maybe the dream could come true. After I graduated, I worked for Bell Canada for a while, writing and producing commercials. I soon decided, however, that what I really wanted was to be on camera.

I went to the CBC and CTV and applied for a job. They both said the same thing: "We love your education, but you don't have any experience. Come back when you get some!" And I kept saying, "How can I get this experience? I've been busy getting an education." They both turned me down.

Luckily, Global Television had just started broadcasting in Canada that year. I thought to myself: *I'm new and they're new. I don't know a soul there, so if I'm going to get to know one person at Global, it might as well be the president.* It really boiled down to how badly did I want a job, and what was I willing to do? I found out who the president was and decided to call him cold. What could I lose? I was scared, but I knew deep down inside that this was what I wanted. When I called my dad and told him my plan, he said, "Good, Faye. That's exactly what you should do."

With my heart just about pounding out of my body, I called up the president of Global Television, spoke to his secretary and asked if I could speak to Mr. Slate. She said sure! Suddenly Mr. Slate was on the phone. I had practised what I was going to say. I had focused on and visualized my goal. I said, "I've heard that your studio facilities are amazing. I could come at eleven o'clock on Tuesday or eleven o'clock on Wednesday for a tour. What would suit you better?" I caught him totally off guard. He stuttered a bit, then picked a day. When I hung up, I was scared but elated.

At 11 o'clock on the appointed day, I arrived at the studio. Mr. Slate took me around and introduced me to everybody. They must have thought I was someone very important—but I was just a girl from a small town of only seventeen hundred people. I had picked eleven o'clock on purpose, because I thought Mr. Slate might invite me to lunch. Sure enough, after the tour he said, "Are you free for lunch?" Of course, I accepted.

We went to lunch at The Inn on the Park. When we sat down, he looked and me and said, "What do *you* want?" He sounded a little angry and frustrated—but very curious.

"All I want is a chance," I said. "I just want a chance. If something on camera comes up at Global—I don't care what—I want a chance to audition. I just want you to know my face, so that when my resume comes in you can put a face to it. That's all I'm asking."

I didn't know whether I'd ever hear from him again, but three months later, his secretary called. "Mr. Slate wants to know if you'd like to come and audition for a new game show," she said. And I answered, "Sure I'll come!"

When I arrived at the station, I went right into an audition for a new show called *Wintario*. Fred Davis, who was Mr. Canadian Television to me, was there along with various high-level management from the Ontario Lottery Corporation. They were looking for a certain chemistry between Fred and me, and had to make sure we would work well together on camera.

Everything went beautifully. Fred and I hit it off right away. I didn't realize it until the next day, but they had hired me on the spot—but nobody told me! When I went back to the studio the following day, for what I thought was another reading, I was instead handed an airline ticket to Sault Ste. Marie to do the very first *Wintario* show. No one even told me officially that I had the job, but I had the job!

The next week Fred and I did the first *Wintario* show in Sault Ste. Marie. I was nervous. *What if I make a mistake? What if I forget where I am?* This was live TV, and I didn't want to make a fool of myself. And I was still in awe of Fred Davis. When I began to walk out on stage, however, and the negative thoughts entered my head. I replaced the negative thoughts with positive ones: *This is going to be the best show ever,* I told myself. *You are going to just shine!*

My positive thinking worked. It was a good show, Fred and I were great together, and I began to realize that night just how wonderful a man he really was. Fred has since passed away, but he was a great friend for many years.

At that time, 85 percent of Ontario households bought lottery tickets, so on Thursday nights, everyone tuned in to the show. With the proceeds of the lottery, *Wintario* helped build community centres, arenas and art galleries. And the people in small towns throughout Ontario just loved us.

During that first show, I thought of my parents at home watching, and said to myself, *Look at me now, Dad!* My parents later came to any shows nearby, but that first show in Sault Ste. Marie was just too far.

That was the beginning of the weekly travelling show that Fred and I did for the next twenty-two years. Altogether, I did 660 shows.

During the early years of *Wintario,* I also hosted a talk show and had about twenty commercials running at the same time. I had a lot of TV coverage. My dad would often say, "Faye, I knew all along you had this in you."

When people came into his store he would ask, "So, did you watch *Wintario* last night? Did you see my daughter?" He talked to everybody about me being on television. I would hear about this from my mother, who is more quietly proud of me. When my parents went to Florida, dad would say, "I see you have Ontario license plates on your car. Do you watch *Wintario?* Well, that's my daughter!" That's how proud he was.

From *Wintario*, everything happened for me. I did a talk show at Global, I hosted the National Santa Claus Parade for fifteen years, I did hundreds of television commercials, a number of movies, training videos, travel shows and a business show. And everything came from finding the courage back in 1975 to make that one phone call.

Faye Dance
Etobicoke, Ontario

The Magic Skates

It's okay if you fail at something, as long as you don't give up, as long as you say—okay, I will try it again!

Marilyn Bell Di Lascio

We had one hour left before skating the program we'd worked toward for years. I tried to stay focused, but in an hour we could be the Olympic pairs champions!

I thought back to the end of 1983, and how we had finished the season on a high—taking the bronze medal at the World Championships in Helsinki. Some people, however, felt we should have taken the gold. Now, suddenly, Underhill and Martini were one of the favourites going into the 1984 season—and the Olympic year.

I was nineteen and Paul was twenty-two. Here we were, with all these extraordinary expectations for us, and the additional pressure of knowing that this would be our last year. No matter what the outcome of our competitions, we would be leaving amateur skating at the end of the season. Along with our coaches, Louis Strong and Sandra Bezic, we had made the decision to focus exclusively on preparing for the Canadian Champion-ships in January, then the Olympics, and finally, the World Championships in Ottawa.

From the beginning of the season, however, things just started to unravel. My skates had always allowed me to fly, but now they were failing me. I struggled with my equipment for the entire season, never feeling totally on top of my game. Nothing would flow, and we were both constantly frustrated. Then, in early January, a bad fall left me with torn ligaments in my foot, so we weren't able to skate at the Canadian Championships—our only tune-up event before the Olympics.

By the time we could skate again, there were only three weeks left until the Olympics. On the plane to Sarajevo, we saw the cover of *Mcleans* magazine: "Barbara Underhill and Paul Martini—Canada's Olympic Hopefuls!" Every-body felt we could do it, but we just knew we weren't totally prepared.

Once in Sarajevo, though, we caught the excitement. Our practices weren't the best, but we still felt we could do it when it counted—in front of the judges.

When we stepped onto the ice, we knew this was our one shot at our dream. We skated well, nailing all the hard elements, and I thought to myself: *We did it!* And then it happened. As we were stepping into an easy element (a spin we could do in our sleep), my edge just slid off. I smashed right into Paul as he was coming around, send-ing us both crashing onto the ice. We were very lucky. His blade was just inches from my head, and the fall could have been catastrophic.

We picked ourselves up and somehow finished the pro-gram, but it was just a blur after that. We were totally shat-tered. We finished sixth after that short program, leaving us stunned and without hope. Then, after a sleepless night, we still had to get out on the ice for an early morning practice, which was just terrible.

When we finally stepped onto the ice to skate our long program, we were both just empty shells. We went through the motions anyway, and to add insult to injury, we dropped from sixth to seventh place. We were devastated.

When we arrived home, there was a big crowd waiting for the Canadian team at the airport. Brian Orser walked through ahead of us, and a huge cheer went up because he had brought home the silver medal. We came out next, and suddenly there was total silence. People didn't know what to say to us. They avoided us, and we felt alone and heartbroken. It felt like people had given up on us—like we didn't have their support anymore. I had never been to a funeral, but I thought this was what it must be like. It was the death of our dream.

It was only three weeks before the World Championships in Ottawa. As we began to practice, all the same frustrations continued—no matter what we tried. Everything was a struggle, and we just couldn't figure out what was wrong. Communication was difficult between us, and I had never felt so alone. We'd always had fun skating, but this was more like torture with so much tension.

About a week before the World Championships, we were at the rink for our daily practice. Paul was sitting in the coffee shop, with his feet up, and I was circling the ice—tears streaming down my face. Our coach, Louis, called us into his office and said, "Look, there's no point in embarrassing ourselves. I'm going to phone Ottawa and just call it off. There's no point in going."

He later told us he had been bluffing, but I didn't think so then. We'd never given up on anything before, and I just couldn't handle the thought of giving up now. I left his office.

It just happened that Brian Orser was at the rink that day. He came down every couple of weeks to train at the Granite Club. He and I had started together at the Junior Worlds back in 1978, and we were very, very close friends. He was still tying on his skates, so I sat down beside him, put my head on his shoulder and just started to sob. "It's over," I managed to get out. "We're not going."

He looked at me, thought for a second, and then said, "Why don't you go back to last year's boots?" He said it *so easily*.

Now I had thought those boots were totally done. But it just so happened they were in my car with all my other stuff, because I was moving. I probably wouldn't have done it if they hadn't been out there—but they were. I thought to myself, *Why not? What do I have to lose?* I retrieved them from the car, Paul switched my good blades to the old boots—and then I stepped out onto the ice.

What happened then was like magic! Within five minutes I knew. The wings were back on my feet, and I was flying again. Paul came out and joined me. He was so excited. After working so hard all season, everything was suddenly effortless, just the way it used to be! I didn't know whether Louis had made that telephone call yet or not, but I wasn't even going to talk to him. We were just out there skating, making him watch. The first time we tried a run-through, it was perfect! We hadn't done that all year. We stayed on the ice that entire day, skating right until midnight!

It was suddenly clear that everything that had happened was all a result of firmly believing that my new skates would eventually "break in" like any other pair of skates. But they hadn't, and they never were going to.

The rest of the week was unbelievable. Every day, it was all just there: the excitement, the energy, the fun! In one instant we'd gone from the most devastating low to believing that maybe this could still happen.

We went to Ottawa, and every practice was perfect. Our routines flowed and clicked just the way they used to. People couldn't believe the difference in our skating.

The day of the World Championship finals arrived. When we stepped onto the ice, we knew, right from the first moment. We were in such a zone. Everything happened so easily. We skated flawlessly, effortlessly— and I wouldn't allow myself to look at the crowd and get caught up in their reactions. However, about thirty seconds before the end of our program, as I was coming down from the top of a lift, I allowed myself a peek at the crowd for just an instant. The people were on their feet, and the building was starting to erupt—something I had never experienced in my life. It felt like the roof was about to come off!

When we finished, the feeling of relief was indescribable. To top it off, everyone who had ever played a role in our career was there in Ottawa that day. We were able to share this incredible moment with all of them. As I looked into the audience, I saw my two sisters sobbing, with their arms wrapped around each other.

It was a long two minutes while we waited for our scores. We were in the "kiss and cry" area with Louis and Sandra, jumping up and down. Everyone was screaming. We kept looking up to Johnny Esaw—he always had the results first on his monitor—but he was so excited that he pulled the cord out of his computer by accident, and the screen went blank! Everyone was wondering: Did we do it? Did we do it? I think we all knew in our hearts that we had, but it wasn't until we saw and heard the string of 5.8s and 5.9s that we really believed it.

Our dream had come true: we were the new world champions! It was so amazing to realize that we had gone from the lowest possible low to the highest possible high in just three weeks. We had defeated the Russian team that had taken the Olympic gold only three weeks earlier, and the East Germans who had been world champions two years previously.

We stood on the podium with two sets of world champions and the Olympic champions. The flags began to go up. We waited, hearts beating, for the Canadian flag to rise to the top of the pole—but it became caught on something and was lowered again! I thought, *No, no, no. This is such an amazing moment. Don't ruin it.* But they unhooked the flag, sent it back up and then the sounds of "O Canada" spread across the arena. As we stood there listening to our national anthem, it felt like we had ten thousand friends sharing this special moment with us. After all we had been through, it seemed like a miracle that we had managed to deliver two perfect programs. We both had tears running down our faces. It was amazing going from what we were feeling a week earlier to being part of this incredible celebration! To this day, every time I see a Canadian flag go up, I relive that moment at the World Championships.

All these years later, people will stop one of us in a mall or on the street—they recognize us—and say, "I was there that day. . . . I was there." And we instantly know that they mean they were there in Ottawa, when we skated that miraculous, memorable skate.

Barbara Underhill and Paul Martini
Mississauga and Aurora, Ontario

To The Top Canada!

I have one love—Canada; One purpose—Canada's greatness; One aim—Canadian unity from the Atlantic to the Pacific.
Former Prime Minister John G. Diefenbacker

I could not sleep. I quietly stared at the ceiling. Ten hours left before the media conference that would begin the To The Top Canada! expedition. Like a racehorse in the starting gate, I was ready to go. I knew I was about to start the most challenging year of my life.

A short time later, in the cold morning air, I pushed my heavily loaded mountain bike from the beach up to the road. Accompanied by an army of local cyclists, I pulled out of Point Pelee. It was March 1, 1997, and the To The Top Canada! expedition had begun! A large contingent of media was there to see me off, and I pulled out the big Canadian flag that I'd bought for the Montreal Rally back in 1995. People cheered and waved as I went by, and cars honked their horns. As they followed my progress across Canada, the media quickly dubbed me "The Unity Guy."

The emotional rally in Montreal before the Québec

Referendum in October 1995 had changed my life. My eleven-year-old son, James, was at my side. Like so many Canadians, we were filled with anxiety about the referendum's outcome. That day, tens of thousands of Canadians made a difference by coming to Montreal and standing tall for Canada. I knew then that I had do something myself. Something personal, something to help make Canada a better country.

And so it was that the To The Top Canada! expedition was born. By cycling, alone, the 6,520 kilometres from Point Pelee to Tuktoyaktuk, I'd be the first person in history to travel from the bottom of Canada to the very top—under his own power. The second and more important goal of the expedition was to get Canadians' attention and ask them one question: "What will you do to make Canada a better country than when you found it?" The expedition wasn't so much about being the first to travel to the top of Canada, as it was a dream to take Canada to the top of its potential.

As a professional speaker I'd travelled to many countries, and I knew Canada was the best of them all. I knew the greatest legacy I could leave my son was a strong, united Canada. Even at his age, he realized the growing pains we faced as a nation. That rally in Montreal changed his life, too, and when I announced I was leaving home for almost a year to fight for Canada, he understood. My wife, Carol, also understood my passion, and as a family we decided to cash in our life savings to allow the To The Top Canada! expedition to go forward. I believed if thirty million Canadians each did one personal project to make Canada better, the result would be a synergy that would empower our country and exceed everyone's expectations.

I didn't look like a cyclist; at 272 pounds I looked more like a retired linebacker for the Hamilton Ti-Cats. And at age forty-one I was about to start a near-impossible journey. Roads in Canada go only as far north as Inuvik in

Canada's Arctic, and then they stop. Once in Inuvik, I would have to wait for the middle of the Arctic winter when the mighty Mackenzie River froze. Then, in total darkness and temperatures of -50°C, I would ride my mountain bike on an ice trail down the centre of the river, then out onto the Arctic Ocean to reach Tuktoyaktuk. Many cynics and critics thought I could never pull it off, but I was determined to prove them wrong.

As the days passed, and I rode in and out of communities, people would recognize "the unity guy" they had seen on TV. The month of May found me along the shores of Lake Superior, and by early June, I was approaching Thunder Bay. As I passed the Terry Fox Memorial, I remembered the emotional day when I'd seen Canada's greatest hero sprint to Toronto City Hall, and it inspired me on. After that, when things got very rough and discouragement set in, I'd think of Terry—he never gave up, and neither would I.

On July 1, I reached Yorkton, Saskatchewan, did a radio interview and participated in Canada Day celebrations. The local high school band played "O Canada," and I spoke passionately to the crowd about my love for Canada. They came alive when I had them cheer, "I Am Canadian!"

After the blistering hot days of the prairie summer, I rode through the Rockies and into the beautiful fall days of British Columbia. After that I faced weather that got progressively colder. On September 17, I rode into Dawson City, Yukon. It was eighty-two kilometres off my route, but its history seemed too important to miss. The city still had the spirit of the Klondike—all the buildings, the dirt roads and the wooden walkways looked like they were fresh from 1898.

I had now cycled over 6,000 kilometres. The gears on my mountain bike were stripped, and I was exhausted after fighting hundreds of kilometres of mountains and mud on the dirt trail called the Dempster Highway. I was tired, wet, hungry and cold, and very glad to arrive in Fort McPherson, a Gwich'in First Nation community just north of the Arctic Circle. So far I'd spoken from my heart in forty-seven cities, to over five million Canadians. Now, during a radio interview with Bertha Francis, radio host for Gwich'in station CBQM, I spoke enthusiastically about the U.N. Report that had ranked Canada "number one"—the best country in the world in terms of education, health care and income—not just once, but three years in a row!

That's when Bertha jumped in with excitement and exclaimed: "Canada is the best country in the world, and we should all be thankful we have been blessed with an abundance of caribou and berries!"

It took a moment, but then the significance of her words struck me like a bolt of lightning. For people who lived off the land, caribou and berries meant the difference between life and death. Bertha hadn't said to be thankful for nice clothes, or a new car, or a big house. What she had really said was to be thankful you are alive, and living in this great country!

On September 29, I awoke to a heavy blanket of snow, and once back on the road, the mud was even worse than before. With all my dry winter clothes gone and almost no food left, I decided to ride straight on to Inuvik, still 112 kilometres away. Around 8:00 P.M., hungry and thirsty, I met a family who called out, "You've made it! You've made it to the top!" And the whole family clapped and cheered from their truck.

Now I had to rest my expedition until the Mackenzie River froze. Finally, on January 5, in the midst of the total darkness of the Arctic winter, I began the last leg of my journey. With special protective clothing, goggles and a face mask, I battled Arctic winds and ploughed through snow in temperatures colder than -50°C. I was startled to discover that rather than hugging the coast, the ice trail actually went five to ten kilometres out into the Arctic Ocean. There were cracks in the ice with seawater gushing out, and as I rode on alone, the cracking sounds made me shiver. Even so, I marvelled at the incredible beauty of the northern lights as they glowed fluorescent green and looked like shimmering curtains that danced in the sky. I was exhilarated and thankful to be alive.

On Wednesday January 7, 1998, I proudly carried my Canadian flag over the last few metres, and was welcomed by a mass of media and community elders when I arrived at a school in Tuktoyaktuk. It was packed with young and old, and as I wheeled my bike into the gym, they made a tunnel for me through the crowd. It was lined with Tuktoyaktuk drummers, and everyone was clapping and cheering. A giant multicoloured "CONGRATULATIONS!" sign ran the length of the gym. Tears came to my eyes from the warmth that poured from the entire community. After the formalities, the mayor of "Tuk" introduced the drummers, and then the dancers performed in my honour.

As I left the gym, a crowd surrounded me—people shook my hand and patted my back. It was a moment that money could never buy. I let the feeling sink in, knowing I'd treasure the memory for the rest of my life. Later I called my wife; she had already heard me on the CBC, and friends were calling to say they had as well. I was thrilled to know my Canadian unity message was spreading across Canada like wildfire. I'm proud to say my journey was a success—it sent a message to all Canadians that any dream is possible to make Canada the best country in the world during the twenty-first century!

Chris Robertson
Hamilton, Ontario

Our Olympic Dream

People talk about world peace, and I wish that there was some way to extend the experiences of international athletes to everyone. Thus enlightened, we would have a much better chance at achieving that world peace.

Brian Orser

It didn't start out as an Olympic dream. Back in elementary school in Montreal, we were a pair of overweight, uncoordinated twins. During gym class, when teams were chosen, it didn't matter if the game was baseball, dodge ball or lacrosse, we were always last to be picked.

It was so bad, our teacher said to us one day, "Penny and Vicky, you have been chosen, along with four other kids, to miss music class and go to remedial gym." This was because neither one of us could catch or throw a ball. We were totally mortified.

Although this humiliation whittled away at our self-esteem, we continued to try other sports and activities outside of school. Then, at age eight, we discovered synchronized swimming. It was as if the sport had chosen *us,* since it was the only one we were good at, and we loved it.

It was an ideal sport for identical twins, and we had great fun creating routines to music. We passionately loved working with other swimmers and our coaches and practiced incredibly hard. Each year we set higher goals and became more successful. Then, in 1979, at the age of fifteen, we were thrilled to represent Québec at the Canada Games. Subsequent victories allowed us to travel all over the world, and our dream to participate in the Olympics was born.

We achieved many of our goals, including being seven-time Canadian synchronised swimming duet champions, and World champions in Team. We were thrilled to be the first duet in the world to ever receive a perfect mark of "10".

But to our great disappointment, the 1980 Olympic Games eluded us when they were boycotted by many countries, including Canada. Then, in 1984, we didn't make the team. After fourteen years of training and striving, we had to accept that our Olympic dream would remain out of reach. We retired from swimming to finish our degrees at McGill and start our careers.

Then, one day five years later, while watching a synchro competition, we both experienced an unexpected sensation. We suddenly realized our Olympic dream was still alive, and we could no longer ignore it. On April Fool's Day, 1990, we decided to make an unprecedented comeback and shoot for the 1992 Olympics. We were afraid to announce our plans in case we didn't make it, but in the end, we were more afraid of not trying and having to live with the thought of "What if?" We decided to give it our all, and take pride in simply doing our best. *"Si on n'essaie pas, on ne le saura jamais!"* we said—"If we don't try, we'll never know!"

Everyone said it would be impossible. But our intense desire provided the energy needed to persevere. We only had two years to get back in shape and be among the best in the world. No swimmer had ever come back after a five-year absence, especially not at the age of twenty-seven! We weren't eligible for any funding, so we both maintained full-time jobs and trained five hours every day after work. We still had to support ourselves and fund all our travel to international competitions. We were determined to succeed, vowing, "Nothing will stop us this time." For two full years we maintained that gruelling schedule without ever knowing if we'd make it.

Thankfully, we had four dedicated coaches from Québec who poured their hearts and souls into helping us achieve our dream. Julie was our head coach, André directed our weight training, Richard helped us improve our conditioning and Denise helped with our accuracy in the water. We never could have done it without them.

We were pushed to our physical limits during training since we had to make up for the five years off. Through it all, however, we still loved it and maintained our sense of humour. Sometimes we laughed so hard with Julie we ran out of air and ended up sinking to the bottom of the pool. Julie helped us to continue believing in ourselves. We can still hear her saying: *"Okay les jumelles, vous êtes capables!"*— "Okay, twins, you can do this!"

The day of the Olympic trials finally came. We were confident but nervous. We could hardly breathe as we waited to hear our marks in finals. When they were announced, we jumped up and down hugging each other—we had won by 0.04! In that incredible moment we realized we were finally going to live our Olympic dream!

We could hardly contain our excitement as Canada's '92 Olympic team gathered in Toronto, en route to Barcelona. When we received our Olympic outfits, we felt just like kids at Christmas! Then Ken Read, our chef de mission, called a meeting and said to the group: "Congratulations and welcome to the Canadian Olympic Team! You are now Olympians and no one will ever take that away from you."

Our Olympic experience was unforgettable. During the opening ceremonies, we were thrilled to walk into the packed stadium to thunderous applause, with hundreds of Canadian flags being waved. We also found out how much support we had from Canadians everywhere. Thanks to the Olympic Mailbag Program organized by Canada Post, our spirits received a tremendous lift during those last few stressful days of training. Many Canadians wrote their thoughts and wishes on a postcard simply addressed to "Penny and Vicky Vilagos—Barcelona." After practice each day, we rushed to dig through the giant pile of bright yellow postcards sent to the Canadian team, and pick out those addressed to us. They came in French and in English, from old childhood friends in Montreal and Québec, complete strangers, former athletes, and proud Canadians young and old. They inspired us, made us laugh and even made us cry. Imagine how we felt when we read this incredible message:

> *Dear Penny and Vicky: You are swimming my dream. I used to be able to swim two lengths of the pool in a single breath. I am now disabled and can no longer swim at all. I am sending you my strength—May the sun shine on you.*

And the sun did shine on us in Barcelona.

Finally, our big day came. We felt considerable stress knowing millions of viewers would be watching, but we were ready. As we stepped onto the pool deck and heard, "Competitor #9 . . . Canada!" we almost burst with pride. As the Canadians cheered and waved their flags, we looked at the water to focus on the job at hand. The temptation in the moment was to reflect on the 30,000 hours of training it had taken to get here, but there would be time for that later. . . .

Swimming for Canada that day was magical. Despite the stress, we enjoyed every moment. As the music ended and the applause began, we looked up at Julie, and her expression told us what we already felt—we had given the performance of our lives!

Finally, wearing our Canada tracksuits, we marched around the pool for the medal ceremony. As we stepped on the podium to receive our silver medals, in our minds our coaches were there with us to share this special moment. As we watched the flag go up, the awareness that so many Canadians were proud of us made it that much better.

Still floating on a cloud, it was soon time for the closing ceremonies. We'll remember forever the electric atmosphere in the stadium as everyone swayed back and forth and joined in singing "Amigos Para Siempre," or "Friends for Life". And then it began to sink in—after twenty-one years, our Olympic dream had finally come true!

Penny and Vicky Vilagos
Montreal, Québec

3

OVERCOMING OBSTACLES

The greater the difficulty, the more glory in surmounting it.

Epicurus

The True Story of Lake Ontario

*Never give in—never, never, never, never, in
nothing great or small, large or petty, never give in
except to convictions of honour and good sense.*

Winston S. Churchill

There were no stars at eleven o'clock that September
night, and no moon. It was overcast and windy, and very,
very black. Taking a deep breath, I dove in and so began
the night that would change my life forever. When I sur-
faced and looked around, I couldn't see where the lake
ended and the sky began. I couldn't see anything, so I just
started swimming.

When I had said good-bye to my coach, Gus, earlier,
I was very worried about finding him in the escort boat. I
was nervous about getting lost in the dark and not nearly
as brave as I've been portrayed. Gus just looked me in the
eye and said, "When you dive in the water, keep your eyes
open, and swim north, and *I will find you.*"

I believed him. Gus Ryder had been my coach and
mentor ever since I joined Toronto's Lakeshore Swimming
Club. Although I'd been swimming since I was nine—and

always put my heart into it—I was never very fast and never very good. But I was so determined.

In 1948, when Barbara Ann Scott won the World and Olympic figure-skating championships, she captivated me. She became my role model, and I wanted to go to the Olympics and win a gold medal swimming for Canada. When Toronto gave her a ticker-tape parade, I went by myself and stood on the corner of Bay and Queen. As she drove past sitting on the back of the convertible, I thought she was so wonderful—the perfect Canadian girl—and everything I wanted to be. After seeing her, I became even more determined.

When I was eleven, Gus had watched me finish a one-mile race in freezing cold Lake Ontario. He introduced himself, saying, "Marilyn, you have so much determination and so much heart, if you work at it you'll be a fine swimmer." I started swimming for Gus, and was soon totally involved with the club. We trained for hours in open water, and every time I got into the lake, I had to deal with my fears. I was petrified of fish, of weeds, of whatever might be in there. I did it anyway, but no matter how hard I worked, I still came in third or fourth.

By 1952 it was clear I was never going to the Olympics, so I turned professional. I looked forward each year to the competition hosted by the Canadian National Exhibition (CNE), and I just knew I was ready to win. Then, in the winter of 1954, the CNE announced they had challenged the American long-distance swimmer Florence Chadwick to swim the thirty-two miles across Lake Ontario from Youngstown, New York, to Toronto. They also announced that the annual professional swims for Canadians would be cancelled. I was sixteen that year and bitterly disappointed.

In July of 1954, I swam the Atlantic City Marathon. There, I met a young lifeguard named Joe Di Lascio.

Having never been in the ocean before, I was petrified. I said to Joe, "Excuse me, are there fish in here?" Like everybody else, Joe never expected me to win. But when the twenty-six-mile race was over, I had won the women's championship—and Joe had won my heart.

Back in Toronto, there was a lot of controversy around the CNE challenging an American. That's when Gus suggested I challenge Florence in a race across the lake. The idea had never occurred to me, but it had to Gus, and after Atlantic City, he had made up his mind.

The *Toronto Star* agreed to back me, in return for an exclusive. I really had no confidence about completing that swim, and the idea of swimming at night terrified me. But I wasn't sure Florence could make it either. I figured if I could swim one stroke further than her, it would be worth it. I would do it for Gus, and for me, but I would also do it for Canada.

We were to start Monday, September 6, from the Coast Guard station in Youngstown. The forecast was bad, so Florence postponed, and we all went into "waiting mode." My team, along with the many *Star* reporters, waited at the Youngstown Yacht Club on the *Mona 4,* the yacht that would accompany me on my swim. The officials agreed to give us a two-hour notice of when Florence planned to start, allowing us plenty of time to get to the starting point. But, when word came at ten o'clock Wednesday night, there was a mad scramble. They had left us only one hour! There wasn't enough time for me to go to the starting point with Gus in the escort boat. He had to leave immediately, knowing he wouldn't get there in time to be beside me when I started. I would have to start alone. But when he left he said, "I will find you," and I believed him.

Howie, one of the *Star* reporters, took me by car to the starting point. A few minutes after Florence started, he said, "Okay, Marilyn. Now it's your turn." Shortly after that, Winnie Roach, the other Canadian swimmer, began.

It was so dark; the only things I could see were the lights from the boats around Florence. So I did what Gus told me—swam straight out of the Niagara River and just kept going. After what seemed an eternity, I finally heard Gus's voice—they had found me! With him were George, another *Star* reporter and Jack, the boatman. Gus had a big flashlight, and he shone it just ahead of my stroke, saying, "Marilyn, just swim to the light and I will get you across this lake." For the rest of the night, each time I extended my arm for the next stroke, my hand was reaching into that beam of light.

Florence swam for about four or five hours before she quit. But it wasn't until several hours later, when I was having difficulty, that Gus told me that Florence—and Winnie—were out. I was the only one left, and it was up to me to swim for Canada!

It was a long night. I had to deal with horrible lamprey eels, and my fear of the lake and of the dark. Gus kept me going any way he could. But when I realized the dawn was coming, and the night was almost over, everything changed. It was the most glorious sunrise I've ever seen, and one of the most wonderful moments in my life. I thought to myself, *Perhaps I'll be able to do this after all.*

Now Gus began writing messages on a chalkboard to distract me and keep my thoughts positive. Once he wrote, "You know you can do it, you can do it for the team!" Another time he wrote, "All the Atlantic City lifeguards are pulling for you." This referred to Joe, of course. He even wrote, "If you give up, I give up."

Sometime in the morning, a flotilla of boats began to surround me. Interest in my swim had spread like wildfire all across Canada. When Gus held up the message, "All of Canada is rooting for you," I wondered, *How did all of*

Canada know I was in the water? But they did!

At the CNE grounds in Toronto, people had started to arrive by the thousands to watch me come in. I knew nothing about that, however. I was just in the lake, in this little cocoon, moving along.

By midday I started falling asleep and veering away from the boat, so Gus brought out my close friend Joan in a water taxi and said, "Joan, you've got to go and swim with her and get her attention back."

I heard a splash and suddenly Joan was right in my face saying, "I'm here to swim with you Marilyn. Come on!" She swam with me for a while, and I perked right up.

By now the boats that surrounded me were cutting in front of me, jockeying for space. The exhaust, oil and gas began to cause problems. My team fought quite a battle to protect my space. Eventually they were successful, because all the jockeying stopped.

Somewhere on the lake, later in the day, I began to experience a very unusual, hard-to-describe spirit of unity and togetherness. For a short while, competing media or not, it felt like there were no divisions and everybody had only one goal, and that was to get me to Toronto. I learned later that my family and friends were all praying for me, and that the whole time I was swimming there was always a nun in my school chapel praying for my safety.

At 8:00 P.M., after twenty-one hours in the water, I began approaching the shore. I was suffering from sleep deprivation and not really "present," but my arms were still going. I later saw a film of the moment when I touched the break wall and an enormous roar went up from the crowd. But I don't remember that. I remember a lot of confusion, and finally, Gus's voice breaking through the haze. As they pulled me into the boat I said: "What happened? Did I do it?" And that's when I heard Gus say, "Oh Marilyn! You did it, you did it, you finished!" At that point I came out of the zone I'd been in and realized I had actually done it. I was amazed because I hadn't really thought I could. I hadn't really thought anybody could!

I was stunned when I learned the CNE decided to award me the $10,000 prize money. That night, among the many congratulatory telegrams I received was one that thrilled me to pieces—from Barbara Ann Scott!

The next night I was presented with the prize on the CNE Grandstand stage with the show headliners—Roy Rogers and Dale Evans, who had stopped their show the day before to pray for my safety in the lake. On Monday, Toronto hosted a ticker tape parade for me up Bay Street to city hall. It rained, but the people came out anyway. There were mounted police, marching bands and thousands of people crowding the streets—screaming and yelling and waving at me, while the ticker tape streamed down from every window. Gus and I rode in a big Cadillac convertible, and sat up on the back, just the way Barbara Ann Scott had. When we stopped at the corner of Bay and Queen, the same corner where I had watched Barbara Ann Scott's parade, I had a flashback. I saw myself standing there five years before—just a kid—with my dream of swimming for Canada.

For many years after my swim, when I returned to Canada, people would come up to me and say, "The day you swam that lake, I was with you." I hear magnificent stories all the time when I'm home, from people who say things like, "My mother didn't cook dinner that night. We had baked beans on toast by the radio, because my mother wouldn't leave it. And we prayed for you."

All these years later, I am still so deeply touched, and I really think that all *those* stories are the true story of Lake Ontario.

Marilyn Bell Di Lascio

Women Are Persons!

I feel myself equal to high and splendid braveries!

Emily Murphy

Judge Emily Murphy was frustrated. Her last petition had been no more successful than all the others she had sent over the past ten years. It was 1927, and Canadian women were still defined by British common law, which astonishingly stated: *"Women are persons in matters of pains and penalties, but not in matters of rights and privileges."*

Emily was not at all happy about the outrageous indignity of being told she was "not a person." She had set her sights on becoming Canada's first female senator, but because women were not "persons," *no woman was eligible!* Emily was determined to change things.

And so it was that between 1921 and 1927, over 500,000 people, men and women, had signed letters and petitions requesting that Judge Murphy be appointed to the Canadian Senate. For most of them, it wasn't about becoming a senator. Like her, they were upset and offended that women were not considered to be persons. Amazingly, despite all her efforts, two prime ministers had still said "no!" But Emily refused to take "no" for an answer and kept up her relentless pressure. Then one day, after ten years of lobbying, she happened upon a new strategy. Her brother had discovered a legal clause stating that any five citizens acting as a unit could appeal to the Supreme Court to clarify a point in the constitution. So in late 1927, she invited Henrietta Edwards, Louise McKinney, Irene Parlby and Nellie McClung to her Edmonton home. All four of these prominent Alberta women had been active in fighting for women's rights, and all of them were determined that by the end of their efforts, Canada would recognize them and all women as "persons."

That day, the five women signed Emily's petition, and with great hopes and expectations they sent their appeal. Then they sat back and waited. Several months later, Judge Murphy excitedly opened the telegram that arrived from the Supreme Court of Canada.

But her hopes were dashed. "No," read the reply from the learned justices, "Women are not eligible to be summoned to the Senate. Women are not 'persons.'"

Emily and her colleagues were devastated. First two prime ministers, and now the highest court in Canada had formally ruled against them, and they feared they had done irreparable damage to their cause. However, further research revealed one more option. The absolute final court for Canada in those days was still the Privy Council of Great Britain—it could be appealed there. But they were not hopeful. They would have to persuade the Canadian government to appeal the decision, and the rights of women in England were far behind those so far gained in Canada.

Holding her breath, Emily wrote to Prime Minister Mackenzie King, asked for his support, and urged him to appeal this matter to the Privy Council. To her great elation, he responded with his full support, and that of his government, and in addition they would pay for the cost of the appeal!

With their hopes back up, the five women wondered, *Should they go to England? Should they write articles for the newspapers? Contact their friends there?* No, they were advised, only the merit of the case would be heard. Just wait.

Finally, in October 1929, the five British Lords made their historic decision. When Emily and her friends learned that the new definition of the word "persons" would from that day forward always include both men and women, they were overjoyed! They had won!

As the word spread, women around the world celebrated. The five friends were gratified to know that because of their efforts, every woman in the British empire would now be recognized as a "person," with all the same rights and privileges as men.

[EDITORS' NOTE: *On October 18, 2000, a memorial celebrating the Famous 5 and their tremendous accomplishments was unveiled, and our five heroes became the first Canadian women in history to be honoured on Parliament Hill. The monument depicts an imaginary moment when the women received the news of their victory. A joyous Emily stands beside an empty chair and beckons visitors to join the celebration. Today, many come and visit so they can sit in Emily's chair and thank the Famous 5 for what they did. And everyone who does makes a pledge to do their best to participate in the building of a better Canada!*]

Frances Wright
Calgary, Alberta

The Legacy of Terry Fox

I just wish people would realize that anything is possible if you try . . . dreams are made if people try.

Terry Fox

I was a young reporter, not long at *The Toronto Star,* when my editor asked me to find a young man named Terry Fox—he was somewhere in Newfoundland. She told me Terry had lost a leg to cancer and was trying to run across Canada to raise money for cancer research. "See if he's for real," she said. By mid-afternoon, I was speaking to Terry Fox.

His voice was young, hopeful and happy as he told me about his Marathon of Hope. His dream was to run 5,300 miles across Canada and raise $1 million to fight the disease that had claimed his leg. It was April 1980, and Newfoundland weather was harsh and unpredictable. He told me about being buffeted by high winds, about running in snow and freezing rain. His good leg was strong and muscular, and his artificial leg was made of fibreglass and steel. The run was painfully difficult, but he was cheery and confident, and at the end of our interview, I was certain he was unstoppable. He also made sure I understood one more thing: He didn't think of himself as disabled.

After that, we spoke every week, and I learned he was from Port Coquitlam, British Columbia. He was the second of four children, and his parents were Betty and Rolly. His family was close-knit, hardworking and competitive. They all loved to win.

Terry wanted to play basketball when he was in grade eight, and despite his small size, his physical education teacher, Bob, noticed the "little guy who worked his rear off." After three practices, Bob suggested Terry might be better suited to another sport, but Terry persisted, and finally made the team. When Bob said, "If you want something you have to work for it, because I'm not interested in mediocrity," Terry heard him.

So Terry worked hard, and by grade ten, he and his friend Doug shared the athlete of the year award, winning it again in their last year of high school. His first year at Simon Fraser University, he made the junior varsity basketball team—there were more talented players than he, but none with a greater desire to win.

Terry was studying kinesiology and thinking of being a physical education teacher himself, when a pain in his knee he assumed was a sports injury sent him to the doctor. But it wasn't a sports injury. To his great shock, Terry learned he was suffering from osteogenic sarcoma, a rare bone cancer. It was March 1977, and he was eighteen years old.

He hardly understood what the doctors told him. What was a malignant tumour? They explained they would amputate his leg and follow up with chemotherapy to catch any stray cancer cells circulating in his blood. The night before his operation, his basketball coach brought him a story about a one-legged runner who competed in the Boston Marathon. Already Terry began to wonder,

Could he do something like that, maybe even run across Canada, with one leg?

Terry faced the loss of a leg as another challenge. "No one is ever going to call me a quitter," he said. He learned to wear his artificial leg, played golf with his dad and began a gruelling sixteen-month course of chemotherapy. He lost his hair, and was weak from nausea. In the cancer clinic, he heard young people crying out in pain, and he heard doctors telling patients they had a 15 percent chance of surviving.

When Terry left the clinic, he was more than a survivor; he had a new sense of compassion and responsibility. His hair grew back thick and curly. He'd been blessed with life, the greatest gift of all, and he was determined to live as an inspiration so that others might find courage from his example. While still undergoing chemotherapy, Rick Hansen recruited him to join a wheelchair basketball team. And then secretly, quietly, in 1979, he began training for his great dream—running across Canada.

He started with a quarter-mile run around a cinder track. It nearly killed him, but soon he was doing a half-mile, and then amazingly, a week later, he ran a full mile. He was drained but ecstatic. Terry ran and ran and ran. Sometimes the stump on his leg bled, and his mother, rarely at a loss for words, would bite her lip and turn away in tears. Betty and Rolly weren't happy with his plan to run across Canada, but they knew all too well his strong and stubborn will. In a letter he wrote when he began seeking sponsorship, he said he felt privileged to be alive. He said: "I remember promising myself that should I live, I would rise up to meet this new challenge face-to-face, and prove myself worthy of life. That's something too many people take for granted."

With a handful of sponsors, the support of the Canadian Cancer Society, and a camper van donated by

Ford of Canada and driven by his old friend, Doug, Terry began his Marathon of Hope. On April 12, 1980, he gazed for a moment out over the harbour in St. John's, Newfoundland, dipped his artificial leg in the water, turned and started running.

Terry ran through the Atlantic provinces, then through Québec and Ontario, incredibly averaging a marathon—twenty-six miles—every day. Once in his diary he described his running as "the usual torture."

All of Canada fell in love with him along the way. Creating images that will stay in our hearts forever, in sun, rain and early morning mist, Terry's familiar lopsided gait took him through cities, towns and villages. Day-by-day his fame grew. There was something in his good nature, his simple words, sunburned good looks, astonishing strength and the greatness of his dream that brought many who saw him to tears.

He wanted to run, but believing that advances in research had saved his life, he was also determined to raise money for research. And so he often stopped along the way. Standing on picnic tables, he talked to crowds, kids and reporters, even Prime Minister Pierre Trudeau. He'd visit schools and take off his artificial leg and show the children how it worked. As the miles passed, people began calling him a Canadian hero. He didn't like that; he saw himself as just an ordinary person, even though hundreds, sometimes thousands, of people would wait to see him pass on the highways or at city halls, acknowledging his courage and cheering him on in accomplishing his dream.

And so it went that glorious summer of 1980: he ran 3,339 miles in 143 days. And then, on September 1, seven miles outside Thunder Bay, something felt terribly wrong in his chest. The pains were so bad, he wondered if he was having a heart attack. Whatever it was, he needed to see a doctor—quickly. The doctor confirmed his worst fears—

the cancer was back, this time in his lungs. Terry had run his last mile. The Marathon of Hope was over.

Or so it seemed.

Terry was flown home the next day lying on a stretcher, with his parents Betty and Rolly at his side. He'd raised $1.7 million dollars for cancer research. Then, despite the sorrow felt by Canadians everywhere, something wonderful happened. As he lay in a hospital bed with the cancer-fighting drugs flowing silently into his body, the whole country went crazy raising money for cancer research—just as he hoped it would.

Terry bravely fought the disease another ten months, and all of Canada fought with him. Once, while watching a hockey game on TV, he saw a banner that read "KEEP ON FIGHTING, TERRY FOX!" strung along the stands. Despite the prayers of thousands, he died just before dawn on June 28, 1981, his family at his side. But before he died, he knew he had realized his dream. More than $23 million had been raised in his name—a dollar from every Canadian.

Canada was plunged into mourning. Flags flew at half-mast, condolences came from around the world and Prime Minister Trudeau personally paid tribute to Terry in the House of Commons. But the legacy of Terry Fox didn't end there. In 2000, the twentieth anniversary of his Marathon of Hope, the Terry Fox Foundation—with Terry's brother Darrell at the helm—raised $20 million.

Since Terry first dipped his leg in St. John's Harbour, more than a quarter of a billion dollars has been raised for cancer research in Terry's name. He became the youngest recipient of the Order of Canada, our nation's highest civilian honour. In 1990, he was named Athlete of the Decade by The Sports Network (TSN), and has been unanimously proclaimed Canada's greatest hero.

Just outside Thunder Bay, a section of the Trans-Canada Highway has been renamed the Terry Fox Courage

Highway. Along it, on a hill overlooking Lake Superior near the spot where Terry was forced to stop, stands a nine-foot bronze statue of Terry in running stance, facing toward his western home. Terry inspired and united an entire generation of Canadians, and so the monument was designed joining east with west, and proudly displaying all provincial and territorial coats of arms and the Canadian maple leaf and beaver.

Every year in September, Terry Fox Runs are held across Canada and in fifty other countries, so that his dream now spans the world.

I run, or sometimes walk, every year in the Terry Fox Run. My favourite one was September 15, 1991, when I was pregnant and past my due date. I had intended to walk a symbolic kilometre for Terry, but it was a beautiful day, and I kept walking until, to my shock, I'd walked six kilometres. Not surprisingly, little David was born that night. Now he's ten, a beautiful, dark-haired boy who loves soccer and hockey and baseball. He's not the best player on the team, but his coaches love him because he's so determined and works so hard. Just like someone else I knew, whose strong and youthful voice I first heard on the telephone so many years ago.

Leslie Scrivener
The Toronto Star
Toronto, Ontario

One Person *Can* Make a Difference

If a friend is in trouble, don't annoy him by asking if there is anything you can do. Think up something appropriate, and do it.

Edgar Watson Howe

It was the first weekend in June 1985, and I was conducting a weekend seminar at Deerhurst Lodge in Muskoka. Late that Friday afternoon, a tornado swept through the town of Barrie, killing dozens of people and doing millions of dollars worth of damage. On the Sunday night as I was driving back to Toronto down Highway 400, I stopped when I got to Barrie. I got out of the car, about where the Holiday Inn is, to have a good look. The destruction was incredible—it was an absolute mess. There were cars upside down, smashed houses, and many buildings torn apart. I'd never seen anything like it.

Well, the same night, Bob Templeton was driving down the 400 from a fishing trip on the French River. Bob was vice president of Telemedia Communications, which owned a string of radio stations in Ontario and Québec. While at the fishing camp, Bob had heard about the tornado. When he got to Barrie, he also got out of his car, stunned by the devastation. Up on the hill, he saw a house that looked as if a sickle had sliced right through it. The back was totally gone, and in the other half, a picture still hung on the wall. Just a few feet were between total disaster and nothing. Bob only lived about thirty kilometres away in Aurora. Waiting at home for him were his wife and three small children. They were his whole world. *My gosh,* he thought, *that could have been my home.*

On the radio, they were appealing for people to come out and help clean up the mess. The whole thing disturbed Bob enormously. He really wanted to do something to help, but felt that lugging bricks or writing a cheque was just not enough. *There has to be something we can do for these people with our string of radio stations,* he thought.

The following night, he and another vice president with Telemedia came in and stood at the back of the room to evaluate a seminar I was doing to see if he wanted me to work with his company. During my presentation, Bob got an idea and after the seminar, the three of us went back to his office. He knew if you can visualize something, and really believe it and attach to it emotionally, wonderful things can happen. He was now excited and committed to the idea of doing something for the people of Barrie.

The next day he went to see the president and CEO of Telemedia, a marvellous man with a huge heart. When Bob told him his idea, he was given carte blanche with the company to make it happen. He put together a team, and the following Friday he hosted a meeting. He told them he wanted to use the awesome power they had right across Canada, and create something that could raise a serious amount of money.

Bob took a flip chart, and wrote three "3s" on the top. And then he said to all these executives, "How would you like to raise three million dollars in three hours, three days from now, and give it to the people in Barrie?"

Now they were acutely aware of the situation because their own radio station had been broadcasting it every few minutes. At first, they all said, "Templeton, you're crazy, you couldn't raise three million in three hours in three months from now, let alone in three days from now!" And Bob said, "Now wait a minute, I didn't ask you if we could, or even if we should. I asked 'Would you like to?'"

So he said, "Here's how we're going to do it." Under the three 3s he drew a line, and then he put a line right down the centre of the flip chart. On the left side of this "t" he wrote, "Why We Can't," and on the other side he wrote, "How We Can." Underneath 'Why We Can't,' he put a big "X". Then he said, "Every time an idea comes of why we can't do it, we're not going to spend any time on it. That's of no value. We're simply going to say, 'Next!' and we're going to spend the next few hours concentrating on how we can do this. And we're not going to leave the room until we have it figured out."

At first he didn't get much cooperation. And then somebody said, "We can have a radiothon right across Canada." So he wrote that down, under "How We Can", and then somebody else said, "We can't do that—we don't have radio stations right across Canada!"

Well, someone in the back of the room quietly said, "Next!" And Bob said, "No, a radiothon is a good idea— that will stand." Once they started buying into the process, it was magical. The creativity that began flowing from these broadcasters was really something to see. At that time, they had the sports rights for the Toronto Maple Leafs and the Blue Jays, and the people from that wing of Telemedia said, "We can get you the celebrities and the hockey players!" Somebody else was in network broadcasting and had contacts all across the country. Once they were locked into it, it was amazing how fast and furiously the ideas kept coming. The project took off like a brush fire!

Then someone said, "We could get Harvey Kirk and Lloyd Robertson, the biggest names in Canadian broadcasting, to anchor the show." Someone else replied, "We'll never get these guys to anchor the show; they're anchors on national television. They're not going to work on radio!"

And then a few of them said all together, "Next!"

So they put the thing together. Radio stations rarely work together; they're extremely competitive, and they're very cutthroat in every market. But somehow they got fifty radio stations across Canada to participate, based on the idea that it didn't matter who got the credit, as long as the people in Barrie got the money. The following Tuesday, they had a radiothon that went right across Canada. And yes, Harvey Kirk and Lloyd Robertson anchored it—on the radio. The dynamic duo had been apart for a number of years, but Bob and his team reunited them. When asked, they both responded "Absolutely, count on me."

Many legendary Canadian performers were asked to participate, and each one said, "I'll be there," "Count on me." If they were in town, they were there. One after the other they showed up at the station, and Lloyd and Harvey would talk with them about the tornado, and about their experiences living in the area. Some were on tour and phoned in from wherever they were. A lot of them were from the Toronto area, and of course, they were all shocked. It was kind of like, "This is something that happens in Kansas, not in our backyard!" It was very emotional.

The radiothon drew a huge audience. Lloyd and Harvey received nothing for their efforts; it was all out of the generosity of their hearts. But they raised the three million in three hours, three days after they began.

Back then, those homes were worth about 100 thousand dollars each. So Bob and his team like to think that instead of each of them writing a cheque to help out, they built thirty homes! Bob told me how very proud he is of being part of that effort. Obviously, he couldn't have done it alone. But one idea by one person, with the right people buying into it, can have dramatic and magical effects and produce something of greatness!

Bob Proctor
Willowdale, Ontario
with Bob Templeton
Halifax, Nova Scotia

Rise Again!

. . . There's one of the finest voices to ever express what Canada is. Stan Rogers. May we never forget him.

Her Excellency, The Right Honourable
Adrienne Clarkson, Governor General of Canada

Although my husband, Stan Rogers, died suddenly and tragically back in 1983, his music lives on in the hearts of Canadians. When people who have never heard Stan's music before hear it for the first time, they never forget it. It just somehow gets under their skin, and they recognize it instantly as something uniquely Canadian. They realize Stan is talking about them, and it makes him very special to them.

Although Stan was born and raised in Ontario, his family ties and his cultural roots were in the Canso area of Nova Scotia's Chetabucto shore. He travelled all over Canada and the United States, and he loved the excitement of playing gigs with other musicians, meeting different people, listening to their stories and always creating a great deal of emotion with his music. Wherever he sang, he connected with the people. But he always loved to go back to Nova Scotia and to the sea.

Often, Stan and his band members would end a concert with a rousing rendition of "The Mary Ellen Carter." This is a song about a group of fishermen, possibly Nova Scotian, who get caught in a violent October storm. Despite their desperate attempts to save the ship they love, which served them well, they are devastated when she goes down, due to the negligence of the captain. They hope she can be salvaged, but the owners are not interested. The men, therefore, vow to raise her themselves. Despite the difficulties they have to face, they are determined to make the *Mary Ellen Carter* rise again. In the last verse and final chorus of the song, the power of the human spirit to triumph over adversity is proclaimed with such great passion, everyone gets involved. With the crowd singing along, and Stan belting it out with everything he had, it was always one of his most popular songs.

One dark and stormy night, that song literally became a lifesaver. After a concert one evening, a man who had gone down with his ship—but who was ultimately saved—came up to Stan.

"Stan Rogers, I'm alive and here today because of you and your song, 'The Mary Ellen Carter.' I was on an old ship," he continued, "and we were carrying a load of coal when we got caught in a very bad storm. We didn't have very much warning. At about two o'clock in the morning, the ship was starting to get in trouble, then at about 4:15 in the morning, she cracked up and rolled over. I didn't want to be sucked down by the vortex when the ship sank, so I started swimming away as fast as I could. After about an hour, I ran across a swamped lifeboat, and I managed to get in. It was very cold, and as the night wore on, and the sea kept smashing down on top of me, I finally got to feeling I just couldn't take it any more. I was just about ready to give up, when all of a sudden, the words of your song came into my mind: 'Rise again! Rise again! No matter what you've lost, be it a home, a love, a friend, like the *Mary Ellen Carter*—rise again!'

"And I kept saying it over and over, and then the water would clear away, and then I'd shout it out, and then I'd sing it out, and then another wave would crash down on top of me. Stan, I firmly believe that if it weren't for me remembering those words, I had just reached the point where I couldn't have survived. There's no question in my mind that your song was the reason I lived through that night."

> "... *And you, to whom adversity has dealt the final blow,*
> *Turn to, and put out all your strength of arm and heart and brain,*
> *And like the* Mary Ellen Carter, *rise again!*
> *Rise again! Rise again!—Though your heart it be broken*
> *And life about to end.*
> *No matter what you've lost, be it a home, a love, a friend,*
> *Like the* Mary Ellen Carter, *rise again!*"

When we lost Stan, those of us who knew him and loved him faced our own dark night on the water. To think that such a vibrant spirit and voice could just be wiped out in seconds was almost too much to bear. But Stan's spirit lives on in his music, and like that sailor who saved his own life by hanging on to the song inside himself, we were able to find strength in the memory of who Stan was and in his inspiring words of determination and hope. Stan's own words helped us find the courage to go on— "And like the *Mary Ellen Carter*, rise again!"

Ariel Rogers
Dundas, Ontario

Gift of Wings

I have a sense of euphoric well-being when I fly, and I suspect that the same private ecstasy rises in the hearts of all pilots. Humans are shattered beings, but pilots heal themselves in the sky. Flying is an impudent act, a metaphor for freedom.

June Callwood

It happened on a perfect autumn day. It happened in a fraction of a second. Our love of hang gliding had brought about twenty-five of us to an eight hundred-foot ridge in upper New York state, one of my favourite sites. Just two years earlier, I had done my first high-soaring flight here, wheeling and dancing in the skies for almost three hours. The experience was overwhelming. Over the years I had pursued motorcycling, scuba diving under ice, barefoot waterskiing and skydiving. But after that first flight, I was totally captivated. Nothing could touch this. I knew I had found my sport.

September 12, 1981. As one of the instructors, I was first to launch and verify wind and thermal conditions. It had been gusty, but by two o'clock it looked settled enough. "Clear," I yelled, eager to fly. But just as I pushed off, a gust of wind stalled my wing. Moments later I smashed through the low-lying bushes, and then . . . total, surrealistic quietness.

It wasn't a violent crash, but at the moment of impact I felt a "twang"—as if some internal rubber band had snapped off its hooks. I had the sudden, sickening feeling that something overwhelming had happened. I ran a quick body check and then tried to flex my leg muscles. Nothing. When I reached down to touch them, there was no sensation. Then it hit me. I had broken my back. I was paralyzed.

Less than a hundred feet away, my friends awaited my call that everything was okay. But first I needed to grasp what had happened. My thoughts for the next thirty seconds were planted indelibly in my brain. *I've broken my back. I'm going to spend the rest of my life in a wheelchair. I don't think I can handle this. I don't think I want to live.* There was a short pause, and then I found myself insisting, *No! I still have my mind. I need to see this as a challenge. The issue here is not my broken back; it's my attitude. How I handle this is up to me.*

It was the most dramatic turning point of my life. In the space of a few seconds I had to make the transition from a world that celebrated physical activity to being in a wheelchair. Only then did I finally yell for help.

My new home following the accident was an electric circle bed in Kitchener-Waterloo Hospital. "You'd better get used to it," the staff informed me. "You're likely to be here for a couple of months."

While in the hospital, I asked myself the same questions repeatedly: *Who am I? Could this still be me? From Mr. Jock to this, all because one connection had been broken?* It seemed impossible. I had always known intellectually that I was equal parts body, mind and spirit. Now I began to feel that belief in my heart as well. If the most important part of my essence was spiritual, I realized that in the greater scheme of things, my broken back was secondary.

One day, I was totally immersed in these thoughts and looking for an affirmation of some kind. My answer came that evening. As I prepared for bed, I was startled to see my big toe move slightly—an unquestionable miracle! The next morning my therapist was awestruck to discover I had weak movement in every major muscle group of my lower body. We hugged and cried together out of sheer joy!

I had been told I would never move my lower body again, and yet I had. "A significant, spontaneous improvement in the lower extremities," was noted on my file. It seemed to me the word "miracle" was easier to spell.

The gift of healing continued, and within a few days, by supporting myself with parallel bars, I could stand. After four months of therapy, I could walk short distances using canes. By now I was in the rehabilitation wing. Two weeks after arriving, my old hang-gliding buddy Bob came to visit on a lovely, warm Saturday morning in October.

"We're going out to the parking lot to get some air," I told the nurse as I wheeled down the hall. I didn't tell her about the sign on my door, "Gone Flying." Our supposed "parking lot" was really a three hundred-foot grass strip behind a farmer's barn. There, resplendent with its rainbow-coloured wings, was Bob's gift of magic—his single-seat, ultralight plane, fully gassed and ready to fly.

Was I afraid? Yes, absolutely. This was not a flight to be rushed. But after several high-speed taxi runs to reorient myself, I felt ready. With heart-pounding anticipation, I pulled back on the throttle and took off. I was in the air. I was flying!

I flew that day. And flew and flew. As I buzzed the field and saw my empty wheelchair below, I was overcome by this serendipitous moment. Even if I couldn't walk, I could still fly! In that moment, I knew I would again find meaning and excitement in my life. I was ecstatic! I could fly! I would fly!

Two-and-one-half hours later, utterly euphoric, I headed back to the hospital. It had been the most memorable flight of my life. The sight of my empty wheelchair brought with it a leap of hope. Things could only get easier from now on.

My romance with flight continued. Within eight months of my accident, I was teaching eager students to fly in a new, two-seat ultralight. By the following summer, I had opened my own flight school. One day, an idea suddenly came to mind. *Why not fly one of these machines across Canada? If you can go twelve miles, why not 5,000?* And so the dream was born. Soon it became a clear conviction, not just a crazy idea—I knew I had to do it.

I decided to make the flight a fund-raising venture for the Canadian Paraplegic Association and tie it into Expo '86, the World's Fair in Vancouver.

"Forget it Carl," was the message from conventional pilots I spoke to. "This has never been done before with an ultralight." Not stated, but sometimes implied were the words ". . . let alone by someone in a wheelchair." And then there was the money. I calculated the cost would be over $100,000, and now I had to find the funds. But when Air Canada committed itself as a major sponsor, and Expo '86 endorsed my flight, I knew it was going to happen.

The planning was so endless, at one point I became overwhelmed and began to doubt myself. *Why am I taking this chance? What if the experts are right and this just isn't possible?* It was then I had to forgo my programmed need for security and make the deliberate decision to take a risk. Without that decision, the dream might have died at this point.

The big day finally arrived. Just outside Halifax Harbour, my ultralight bobbed gently in the Atlantic Ocean. I taxied out to open sea, took a deep breath and shoved the throttle full forward. Moments later I was airborne! At three hundred feet I banked right, gave a final wave—a dip of the wings—and then headed west to Vancouver, five-thousand long miles away. With a ground team travelling with me, I had to land every couple of hours to refuel. My memorable journey included moments of great euphoria and incidents of near disaster. Once, my engine failed at two hundred feet, resulting in a forced landing on the Trans-Canada Highway in northern Ontario. Often, it was fear that occupied the second seat of my craft. Had I chosen to remain focused on my fear, however, there were many places that the flight might have ended. Instead, I chose to keep my thoughts on my goal—Vancouver and Expo '86—and carry on. The media followed us on our journey, and CTV produced a one-hour documentary for Canadian television. In the end, my flight raised more than $100,000 for the Canadian Paraplegic Association.

If there was a moment of pure joy on this flight, it happened in August in the middle of the Rockies. At five-thousand feet I suddenly encountered a thermal, a column of warm air rising upward. My reactions were instinctive, and I was soon spiralling up higher and higher until I had passed eleven-thousand feet. Then magic happened. Off to my left, a bald eagle, less than one hundred feet away, drifted past my wing in effortless flight, silent as a shadow. For one brief moment, he turned toward me and our eyes locked. Time was suspended as this master of flight and I shared an almost sacred encounter. The spell broke just as quickly when the eagle dipped a wing, veered gracefully and disappeared. I flew on alone, overcome with a sense of wonderment and oneness with the sky.

August 28, 1986. It had been fifty-eight days and five-thousand miles, and now there were just thirty more miles to go. My heart was full with emotion as the Pacific Ocean slid into view.

"Gift of Wings, give us a smile on your left," my headset suddenly crackled. I jumped, startled by this intrusion. Off my left wing tip hung a huge helicopter with a photographer perched in its open door. A television news crew was filming this last chapter of my journey. We flew in formation over the city toward the coast, where I circled over the pavilions of Expo. I was suddenly tempted to turn and head back to the mountains. I wanted to keep flying. I had finally realized that the joy was not in reaching my destination, but in the journey itself.

The dream had come full circle. The journey from a simple idea to the actual flight had taken five full years. I pulled back the throttle for the last time and began my descent. Just off the beach of English Bay, I eased back on the stick and after a light bounce, splashed down for a perfect landing. I smiled as again the ultralight rocked gently in the ocean waves—this time the Pacific Ocean. I had done it! A coast-to-coast flight in an ultralight aircraft. I had been given my Gift of Wings!

Carl Hiebert
Waterloo, Ontario

Ultra light aircraft photo by Alan Ralston from Gift of Wings: An Aerial Celebration of Canada *by Carl Hiebert. Reprinted by permission of Alan Ralston. ©1981 Alan Ralston.*

David's Run

*P*erseverance *is not a long race; it is many short races one after another.*

Walter Elliot

It was the day of the big cross-country run. Students from seven different elementary schools in and around the small town of 100-Mile House, British Columbia, were warming up and walking the route through thick evergreen forest. In the five years I had been teaching at Horse Lake Elementary School, I had come to respect the tough pioneer spirit of the local people. Named for its location 100 miles from Lillooet, (mile zero on the old Cariboo Gold Rush Trail), and dotted with active cattle ranches, 100-Mile House sometimes seemed like a place out of time, with its horses, cowboys and cattle drives. At an elevation of 930 metres, 100-Mile House is a community in which spring comes late, snow comes early and winter sports are a local passion.

It was now late May and the ground had only just dried enough from the melting snow to hold the race. I looked around and finally spotted David, standing by himself off to the side by a fence. He was small for ten years old, with freckles and unruly red hair. But his usual big toothy grin was absent today. I walked over and asked him why he wasn't with the other children. The only response he gave me was he had decided not to run.

What was wrong? He had worked so hard for this event!

I quickly searched the crowd for the school's physical education teacher and asked him what had happened. "I was worried the other kids would laugh at him," he explained uncomfortably. "I thought there might be a fight if our kids tried to defend him. I gave him the choice to run or not, and let him decide."

I bit back my frustration. I knew the coach meant well and sincerely thought he was doing the right thing. After being assured David could run if he wanted, I turned to find him coming towards me, his small body rocking from side to side as he swung his feet forward, awkwardly walking on his toes.

David's cerebral palsy prevented him from walking or running like other children, but at school his peers thought of him as a regular kid. He always participated to the best of his ability in whatever they were doing. Which is why none of the children thought it unusual that David had decided to join the cross-country team. It just took him longer, that's all. David had not missed a single practice, and although he always finished his run long after the other children—he did always finish. He had stubbornly run a total of twenty-three kilometres in practice runs to prepare for that day's two-and-a-half-kilometre (1.5-mile) run, and he had asked me to come and watch. As a special education teacher at the school, I was familiar with the challenges David faced and was proud of his dogged determination.

We sat down together on some steps, but David wouldn't look at me. I quietly said, "David, if you don't want to run today, no one is going to make you. But if you're not running because you're afraid someone is going to laugh, that's not a good enough reason. There will always be someone who will laugh and say mean things. There are people like that, and that's just the way it is. The real question is whether you are going to let those few people stop you from doing something you really want to do. Are you going to let them get in your way? If you really want to run, David, then you run!"

I held my breath as David took this in. Then he looked at the field and said with a fierce but quiet determination, "I'm gonna run."

I stood on the sidelines with the excited crowd as David moved up to the starting line. The starter's gun sounded, and David lurched forward with the other children. But he had only gone a few metres before he tripped and fell flat on the ground. My heart sank. As I started to shout encouragement, other voices around me took up the call. "Come on David, you can do it!" I knew without even looking that these voices were not just those of his schoolmates. They came from parents, teachers and kids from other schools, who quickly understood the courage it took David to attempt this run.

David picked himself up and started again. All the other runners had disappeared over the hill. But it didn't matter. This was David's run. He had worked for it, and he wouldn't give up! As long as he was in sight, David heard people calling his name.

I waited anxiously by the finish line as the first runners completed the two-and-a-half kilometres of forest trails. Soon all of the other runners had come in and another race had begun. Still no David! I started to feel sick. Had I done the wrong thing? He hadn't checked out the trail with the other runners. Could he have become lost? Finally, a small figure emerged from the forest. With heels kicking out to the side and his body rocking with the rhythm of his run, David plodded toward the home stretch. He raised his arms in triumph as he crossed the finish line to wild cheers and applause.

Then, when David's coach slapped him on the back and said proudly, "Good job, David!" he caught my eye, flashed me a toothy grin and said, "That was easy!"

At the end of the year, the track coach asked the class to nominate one of their classmates for the athletic award for their grade. Without hesitation the whole class voted for David, saying that no one had worked harder for that award than he.

It was an amazing moment at our year-end assembly. The auditorium resounded with cheering and applause when David came forward and received his award for outstanding athletic achievement—from his beaming coach.

Linda Chamberlayne
Kelowna, British Columbia

The Making of a Miracle

To the immigrant who comes on dreams and bears the mirror that reflects us all. Keep faith— this place is capable of miracles.

Lindalee Tracey

A Scattering of Seeds

It had been five long years without our little daughter. How can I explain the desperate feeling? The situation seemed hopeless. We'd been in Canada for five years and had just received our fourth rejection letter from the Hungarian government. There was no explanation—as usual—just a short statement: "Your request cannot be fulfilled at this time."

In 1945, while fighting in Hungary against the invading Soviet forces, I was captured and forced to spend the next six years in a Soviet camp doing hard labour. My wife and I had been married only two months when I was captured, so we weren't reunited until April 1951. After my release, I was forced into exile as a state farm worker. Although she did not have to, my wife went with me voluntarily. Our beautiful baby daughter was born on August 15, 1952, while we were in exile.

After Stalin's death in 1953, my exile ended. My wife had a residency permit back in Budapest, Hungary, but as a former deportee, this status was denied to me. So I lived illegally with her in Budapest—where I worked as a bricklayer—in constant fear of being found out and arrested. In order to protect our beloved daughter, we sent her to live with my parents in a town close to the eastern border.

I was a strong supporter of the Hungarian freedom fighters, and in 1956, when they were subdued by the Soviets after a spontaneous uprising, we were suddenly forced to flee. First we headed for my parents' home to get our daughter, but our attempts to reach her failed. The Danube River flowed between Budapest and the town where my parents lived, and all the bridges that would have allowed us to cross the river were guarded as a result of the uprising. Budapest was now under siege, and we were in great personal danger. Despite our terrible despair over leaving our daughter behind, we had to leave.

With the help of some very good people, we made our escape from Hungary to Austria and eventually to Canada and to freedom. We settled in Winnipeg and started a new life. Our beautiful little daughter was only three years old when we came to Canada and began the process of applying for her to come join us in Winnipeg. Little did we know how many years it would take.

When we received our fourth rejection from the Hungarian government, I feared for my wife's emotional health. First she had waited six years for me to return from captivity; she had now been waiting another five years for our daughter to return to us. How much could one person endure? The most frustrating part of it was that with each rejection we were required to wait another six months before making another application.

Another six months! I couldn't bear waiting one moment longer. We had become Canadian citizens and were so very grateful for that, but the seemingly simple matter of reuniting our family remained out of our reach.

One day my wife said to me, "I'm going to pray for the intervention of St. Jude. He is the patron saint of hopeless causes."

"Fine with me," I replied. But I had lost faith in such supernatural intervention long ago. At that time, I was working in the basement of a downtown building in the evening as a sculptor. Day after day, after finishing my regular job, I went to work for a church supplies company for a few extra dollars. The bonus was, I was allowed to use the facilities for some of my own work—and sculpture is an art form that really requires a work space. In the church basement I was surrounded by dusty plaster fig- ures of various saints. My job was to finish them and pre- pare them for painting. *Hollow lifeless figures,* I thought to myself. *Ridiculous to expect any help from them.*

But what did I have to lose? Why not take a chance? One evening I made a sudden decision. I dropped my work pail and went to the heap of wood where I often chose pieces for my own carvings. There I found a nice block of basswood that seemed to offer itself up for the task I was planning.

I began to envision the features of St. Jude. I had to see him first in my imagination. In a sudden flash, I saw a bearded face full of dignity and hope. *That's it!* I thought. I put my chisel to the wood and started carving like I'd never carved before. The hours slipped away. Usually I arrived home at eight every evening, but on this occasion it was well past ten when I finally entered our little attic apartment.

I realized immediately that my wife was very agitated. "Where have you been?" she cried. "I was anxious to reach you, but there is no phone in that basement!"

"Why, what happened!" I asked.

"Look!" she said excitedly. "A new response from the Canadian government. They put some pressure on the Hungarian government, and they have finally relented. They're letting her go! Our daughter is coming to us in six weeks!"

I was speechless. Suddenly feeling weak, I reached for a chair to sit down. I gently placed my new carving on the kitchen table.

"What is that?" my wife asked.

"Don't you see? It's a statue of St. Jude," I replied. I told her then the reason why I was late, about my sudden impulse to carve and about my vision of St. Jude's face.

We looked at each other. There were no words to express our emotions. Joy, disbelief, shock—all of these and more were wrapped into one.

Six weeks later, my wife and I stood at the Winnipeg Airport waiting for the plane that would bring our daughter home to us, to Canada and to freedom. Back then, the airport was more like a barn in a large field. We saw the plane land, but it was far away across the field. I could see people disembarking. Guards were placed there to keep the waiting people back. And then, suddenly, I saw her! Our little girl—now almost ten years old! In an instant, I broke free of the guards. I ran to her and in one miraculous moment, embraced her. My heart was overjoyed. Our beloved daughter had finally come home!

Alex Domokos
Winnipeg, Manitoba

Liberation Day

To those who fall I say: You will not die but step into immortality. Your mothers will not lament your fate but will be proud to have borne such sons. Your names will be revered forever and ever by your grateful country, and God will take you unto Himself.

Lieutenant-General Sir Arthur Currie
Address to the Canadian Corps, March 1918

For the citizens of Mons, a small Belgian city south of Brussels on the French border, it seemed like the horrors of the Great War would never end. Since the German occupation endless years earlier in 1914, their lives had changed forever.

For the youngest, their memories were only of bombs and artillery shells shaking their beds and making their homes fall down around them. They dreamed of tanks and guns, and of strange men in uniforms walking through their streets. They knew the smell of death better than the smell of baking bread.

For the older Belgians, their memories were of a time

long-since passed . . . a time of peace that seemed a lifetime away . . . a time they feared they might never see again. Yet they lived in hope.

The first glimmer of hope arrived just after Easter in 1917 when they learned the Canadians had successfully taken Vimy Ridge. About eighty kilometres west of Mons, the Ridge had been occupied by the Germans in September of 1914. Rising over 130 metres above the surrounding land, it offered an unobscured view of all activities below. It was protected by many kilometres of trenches, underground tunnels and impenetrable walls of barbed wire. Concrete bunkers sheltering machine guns were constructed on top. Vimy Ridge became a virtually impregnable fortress.

Every Allied attempt to take Vimy had failed, but the Ridge was crucial to the Allies if they wished to win the War. The challenge was finally handed to the Canadians. In every battle they waged, the Canadian forces had been victorious, even against impossible odds. Certainly nothing seemed more impossible than conquering Vimy.

Arthur Currie was not a soldier by nature. He was, in fact, a British Columbian Realtor. But when the approach of war caused real estate to collapse, Currie joined the Canadian militia, and then devoured every book on military strategy he could find. As a result he was quickly promoted through the ranks, and by 1917, he was commander of the First Canadian Division. The burden of capturing Vimy Ridge from the German armies now fell on his shoulders.

When Currie studied past attempts at taking Vimy Ridge, he was convinced they had all been doomed to failure before they began. A completely new approach was needed—something totally unexpected. Vimy Ridge was impregnable, but he was determined to find a way to break it.

Arthur ordered intensive surveillance photos to be taken of the Ridge and all the surrounding land. These photos were then compiled into one large image of the entire area. For the first time in military history, detailed maps were made and distributed to every soldier. Meanwhile, with the help of the Allies, an exact replica of the Ridge complete with tunnels, trenches and caves, was constructed behind the front. There, Currie trained his men. After two months of intense training, the Canadians knew the Ridge as well as the Germans. Each man knew exactly where to go, and precisely what he would find when he got there.

On April 9, 1917, at 5:30 A.M., the assault began. It was daring and risky, and the Allied commands could only watch in amazement as events unfolded. Arthur Currie's unusual offensive left the enemy scratching their heads in wonder. Instead of being bombarded by artillery as they expected, the shells fell in a solid line far across the land below. The attackers appeared either very inept or extremely cunning. At predetermined times, the bombardment advanced 100 metres toward the Ridge, and behind it, with carefully paced steps, advanced the Canadians in what would be named the Vimy Glide. Every three minutes the army moved steadily forward, 100 metres at a time, shielded by the ever-advancing artillery fire.

The advance moved forward through all the barriers, and incessantly up Vimy Ridge. Bodies lay where they fell; they would have to wait for the stretcher-bearers and medics following behind. The advance must continue, and it did. When it was over, Vimy Ridge belonged to the Allies for the first time since the beginning of the war.

On that day, 3,598 Canadian soldiers died and 7,004 more were wounded, but this victory marked the "beginning of the end." For his efforts, General Arthur Currie was knighted by King George V on the Vimy battlefield and named commander in chief of the Canadian Expeditionary Force. Canadians were finally no longer considered simply colonials or subordinates. For the first time, they were now regarded as full Allies.

While the Germans regrouped, the Allies began forming their final offensive to liberate all of France and Belgium.

August 4, 1918, to November 11, 1918, became known as Canada's Hundred Days. Flanked by Australian and French troops, the Canadian "spearhead" advanced steadily eastward from Amiens (northeast of Paris) through France and into Belgium. Realizing defeat was imminent, the German High Command was devastated.

The advance continued incessantly. Losses were heavy on both sides, but in the end, freedom for the beleaguered French and Belgians lay in the wake of the terrible battles and bloodshed. Finally, in the early morning hours of November 11, Canadian troops marched into Mons. The words of Victor Maistrau, bourgmestre (mayor) of Mons, describe that moment:

> *At five in the morning of the 11th, I saw the shadow of a man and the gleam of a bayonet advancing stealthily along that farther wall, near the Café des Princes. Then another shadow, and another. They crept across the square, keeping very low, and dashed north toward the German lines.*
>
> *I knew this was liberation. Then, above the roar of artillery, I heard music, beautiful music. It was as though the Angels of Mons were playing. And then I recognized the song and the musician. Our carillonneur (church bell ringer) was playing 'O Canada' by candlelight. This was the signal. The whole population rushed into the square, singing and dancing, although the battle still sounded half a mile away.*

In the city hall at six in the morning I met some Canadians and we drank a bottle of champagne together. We did not know that this was the end of the war.

The dawn revealed a strange sight in the square. The Canadian troops, exhausted from their long offensive, lay sleeping on the cobblestones while all Mons danced around them.

That same morning, on the eleventh hour of the eleventh day of the eleventh month, the Armistice was signed. World War I, "The Great War," was over.

Neil Simpson
Peterborough, Ontario

4

ON LOVE

*From the beginning of life to its end,
love is the only emotion which matters.*

June Callwood

For Better or For Worse®

by Lynn Johnston

One True Love

When Henri Bissette of Sherbrooke, Québec, went off to fight in World War I in 1917, he left behind his love of four years, Émilie Chevrier. The two wrote to each other faithfully. Letters could not always cross the battle lines, however, and eventually their writing became less frequent.

Émilie missed Henri terribly and constantly prayed for his safe return. One day in April 1918, Henri's family received a letter informing them that their son was "missing in action." When Émilie heard the report she was devastated and refused to believe that Henri was gone. Six months later, when no further information had been received, Émilie finally realized that she would never see her beloved again.

Five months after the armistice was signed, ending the Great War, Émilie received a letter that Henri had written almost one year earlier. In it, he wrote about his feelings of desperation and his longing to leave the horrific war. His only desire was to return home to Canada so that he and Émilie could be married. The letter reassured Émilie that Henri's love was a true one, and although she kept all his letters, she treasured this one the most.

Émilie felt deep in her heart that she could never love another man as much as she loved Henri. He was her one true love, and she promised herself that she would never marry. In 1921, however, she met a kind, caring man named Joseph who she married shortly thereafter. They moved to Ottawa, where they raised a family of four children and lived happily until Joseph passed away in 1959.

Émilie was sixty years old when Joseph died, and her full-grown children were living lives of their own. Finding herself alone, she decided to return to her hometown of Sherbrooke, Québec, to enjoy her retirement years.

One day while out shopping, Émilie met an old school friend and the two reminisced about their past. During their conversation her friend mentioned Henri—she hadn't known about his war experience or his being "missing in action." When Henri's name came up, Émilie told her friend about everything that had occurred over forty years ago.

When she heard the story, her friend replied, "How odd! I'm sure I remember hearing that Henri bought a farm up north in the 1930s."

Émilie assured her friend that she must have been misinformed. After the two parted company, however, Émilie couldn't help wondering about the woman's story. *Could it be true?* she wondered. Surely, if Henri were alive, the two of them would be together now. Émilie needed to know the truth, but Henry's family had long since passed away. She began to investigate on her own and soon discovered that there was a Henri Bissette—he owned a farm just west of Trois-Rivières, Québec. Émilie decided to visit Trois-Rivières and make a trip out to the farm. She did not hold out much hope that she would really find her Henri. It was over forty years since she had received word of his death. In all likelihood, when the farmhouse door opened, she would simply find some farmer standing there—one who might be amused by her story.

When Émilie arrived at the farm and knocked on the door, however, she received the shock of her life. As the door opened, a farmer indeed stood there, but it was her own beloved Henri! He was greatly aged, of course, but still as handsome as she remembered. Henri gasped, recognising her instantly, and whispered, "Émilie!"

The two fell into each other's arms, so overcome with emotion that for several minutes all they could do was hug each other, crying and trembling. A lifetime had passed since they had last seen each other, but now it felt as if no time had passed at all.

When they calmed down, they both started to talk at once about what had happened over the years. Henri explained that after being wounded, he had spent over a year and a half recuperating in a hospital in Europe. When he finally did return to Sherbrooke, his family told him that the heartbroken Émilie, believing he was dead, had married and moved to Ottawa. They had no other information about her whereabouts. Henri was greatly saddened, but didn't want to disrupt Émilie's happiness in her life. He bought his farm shortly after, and had lived alone there all these years. He had never married because he knew that Émilie was his one true love.

With tears running down her face, Émilie pulled Henri's wartime letters from her purse.

"I never forgot you either, Henri," she said. "These letters have meant more to me over the years than you can ever know. I would always read them over and over when I began to feel sad, and it made me so happy to remember that you were the most special part of my life."

All at once the forty years of separation melted away. Finding each other had made them happier than they had ever been. Shortly after their reunion, they were married, and spent the rest of their days together on Henri's farm.

Crystal Wood
Winnipeg, Manitoba

Letters of Hope

Life holds us like the moon and the sea.
Far, far apart;
The image of the moon shines in the sea.
Yours in my heart.

Laura Thompson

"Love is patient, love is kind. . . . It always protects, always trusts, always hopes, always perseveres." (1 Corinthians 13:4,7). Our Gran Lindsay, who lives in Burlington, Ontario, has this scripture printed on a magnet on her fridge. To visitors it is only a magnet; to our family it is a gentle reminder of a cherished family story.

It all began with a message in the town newspaper: "For Lindsay—Darling, I am well. Hope you and the children are fine." The year was 1943. A ham radio operator had picked up the fragmented message and directed it to the small-town newspaper.

Martha Lindsay had waited thirteen long months for word from the Red Cross that her husband, William Lindsay, had survived the sinking of the HMS *Exeter* on March 1, 1942. She did her best to stay busy with the children, always keeping William in her prayers. One afternoon, the Red Cross finally contacted her with the news that she had been praying for—a William Lindsay had been located and was presently a prisoner of war.

Martha's heart soared: William was alive! She had never given up hope. The Red Cross told Martha to begin writing messages to William—short messages, no more than twenty-five words, on a plain, white postcard—and forwarding them to Geneva. From there, the Red Cross would try to get the postcards to William.

Only one postcard a month was permitted. Martha began by telling William about the antics of their children, Billy and Catherine, who had been babies the last time he saw them. She also did her best to express her love and devotion to her husband on the small, white postcards. In just twenty-five words, she kept reminding him that he was loved. Two and a half agonizing years came and went without receiving an answer from William, but Martha's faith and hope never faltered.

One September morning in 1945, as Martha was getting ready to take the children to school, the mail carrier delivered a small scrap of paper through the mail slot. It had no envelope and no stamp. As she turned the paper over her heart began to pound. Soon her eyes filled with tears as she recognized William's handwriting: "Martha, I've been released. I'm coming home."

On a beautiful day in October 1945, William Lindsay returned home to his family. After their tears and joy had subsided, Martha asked William if he had received her cards. Sadly, she learned that not one card had found its way to him in the prisoner-of-war camp.

Shortly after William's return home, there was a knock at the door one day. Martha answered and found a young sailor standing in the doorway.

"Excuse me, are you Martha Lindsay?" he asked.

"Yes I am," she replied.

"Was your husband a prisoner of war?"

"Yes," she whispered.

With tears in his eyes, he introduced himself. "My name is William Lindsay. I was a prisoner of war, too." He reached into his pocket and, very gently, handed her thirty tiny white postcards tied in a ribbon.

"I received one of these every month," the sailor told her. "They gave me the hope that helped me to survive. From the bottom of my heart I thank you."

Martha just as gently placed the cards back in his hands, and he held them to his heart.

"Love is patient, love is kind. . . . It always protects, always trusts, always hopes, always perseveres" (1 Corinthians 13:4,7).

Shelley McEwan
Sarnia, Ontario
as told to her by Gran Martha Lindsay

That Sunday Afternoon

The plan on which this life is built is somewhat like a patchwork quilt.

E.J. Pratt

It was the first warm day of spring, about 20° C with a clear Calgary sky and full afternoon sun. Only a handful of people were around as I jogged through the park. Ahead was an elderly gentleman in a worn cardigan, sitting on a wooden bench a few feet off the path. He was somewhat secluded, nestled among the poplars and aspens, which were leafing out and stretching their wings. He had found a shaft of sunlight wending its way among the branches; he was enjoying the radiant sun on his face.

I was ready for a break to catch my breath and check my pulse. I sat next to him, looked at my watch, and started counting my heartbeats. After a few seconds, he interrupted my focus by asking how often I jogged. Being somewhat preoccupied with counting, I responded without making eye contact and muttered, "Two or three times a week." He persisted and attempted to engage me in the small talk that one engages in with a stranger.

His genuineness and comfortable smile eventually won me over, and soon we were talking about everything under the sun. We first discussed the timing of spring, our favourite television programs and great places we had visited in Canada. Unexpectedly, we began revealing our politics, exchanging our different experiences as parents, and expressing deeper feelings about the people we loved. He mentioned that his daughter and her ten-year-old son, Jason, were coming to Calgary in a couple of weeks to visit him; he hadn't seen them for two years. How he looked forward to their visit! "You know," he said, touching my arm, "family shouldn't be separated. We should be with people we love and who love us." I nodded.

In-and-out, back-and-forth we went, revealing meaningful moments in our lives, paths taken and not taken, laughing, and occasionally misting at the corners of our eyes. We touched one another, emotionally and physically; a sense of mutual "knowing" washed over us. I learned that he was a widower and gently poked him when he mentioned a certain woman he had recently met in the nearby retirement village. He smiled at the compliment; I could see the face of a young man in his eyes.

I think it was the late afternoon chill that broke the moment between us. I looked down at my watch. What seemed like a half-hour had actually been three hours! We had been captured in a moment, totally unaware of time and place. We who were strangers had somehow become soul mates. It was a serendipitous meeting and yet magical in the "connection" that occurred.

We bade our gentle farewells, "See ya around," smiling and waving as we parted. We knew we probably wouldn't meet again, and why should we? We had never met before despite having engaged in the same activities in the same park many times before.

Several days later, while putting newspapers into a recycling bin, I chanced to see the old man's picture in *The Calgary Herald*, on the back page, in the obituaries: "Mr.— is survived by. . . . In lieu of flowers, please send donations to the Canadian Heart and Stroke Foundation." Tears welled up in my eyes. They trickled down my cheeks as I drove home; I didn't brush them away. I was also crying for his daughter and her not having had that moment of closeness with him that I just had on that Sunday afternoon. Arriving home, I sat down and wrote her a brief letter, describing the chance meeting and what we had talked about. I hoped it might ease her grief knowing that she was loved and in his thoughts before his passing. I addressed it in care of the funeral home.

It was almost eight months later when an envelope arrived postmarked "Brandon, Manitoba." I didn't know anyone from Brandon, at least that I could recall. As I began reading, I realized it was from the old gentleman's daughter. There was a carefulness and kindliness in the letter that brought him vividly back to mind:

Dear Mr. Fouts,

Please excuse the tardiness of this letter. I'm sure you can understand. I wish to acknowledge your warm generosity of spirit for letting me know that Dad had Jason and me in his thoughts just before he died. You were probably the last person that he talked to in his life, since he was found in the park later in the day where you said you had met. It was close to his apartment. I wish to thank you for being the kind of person you are to talk to an old man sitting alone on a park bench. I take comfort in knowing that you were there with him—if only for a brief time—to share the sunshine and a few thoughts. Thank you so much.

I put her letter away with the picture of the old gentleman from the paper. Later, as I went for my jog through the park, I approached the same bench where we had met eight months before. No one sat there now on this cold December day, but as I jogged past, I was filled with the memory of our special connection and all the things we had shared on that Sunday afternoon. With a warm feeling in my heart, I gave a little salute and carried on.

Gregory Fouts
Calgary, Alberta

My Dad and Little Joe

A good dog is so much a nobler beast than an indifferent man that one sometimes gladly exchanges the society of one for that of the other.

William Butler

Dad and Mom both immigrated to Canada from Iceland, their families settling in Lundar and Gimli, Manitoba. After they met and married, they moved to Winnipeg where Dad started his boat-building business in a shop attached to our house. Putting in nails was our job: As kids we were small enough to get to the underside of the boat, and it saved dad a lot of time.

Like many families, eventually we had a dog. Little Joe was a brown, short-legged, sausage-shaped dog of dubious ancestry who supposedly belonged to my sister Anna. I use the word "supposedly" because, with great tail wagging and thumping, Little Joe came to anyone who paid attention to him. We all loved him dearly, as did the rest of the neighbourhood kids.

Little Joe's lack of pedigree caused him no discomfort, nor did it cast any stigma. He trotted around the streets as though he were nobility, his foolish little head held high, bestowing an innocent doggy smile on all he met— including vehicular traffic. We tried to teach him about the dangers of the road, and finally resorted to locking him in the yard. However, on one unforgettable day, Little Joe dug a hole under the fence and bounded out to visit all the friends he knew.

Sometime later, a tearful delegation consisting of the younger members of our family augmented by excited neighbourhood children brought home the alarming news that a truck had seriously injured Little Joe. He now lay down the road awaiting death by a policeman's bullet, the accepted method in those days of dispatching injured animals.

We children ran to the scene of the accident, where a small crowd had gathered around our hapless Joe. Though his eyes were open, he lay pitifully stretched out, apparently unable to move. Tears filled our eyes and also the eyes of some of the bystanders as Little Joe showed that he recognized us with a feeble wag of his tail. We huddled around him, frustrated by our inability to respond to the appeal for help we read in his eyes. And we were terrified by the pistol in the holster of the approaching policeman. He motioned us away from the dog and drew his gun.

Wide-eyed, and with the defenselessness of small children looking up into a tall adult world, we began to back away with feet that seemed to be made of lead. We looked into the faces of those around us. No one could help us, and no one could help Little Joe.

Suddenly we became aware of a commotion, and the crowd parted. My father was elbowing his way through the circle of onlookers. He spoke with authority to the young policeman. "Put that thing away! You don't use a gun around children!"

Then, bending on one knee on the road, he removed his worn work jacket and carefully wrapped it around Little Joe. Perhaps many events in a child's life reach exaggerated proportions as time passes, but to this day I remember that had my father's rough, work-worn hands been those of a great surgeon, Little Joe's broken body could not have been moved with more gentleness. I cannot swear that the emotion that I saw in our dog's eyes was gratitude, but I like to think that it was.

I'll never forget that homeward journey. My father was the master of the situation. With Little Joe wrapped in his jacket, he led a procession of admiring children, tear-stained but no longer crying. We held our heads high with pride as we marched behind the man who had stopped an execution and saved our dog. He might have been a great general leading his troops but for the fact that his uniform was baggy-kneed overalls, his sword a carpenter's rule.

For many nights we thought Little Joe's life was over. In fact, the veterinarian we summoned did not even bother to return, he was so certain our dog would not survive. But my father spoke with resolution as he knelt beside the wooden nail box that served as a makeshift hospital bed.

"He has fight in him. Wait."

So we waited. Sure enough, Little Joe survived. He went on to live a long life, and my dad—he built many more boats.

Our ostensibly stern father would probably not have stood out in a crowd; in stature he was a little above average. But I know of an army of kids and a sausage-shaped dog who, on that one special day, watched him become a giant.

Sigrun Goodman Zatorsky
Winnipeg, Manitoba

Big Red

The first time we set eyes on "Big Red," father, mother and I were trudging through the freshly fallen snow on our way to Hubble's Hardware store on Main Street in Huntsville, Ontario. We planned to enter our name in the annual Christmas drawing for a chance to win a hamper filled with fancy tinned cookies, tea, fruit and candy. As we passed the Eaton's department store's window, we stopped as usual to gaze and do a bit of dreaming.

The gaily decorated window display held the best toys ever. I took an instant hankering for a huge green wagon. It was big enough to haul three armloads of firewood, two buckets of swill or a whole summer's worth of pop bottles picked from along the highway. There were skates that would make Millar's Pond well worth shovelling and dolls much too pretty to play with. And they were all nestled snugly beneath the breathtakingly flounced skirt of Big Red.

Mother's eyes were glued to the massive flare of red shimmering satin, dotted with twinkling sequin-centred black velvet stars. "My goodness," she managed to say in trancelike wonder. "Would you just look at that dress!" Then, totally out of character, mother twirled one spin of a waltz on the slippery sidewalk. Beneath the heavy, wooden-buttoned, grey wool coat she had worn every winter for as long as I could remember, mother lost her balance and tumbled. Father quickly caught her.

Her cheeks redder than usual, mother swatted dad for laughing. "Oh, stop that!" she ordered, shooing his fluttering hands as he swept the snow from her coat. "What a silly dress to be perched up there in the window of Eaton's!" She shook her head in disgust. "Who on earth would want such a splashy dress?"

As we continued down the street, mother turned back for one more look. "My goodness! You'd think they'd display something a person could use!"

Christmas was nearing, and the red dress was soon forgotten. Mother, of all people, was not one to wish for, or spend money on, items that were not practical. "There are things we need more than this," she'd always say, or, "There are things we need more than that."

Father, on the other hand, liked to indulge whenever the budget allowed. Of course, he'd get a scolding for his occasional splurging, but it was all done with the best intention.

Like the time he brought home the electric range. In our old Muskoka farmhouse on Oxtongue Lake, Mother was still cooking year-round on a wood stove. In the summer, the kitchen would be so hot even the houseflies wouldn't come inside. Yet, there would be Mother—roasting—right along with the pork and turnips.

One day, Dad surprised her with a fancy new electric range. She protested, of course, saying that the wood stove cooked just dandy, that the electric stove was too dear and that it would cost too much hydro to run it. All the while, however, she was polishing its already shiny chrome knobs. In spite of her objections, Dad and I knew that she cherished that new stove.

There were many other modern things that old farm needed, like indoor plumbing and a clothes dryer, but Mom insisted that those things would have to wait until we could afford them. Mom was forever doing chores— washing laundry by hand, tending the pigs and working in our huge garden—so she always wore mended, cotton- print housedresses and an apron to protect the front. She did have one or two "special" dresses saved for church on Sundays. And with everything else she did, she still man- aged to make almost all of our clothes. They weren't fancy, but they did wear well.

That Christmas I bought Dad a handful of fishing lures from the Five to a Dollar store, and wrapped them indi- vidually in matchboxes so he'd have plenty of gifts to open from me. Choosing something for Mother was much harder. When Dad and I asked, she thought carefully then hinted modestly for some tea towels, face cloths or a new dishpan.

On our last trip to town before Christmas, we were dri- ving up Main Street when Mother suddenly exclaimed in surprise: "Would you just look at that!" She pointed excit- edly as Dad drove past Eaton's.

"That big red dress is gone," she said in disbelief. "It's actually gone."

"Well . . . I'll be!" Dad chuckled. "By golly, it is!"

"Who'd be fool enough to buy such a frivolous dress?" Mother questioned, shaking her head. I quickly stole a glance at Dad. His blue eyes were twinkling as he nudged me with his elbow. Mother craned her neck for another glimpse out the rear window as we rode on up the street. "It's gone . . ." she whispered. I was almost certain that I detected a trace of yearning in her voice.

I'll never forget that Christmas morning. I watched as Mother peeled the tissue paper off a large box that read "Eaton's Finest Enamel Dishpan" on its lid.

"Oh Frank," she praised, "just what I wanted!" Dad was sitting in his rocker, a huge grin on his face.

"Only a fool wouldn't give a priceless wife like mine exactly what she wants for Christmas," he laughed. "Go ahead, open it up and make sure there are no chips." Dad winked at me, confirming his secret, and my heart filled with more love for my father than I thought it could hold!

Mother opened the box to find a big white enamel dishpan—overflowing with crimson satin that spilled out across her lap. With trembling hands she touched the elegant material of Big Red.

"Oh my goodness!" she managed to utter, her eyes filled with tears. "Oh Frank . . ." Her face was as bright as the star that twinkled on our tree in the corner of the small room. "You shouldn't have . . ." came her faint attempt at scolding.

"Oh now, never mind that!" Dad said. "Let's see if it fits," he laughed, helping her slip the marvellous dress over her shoulders. As the shimmering red satin fell around her, it gracefully hid the patched and faded floral housedress underneath.

I watched, my mouth agape, captivated by a radiance in my parents I had never noticed before. As they waltzed around the room, Big Red swirled its magic deep into my heart.

"You look beautiful," my dad whispered to my mom—and she surely did!

Linda Gabris
Prince George, British Columbia

Hopfstadt's Cabin

Love is all we have, and the only way that we can help each other.

Euripides

The summer of 1944 was the most memorable of my life. It was the year I had my tenth birthday and the last year we lived on the farm: It was the summer when, for the only time in my life, I saw a man cry and the summer I learned der Fuehrer's secret.

The stony quarter section my family owned near Darwell, Alberta, was good for nothing but grazing. To make a living my father followed his trade to the city, leaving my mother and me alone on the farm. My father is a shadowy memory to me, a tall man in a blue serge suit who came home at Christmas and on an occasional Sunday.

I was a shy and lonely child, and I think that's why I liked Hopfstadt so much. Hopfstadt was a big stolid man with a red complexion and blond hair that bristled every which way. He had emigrated from Germany in 1936 and settled about three miles from our farm.

It was my job, twice a week during the summer, to walk

the five miles to the post office, pick up our mail and Hopfstadt's, and deliver his on the way home. I vividly remember that he wore ordinary overalls and a denim smock jacket instead of the bib overalls and bulky sweater the other farmers all wore.

And of course, there was the dog: a great German shepherd, kept on a tether chain in front of the granary that served as a home for Hopfstadt. The dog would bark wildly and lunge on the chain whenever anyone approached. Hopfstadt would quiet him by speaking in German and calling him a strange guttural name that no one was ever able to catch.

I loathed the dog. My greatest fear was that he would break the chain and attack me when I came with the mail. I could never understand why a kind man like Hopfstadt kept a vicious beast like der Fuehrer.

Der Fuehrer was the nickname the neighbours had given the dog. A real killer they all said. Dogs like that are trained to kill.

When the war started, the neighbours made bad jokes about Hopfstadt and der Fuerhrer. The more patriotic ones would have snubbed Hopfstadt if they had been given the chance, but he seldom left the farm.

He worked like a demon from dawn to dusk, eking out a living on the muskeg quarter section he farmed. He'd been a carpenter in the old country; farming was new to him, and he was not good at it.

Whenever I came by, Hopfstadt would smile and hiss a few words I didn't understand. Then he'd disappear inside the granary for a moment and return with a small horehound candy. He'd press the amber circle into my hand, pat me on the head and say, "Iss gute boy,"—along with a few other words I could never understand.

Hopfstadt had a tractor, a huge, steel-wheeled monster that sat in a shed by the gate. One day he was starting it when I arrived. We had no tractor, or car for that matter, and I must have been wide-eyed with curiosity.

"Rhide," said Hopfstadt, taking me under the arms and lifting me onto the iron beast. Four times we rode around the small ploughed area behind the granary, dragging the harrows behind the tractor. The wind was brisk and we were both choked with dust. When we finished, we shared a dipper of cold water from the well. It was one of the happiest moments of my life.

On one of his infrequent visits to our farm, he told my mother that a girl was coming from the old country to marry him. A childhood sweetheart—as near as mother could understand. Shortly after, in the scrub pines behind the granary, there emerged a large, comfortable looking cabin. Hopfstadt continued to live in the granary, apparently saving the cabin for his bride. After the war began, however, the pale purple, parchment envelopes, postmarked Berlin and addressed in a small, neat hand to Herr Eberhardt Hopfstadt, stopped coming. Then one day a dozen of Hopfstadt's letters to Germany were returned in a bundle. Across the top letter were several words written in German, in red ink.

When I approached the farm with the package, all was quiet. Hopfstadt and der Fuehrer were nowhere to be seen. I set the mail on the granary step and walked around to the cabin. The door was unlocked, and I looked inside.

Never had I seen anything like it! The kitchen had a full set of cabinets, polished and decorated in the most ornate manner. Tiptoeing in, I peered toward the living room: there were chairs, tables and bookcases, each piece lovingly carved and beautiful beyond belief. In the bedroom was a large, elaborate, four-poster bed, and beside it, a cradle with kitten faces carved on either end. They were so real I had to touch them, just to be sure.

A low rumbling sound came, and there in the doorway

stood der Fuehrer, with burning yellow eyes. I froze. The fearful growl came again.

Desperately I looked around for Hopfstadt.

If only I knew the dog's name, I could talk to him. Rooted to the spot, I watched him advance. He reached me, his head thrust out, and licked my trembling hand. He was as gentle as his master was.

Hopfstadt appeared a moment later, the package of letters in his hand.

He must have just come from in the fields, and I could see that his dusty cheeks were stained with tears. He tousled my hair with his huge hands, put one arm around my shoulders and pulled me close for a moment. He repeated over and over again a few words in German, his voice so plaintive, so yearning that I was on the verge of crying, too.

Hopfstadt was strong and he smelled like work. I wanted to share his sorrow. I knew at that moment we could have fended off the whole world. We were comrades who together could face anything. In that moment I loved him, but the words of comfort and courage did not come—and what had his words meant? Our moment ended when he turned and slipped from the cabin.

He returned with the remainder of the bag of candies, which he handed to me in silence.

I cried all the way home.

I carried Hopfstadt's parting words in the back of my mind for many years. A short time ago I made a call on a German-Canadian businessman. I repeated the words to him as best as I could remember.

"It must have been someone who admired you very much," he said. "The words mean, 'A son like you'. . . . I wanted a son like you."

William P. Kinsella
Sumas, Washington

When Someone Believes in You

When Marco was a boy, he tried everything to get his father's love and attention. He worked hard to earn exceptional marks; he tried to be obedient, he chose inspiring friends and always tried to behave well.

Sensitive and shy, he was so timid he always wore turtle-neck shirts. He hid behind his hair, which he wore long around his face and ears. To make it worse, Marco was naturally shorter than the other kids. And because his good marks had allowed him to skip second grade—he was younger than everyone else. This added nothing to his already low self-confidence.

When Marco was eight his parents divorced, and Marco was sent to a boarding school. Six years later, he and his young sister Sandra moved in with their dad and his new wife in St-Léonard, a French Canadian and Italian neighbour-hood on the east side of Montreal. Between his work and his new young wife, it felt to Marco that his father had little time for him and Sandra. Except for his demands around chores after school, communication was nonexistent. It seemed to Marco the only time his dad ever spoke to him was to be demanding or critical. He began to dread coming home from school every day.

Marco sank further into his low self-esteem and was overwhelmed with feeling unappreciated, inadequate, depressed and confused. He felt desperately alone and isolated.

One day his father, already tired after a long day, tripped over Marco's bike in the garage. The angry confrontation that followed left Marco feeling violated and humiliated. It seemed no matter how hard he tried he could never do anything right. In despair Marco blurted out, "That's it! It's enough! I'm going to commit suicide."

"You?" replied his dad disparagingly, and without hesitation. " You don't even have the guts!"

For two days, Marco felt so miserable all he could think of was wanting to die so he could leave this enormous pain, those overwhelming feelings of rejection and unworthiness. But then he thought, "If I kill myself, I will never get to live, appreciate life and I will leave my mother, grandmother and sister that I love. They'll be so hurt and I don't want to do that to them. But if I don't, then my dad will be right—and he will win."

Angry, sad and confused, Marco was stuck. He went back to school, and retreated into silent isolation.

Two days later, his aunt called him. To Marco, this seemed like a miracle. Aunt Ginette usually only called once a year, on his birthday. She said she had just seen some young teenagers participate in a public speaking contest called Gala Personnalité sponsored by Club Optimiste—and she thought about him. She thought he should give it a try. She told him she firmly believed he could perform on stage like the other kids, since she had seen him do skits for the family at Christmas.

Marco was startled, and not a little taken aback. Him? Onstage? In a public speaking contest? To agree would be contrary to his entire shy, timid personality. But Aunt Ginette was so confident. She seemed really serious. She was sure it was something he could do. She truly believed in him. And feeling her strong belief, Marco went against all odds, against everything he had ever done or felt, and agreed to enter the contest.

All that winter of 1980 to 1981, twice a week after dinner, he took three different buses in each direction for the three-hour round-trip to practice in Ville d'Anjou, where the competition would take place. Marco was taken by an energy he never felt before. The hours and the obstacles no longer counted. The criticism from his father and his stepmother around his absence for after-dinner chores didn't matter. His father disapproved of this new dream, fearing it would take away from his homework time and impact his marks. But Marco was a top performer in school and never missed a day. His dad really did love him and wanted the best for him, but his own insecurity made him react to anything that might jeopardize his son's future. Even his sister helped to move him towards his dream by taking care of the dishes on those evenings, for "future considerations". She was only twelve, but very perceptive and generous.

Four months later, the big night arrived. His mother, his sister, his grandmother, and yes, his Aunt Ginette, were all in the audience. The nine other contestants were all older than him. Marco was overwhelmed—the whole thing just felt so much bigger than him, and butterflies filled his stomach. But when he stepped onto the stage and began to speak, he felt totally at home, totally at peace, and a kind of bliss stole over him. He was funny, witty and acted extremely natural as he spoke. The audience loved him! He felt energized and very alive—it felt like a real birth. To his shock and amazement, he WON!

When he saw his mother's face, her eyes were glowing—she was so proud. He realized then she believed in him, just like his Aunt Ginette.

As the winner, Marco went on to the regional final, where he won again! His name was published in the local papers, and he knew this was the start of his new life, and a new Marco. He began to believe in himself. His self-esteem and self-confidence started to grow. Not only did he feel he deserved to live, but he began to realize he deserved to be happy and respected. That contest was a truly defining moment in his life.

Today, Marco is one of Canada's rising keynote speakers, educating, inspiring and entertaining audiences around the world. As I travel around the world to speak to thousands of people every year, I tell them Marco's story. I tell them his story because it is my story.

It all happened because of a single phone call, from one single person who simply believed in me. Because of her, I have been able to more than fulfill than my dreams. I've been able to inspire and to touch the lives of so many others—and help them fulfill theirs.

Marc André Morel,
Montreal, Québec

A Son's Love

Where love is, there is God also.

Leo Tolstoy

Our church congregation in Toronto has a way of assisting those who have financial difficulties without making the recipient feel shame or guilt. Money is dropped into an offering box with only the name of the recipient on the envelope. The envelopes are then distributed to those members without them knowing the name of the giver.

There came a time when my husband and I were among those in need. We did not talk about our financial difficulty with anyone. The only reason our children knew was because we had to cut back on many things. Still, we hoped they were not aware of the extent of our need, nor of how much their father and I were suffering because of it. We did not want to burden them with a problem they could do nothing to solve.

Our situation wasn't improving, and my husband and I knew that we would have to look for outside help. Just as we reached the point of despair, our church gave us a gift envelope that had been left in the offering box. We were overjoyed to receive a very substantial amount of money, enough to bring us through that desperate time. We couldn't help but wonder who had given such a generous gift. We were extremely relieved and enormously grateful.

A year later, our seventeen-year-old son was applying for a student loan so he could attend university. It was then we discovered that his savings account was almost empty. His father and I were very disturbed by this. We had trusted him to put part of his wages from his part-time job into the bank towards his education. From the time he was nine years old he had been a paper carrier for *The Toronto Star,* and he had worked very hard for his small earnings. I asked him repeatedly to tell me where the money had gone. At first he would not tell me, which made me even angrier. I would not let the matter alone. I kept hounding him, determined to find out where the money had gone.

Finally, in tears, and with great reluctance, my son admitted that the year before he had put his savings in the offering box for his father and me. I stood there speechless, tears filling my eyes. It had taken my son years to save that money. He had given it to us willingly—without telling us what he had done.

J. P. Bailey
London, Ontario

Kids Can Free the Children

The Inuit have fifty-two names for snow because it is important to them; there ought to be as many for love.

Margaret Atwood

It began on an ordinary day in April 1995. Like most mornings in my Thornhill, Ontario, home, I planned to read the comics while eating breakfast before leaving for school, but a newspaper headline grabbed my attention. "Battled Child Labour, Boy, Twelve, Murdered." The story told how, at the age of four, Iqbal Masih's parents had sold him to a carpet maker in Islamabad, Pakistan, for $16 to pay off a family debt. When he was twelve, he managed to escape and began a crusade to help other enslaved children. For his efforts, he'd been killed by a carpet maker's assassin.

I was stunned and sickened. Twelve, the same age as me! My eyes fixed on the picture of a boy in a bright red vest and a broad smile.

I couldn't get Iqbal's story out of my mind. That night I was consumed with thoughts of children forced to make carpets for endless hours in dimly lit rooms and subjected to horrible cruelty. I knew I had to do something. But Pakistan was so far away. I had to find out more.

The next day, my grade seven teacher allowed me to speak to the class. I passed out copies of the article and told Iqbal's story.

"So here's my idea," I said. "Maybe some of us could start a group and learn more about it together." Eighteen hands shot up, and through that simple action, it began.

During the first meeting at my house that night, we determined our first objective should be to inform people of the plight of child labourers around the world. We read a report about a demonstration in Delhi, India, where 250 children had marched through the streets chanting. "We want freedom! Free the children!"

"That's it," someone shouted. "Free the children!"

And so, Free the Children was born.

Our first action was to participate in a youth fair in Toronto where we proudly set up a makeshift information board we'd put together at my home. The other organizations all had impressive professional displays. We noticed a few high-school students taking part, but mostly it was adults doing things "for" children. We were the only group where children spoke for themselves.

People flocked to our table to hear our message. Twelve-year-old children speaking for themselves on human rights? We were an oddity. That day our second goal emerged—putting more power in the hands of children. Children needed to have a voice and participate in issues that affect them.

I was soon speaking to groups everywhere, and that fall was invited to address two thousand delegates at the Ontario Federation of Labour (OFL) convention in Toronto.

Backstage, I was nervous. When asked how long I planned to speak I said, "Ten or fifteen minutes."

"You're booked for three minutes." I was told. "You'd better cut it down."

I started, as usual, with Iqbal's story. Soon, I was interrupted by loud applause, giving me new confidence. As my voice grew stronger, I pushed aside my notes. I could feel the energy of the audience beyond the bright lights.

Often, I was interrupted by applause. When I finished, the audience was on its feet, and fifteen minutes had gone by! Someone took hold of my hand and held it in the air. Then he announced that the OFL was pledging five thousand dollars to our cause!

It started a chain reaction. One union after another matched what the OFL had given and challenged others to do the same.

After an hour and forty-five minutes, I left the stage. Unbelievably, a hundred and fifty thousand dollars had been pledged to help exploited working children in the developing world. Never in our wildest dreams had we expected it. Free the Children had truly taken flight.

I was constantly being asked, "Have you ever met any of these children? How do you really know this is true?"

Soon, I knew I simply had to go to South Asia to see for myself. But my parents wouldn't even consider it. "It's another world. It's too dangerous. You're only twelve!"

I had discussed the idea with Alam Rahman, a friend I met at the youth fair. At twenty-four, Alam was serious and committed, and my family had grown to admire and trust him. One day Alam said, "Craig, I'm going to visit my family in Bangladesh and then travel around South Asia. Do you want to come?"

"Convince me you'd be safe," insisted my mom.

When UNICEF agreed to help contact people willing to take care of us, everything came together. Alam went ahead of me to Bangladesh to spend time with his relatives. When I arrived in Dhaka twenty-eight hours after leaving Toronto, Alam met me, and we were off.

Before leaving Canada, I had assumed that child labour was something hidden in dark alleyways. But to my shock, within an hour I came upon three instances, all in full view of the world. During my travels, I spoke with eleven-year old prostitutes in Bangkok and children in India who knew no other life than making bricks out of mud. In a remote recycling factory, I met an eight-year-old with no shoes or gloves who sat on the ground separating used syringes and needles for their plastics. She had never heard of AIDS. When I asked these children about their dreams for the future, they looked at me through eyes without expression.

We made plans to meet with a leading human rights activist in Delhi. We wanted to participate in a surprise raid on a carpet factory to release children held in bondage. In our futile attempts to get to Delhi in time, we ended up in Varanasi, about 250 miles away. Disappointed, we resigned ourselves to missing the raid.

The next morning we learned the surprise raid would be right there in Varanasi! But the organizers felt it was so dangerous I had to stay behind and wait for several anxious hours. When they finally returned, Alam's first words were, "Mission accomplished."

I was overjoyed!

Twenty-two children between eight and twelve were rescued from horrible conditions; some with festering sores, all sleep-deprived and malnourished. After the children gave their statements to the police, they were free! I would get to join them on the ride back to their parents. This was the reason for my trip, and my dream came true.

Early the next morning, we piled into two Jeeps for the eleven-hour drive to their village. Soon one of the boys began to sing in Hindi. "Free! We are free!" The others joined in, their voices soaring, their joy erupting to the open skies. When we reached the village, it was two in the morning. "This way, this way," the kids called out. None of us had slept, but we were wide-awake and wildly excited. When the headlights fell on a mud hut, one boy said, "This is where I live." The remote village had no electricity, and the dwellings stood in an unearthly pitch-black silence.

The boy went to his home, knocked and called, "I am freed from the carpet factory. I am back!" The door flew open and a woman stood there, absolutely still. Trembling, she reached for her son. "Is it possible?" she cried, overcome with joy. "Thank you, thank you," she repeated to us. The boy smiled hugely as he waved good-bye and stepped through the door, still hugging his mother.

The same scene was repeated over and over, with parents throwing open the door to the night and the sight of their lost son.

When the last child went to his door, his whole family quickly emerged. "Munnilal, is it really you?" cried out his tearful mother. She pulled him tightly to her, and they stood there motionless, as if the world had stopped.

Putting my arm around his shoulder, I said, "Good-bye."

"*Alvita,*" he said in Hindi. "Good-bye."

"I wish you lots of happiness," I said.

This was the reason I had come to South Asia: To know that change was possible and a smile could return to the face of a child. It was all the inspiration I needed to keep going. I hoped he would remember me, the boy from Canada.

From the moment I returned, our house in Thornhill turned chaotic. Students of all ages from all across Canada wanted to get involved. Speaking requests poured in from everywhere!

Over the past seven years, I've traveled to more than forty countries, visiting street and working children and speaking out for children's rights. During my travels, I've had the great honour of meeting with many world and spiritual leaders, but it is the children who have most inspired me with their courage, resilience and hope for a better life.

Every summer we bring new groups of young people from across Canada to the developing world, including Kenya, Nicaragua, Thailand and India, where they volunteer, help build schools in rural areas and learn from the local people.

In my travels back to India, I've met many of the children who were freed during the raid on the carpet factory, including Munillal. To my great joy, he now attends school and dreams of becoming a lawyer to help other children enslaved in child labour.

Free the Children is now an international organization of children helping children. Hundreds of thousands of youth in thirty-five countries are now involved in our activities. Through lobbying and meetings we've helped persuade governments around the world to tighten laws against those who use child prostitutes and child labour.

We've raised money to build over 300 schools in the developing world, providing education to fifteen thousand children. Our youth have collected over one hundred thousand school and health kits to help children go to school. We've established partnerships with communities in twenty-one countries to provide them with clean water, health care and alternative sources of income to free children from poverty and exploitation. We've done this not with a large bureaucracy but through a revolutionary approach—tapping the heart and spirit of young people who believe they can make the world a better place for other children using speeches, bake sales, car washes, donated birthday money and a lot of positive spirit. An adult board of directors handles legal and financial matters, but youth remain the heart and soul of Free the Children.

To clarify our uniqueness, we recently changed our name to Kids Can Free the Children. New projects include a Youth Ambassadors for Peace training program in 150 schools across North America and the publication of a leadership manual called Take Action that tells children how to get involved in social issues in their communities and in the world. We believe the sky's the limit with respect to what young people can accomplish.

Just before Christmas 2001 we sent nine thousand school and health kits to the children of Afghanistan, along with dolls and blankets. Each kit was personalized from a North American child with drawings and letters saying things like, "We love you" and "We want world peace too!"

We've learned you don't have to be a president or CEO, rich or powerful to change the world. Our actions are simple: Anyone can get involved. All you need is the heart of a child. Who knows? Maybe some day we'll have a United Nations of Children!

Craig Kielburger
Thornhill, Ontario

5

ON KINDNESS

Life is a lonely journey if we take only our bodies on the road and leave our hearts behind.

Doris Hedges

Farewell to the Queen of Hearts

She was only twenty-one years old, a royal rookie on her first visit to Canada, when I met Diana, princess of Wales. Her style at that time was House of Windsor rather than cover-girl glamour. She tended to fold her fingers inward to hide the fact that she bit her nails. But the essence of the woman was as apparent then as it was throughout her public life. She was vulnerable, compassionate, willing to break the rules, take a risk and do what she thought was right.

When I heard the terrible news about her death, and while photos flooded the television screen and commentators serialized her life, I remembered a story about her that I've often shared with family and friends. Although I'd been fortunate enough to meet Diana during royal tours in the 1980s, and later at 24 Sussex Drive in 1991, there was never a story less public or more telling about who this young woman really was. It took place in Halifax in June 1983, just hours after her plane had touched down from England.

The official welcome was being held at the Garrison Grounds, a huge field that on that sunny day was jammed with an estimated 10,000 cheering royal watchers. The crowd was pressed into a U-shape around the edges of the field. The centre was reserved for the trappings of pomp and ceremony. The royal couple was to do a walk-about around the edges of the crowd before proceeding to the centre for the ceremony. I chose a spot near the end of their route and watched what would become a vintage Princess Di walkabout. It turned into a love-in.

Seated near my vantage point were three rows of senior citizens in wheelchairs, who had been positioned to ensure a glimpse of the prince and princess. In the second row, and closest to where I was standing, an elderly gentleman in a pale blue sweater caught my attention. He was watching the princess with enormous pleasure. As the royal couple approached, I thought wistfully, *Too bad, old man. You're in the second row. Royalty only stops to speak to people in the first row.* As Diana approached, he was straining from his wheelchair so forcefully, I was afraid he might tumble to the ground. Like everyone else on the Garrison Grounds that day, he was transmitting waves of warmth and welcome to the young princess.

Then, as if by telepathy, she saw him and apparently couldn't resist returning the warmth. In a rather unroyal style, she reached her arm in over the heads of the people in the first row to shake his extended hand.

That's when it happened. Suddenly, his arm began to flail. A spasm had overcome the old gentleman. His arm was swinging wildly, to the right and left and over his own head. Everyone was watching the discomfiting scene. For a split second Diana looked stunned and then, when an attendant rushed to the man's side and calmed him, she withdrew her hand and returned to her royal walkabout. My heart ached for the old man. He looked so dejected, so disappointed in himself. Now his head drooped down, his shoulders stooped over. It seemed obvious that he knew he'd missed his chance to greet his princess.

Diana continued along the row but kept looking back at

him. Was she concerned? Could this young woman who was just days short of her twenty-second birthday have any idea how he felt? Would she dare to risk embarrassing herself by returning to the man's chair? Surely not. But then there was a space between the wheelchairs and she started moving back toward him. I wondered what she was up to.

You have to imagine the scene: the stiff formality of the entourage, the split-second timing of a walkabout, the royal handlers (aka Royal Canadian Mounted Police officers), the royal household (aka ladies-in-waiting)—all standing around while Diana tiptoes through the uncut grass and takes her royal self to the second row. Although enormously grateful for the bird's-eye view I was getting, even I was bowled over by her decision. The entourage would be held up. The world was watching. It could all go terribly wrong.

When she got to the woman sitting beside the old man she stopped, knelt down and chatted to her for a long time. By now I was certain that she had a plan. The old man was watching her, wringing his hands and still looking distressed. Suddenly, Diana stood up and stepped sideways to his chair. She put her hand on his shoulder, leaned over close to his face and said, "I'm glad to see you. I hope you haven't had to wait too long on this hot day. Maybe they should bring us all some ice cream."

The old man gazed up at her from his chair. Tears were rolling down his cheeks, and his face was wreathed in happiness. She'd touched his heart. And she'd risked a disaster in decorum, not to mention protocol, in the process.

When her life turned upside down in the 1990s, she told a television interviewer she'd never be queen of Britain, but she'd like to be queen of people's hearts. She already was.

Sally Armstrong
Toronto, Ontario

Walls

'Tis friends and not places that make the world.

Bliss Carman

People often talk about the "walls" that some individuals build around themselves. I was one of those individuals. Long after I divorced and became a single parent, I still wore my wedding ring. To this day, I'm not exactly sure why I did that. I told myself that it was because it was too much trouble to get involved with anyone again. It sure beat admitting that men were not lined up to date me. Maybe it was because I didn't want anyone to know that I had failed at something in my life. Wearing that ring helped me pretend that everything was okay.

You think that people can't see through those kinds of walls. But they do. They just know enough to not let you know that they see you are pretending. One day at work, however, pretending didn't come that easily. I was on my coffee break, preoccupied and worried. My car had died. Suddenly. And I didn't have death benefits.

I needed that car to hold down my job. Without it, I would have to walk fourteen miles to and from work in

North Bay. Even I could see the humour in that. Worse, my boys would get home from school before I did. That meant two things: The house would look like a cyclone had hit it, and Ontario Children's Aid would be all over us like a rash.

One of the walls I had built around me was coming down faster than Jericho.

Just before I went on that coffee break, the garage had called and said the car repairs would come to $726. That car and I had a lot in common. We had just been kicked in our rear ends. I not only felt sick, I looked it. I didn't have a credit card, and I certainly couldn't call the $28 in my bank account "savings." But every problem has a solution, and in my case that meant I had to ask someone else for something—even if it was only a lift downtown after work. This might not seem like a big deal to someone else, but I was a hard case: It's difficult to give someone the equivalent of a Heimlich maneuver when they're choking on their pride (as I was). Nevertheless, I got past my pride, and my colleague Jane volunteered to give me a ride to the garage after work.

I spent the rest of the afternoon trying to come up with bright ideas about how to pay my garage bill. I figured I could borrow $200 from my mom and pay her back at a rate of $2.50 a week. I thought of what I had at home that I could live without and therefore sell. I finally decided the best I could do was to offer to type up invoices for the garage—mine included.

When Jane dropped me at the garage that evening, the owner asked me to step into his office. He closed the door and went behind his desk. He cleared his throat and said, "There's something I want you to see." He opened a drawer. In it was a lot of loose change and small bills. "Do you know what this is?" he asked. Before I could say anything, he added, "People you work with have been coming

Loretta

All things bright and beautiful, all creatures great and small: All things wise and wonderful, the Lord God made them all.

Mrs. Cecil Frances Humphreys Alexander, 1848

Wylie Costain seemed destined to save a life.

When I met Wylie in the summer of 1999, he had already lived in British Columbia, on the west coast of Canada, for twenty years. Born and raised in the east, on Prince Edward Island, Wylie knew the harsh realities of a fisherman's life from experience.

I had flown to the Squamish airport in a light aircraft. Planes were stored in the open hangars, but I saw no one about. The flying club was locked and the airport seemed to be devoid of human life. I was thinking of walking into town when a pickup truck drove up.

"How far is it to Squamish?" I asked.

"Eight miles," came the answer. "You'll have a heckuva walk. Wanna lift?"

Without hesitation I said, "Yes!"

in here all afternoon. Must have been 100 of them. Each one put money in this drawer. The lads in the shop have never seen anything like it!" He cleared his throat again. "They even decided to cut their labour costs in half. As it stands now, all you owe me is twelve bucks."

I did three things I had never done before: I cried in public; I baked enough cookies to feed an army; and I stopped wearing my wedding ring.

Mary Lee Moynan
Powassan, Ontario
Submitted by Barry Spilchuk

Loretta

*All things bright and beautiful, all creatures
great and small: All things wise and wonderful,
the Lord God made them all.*

Mrs. Cecil Frances Humphreys Alexander, 1848

Wylie Costain seemed destined to save a life.

When I met Wylie in the summer of 1999, he had already lived in British Columbia, on the west coast of Canada, for twenty years. Born and raised in the east, on Prince Edward Island, Wylie knew the harsh realities of a fisherman's life from experience.

I had flown to the Squamish airport in a light aircraft. Planes were stored in the open hangars, but I saw no one about. The flying club was locked and the airport seemed to be devoid of human life. I was thinking of walking into town when a pickup truck drove up.

"How far is it to Squamish?" I asked.

"Eight miles," came the answer. "You'll have a heckuva walk. Wanna lift?"

Without hesitation I said, "Yes!"

"Wait a minute," I added. "I'll have to get back to the airport."

"Oh, don't you worry about that. I'll bring you back. Hop in."

"Sure you don't mind?"

"Not at all. Hop in!"

That's how I met Wylie Costain. As we drove, Wylie told me an incredible story, backing it up with a couple of newspaper photographs. In 1988 his company, the Atlantic Lobster Company, a wholesaler in Burnaby, British Columbia, had requested large lobsters from the east coast to supply restaurant clients. When they arrived, one of the containers had only a single lobster in it instead of the thirty it normally holds, but what a lobster it was!

Once in town, Wylie stopped at his apartment and returned with two photographs. They showed the largest lobster I'd ever seen—in fact, it weighed twenty-one pounds.

Wylie estimated seven years for each pound. Her twenty-one pounds translated into the age of 147 years. She hadn't lost a claw or a leg during her long life, and she didn't have any scars or scratches from previous battles. In the photograph, she looked perfect.

Someone discovered she had eggs and was still productive. Wylie said that at first he saw only the money the lobster would bring: "Oh boy! That's worth a bit!" But then he began to fight with himself. He thought of her age and the many offspring she must have had, and she seemed to take on a beauty he could not describe. He named her Loretta.

Wylie went on with his story. "Loretta was so old she really deserved to go back in the sea." I nodded in agreement as we drove on.

"I couldn't bear the thought that she'd end her life on somebody's dinner plate. So I decided to free Loretta."

I listened in astonished silence. "But she's an Atlantic lobster and would've died here in the Pacific." He tried to offer her to the Vancouver Aquarium, but the response of the curator of fishes at the time was that the aquarium wasn't "a half-way house for unwanted pets."

"I didn't know how I could pull this off," Wylie continued. "I only knew Loretta had to go home to the Atlantic, so I called Canadian Airlines to get the price of a ticket. I explained I was taking a live lobster home to the Atlantic Ocean, and the lady said they couldn't allow it."

"What did you do?" I asked.

"Well, I called the *Vancouver Province* and told the story to somebody there. The next thing I knew, a reporter and a photographer showed up at my plant in Burnaby. When I told them the airline wanted nothing to do with me, the reporter called them. He must've convinced them 'cause they called and offered Loretta and me a free ride there and back. I had her put in a special container with lots of ice in the cargo hold, and that's how she flew."

From Halifax, Nova Scotia, Wylie and Loretta travelled to the village of Lockeport, where Loretta was probably originally caught.

It was July 1—Canada Day. Wylie, Loretta and some of Wylie's Nova Scotia friends set out to sea aboard a fishing boat. It was a pleasant, calm day. Wylie took Loretta from her container, held her close and tenderly stroked her back. Loretta's tail curled under and straightened out several times.

"That's the way she hugs," Wylie explained.

Then he gently placed her below the surface and let her go. Her tail flicked, the water splashed and she was gone.

"Good-bye, Loretta," Wylie had said, a little choked up. "I'm glad you got back home."

Manuel Erickson
Langley, British Columbia

The Great One

My husband, daughter and I made our way into the small restaurant in our Winnipeg hotel for breakfast. Only two other tables were occupied, one by a family with young children. There was a little girl and a little boy, and the boy was so excited because sitting at the table directly behind us was a face he recognized. "Mom, Mom, look!" he managed to get out. "It's Wayne Gretzky!"

Sure enough, there at the other table was Wayne Gretzky, obviously discussing important business with some gentlemen in suits. They were speaking quietly and just finishing up breakfast. Well, this little boy could hardly contain himself. He was squirming in his seat, wanting to talk to Wayne Gretzky and get an autograph. After all, this might be his only chance! But his mother just kept whispering, "He's in a meeting, honey. He needs his privacy. This is not the time." The poor little boy was almost in tears. You could see he couldn't eat. Instead, he kept indulging in the irresistible thrill of looking over his shoulder and seeing his hero—right in the same room!

Well, it was hard not to notice what was going on. Wayne excused himself from his breakfast and went over to the little boy. He knelt down, put out his hand and said,

"Hi, I'm Wayne Gretzky, What's your name?"

The little boy's face totally lit up! His jaw dropped, and his mouth hung wide open. His eyes looked like they were going to pop right out of his head. He just couldn't believe what was happening. The whole family was thrilled. It was wonderful to watch as Wayne shook hands with the little boy and then signed his autograph on a place mat from the table.

I was so impressed. I thought, *What class. What a wonderful gesture!* It was such a little thing, and yet it said so much. It made me realize that he sincerely meant all the things he has said about encouraging youngsters—and that Wayne Gretzky was as much a hero off the ice as he was on.

Lynn Johnston, creator, For Better or For Worse
North Bay, Ontario

The Way Home

There is no such thing as one's own good. Goodness is mutual, is communal; is only gained by giving and receiving.

Arnold Haultain

I'd spent the night rushing to the window every time I heard a branch fall. Now, looking out into the early morning light, the devastation was obvious. Not one tree in our rural neighbourhood in Kingston, Ontario, had been left untouched. Jagged branches lay everywhere. The Great Ice Storm of January 1998 was upon us.

The house had an eerie silence: no hum from the furnace, no buzz from the refrigerator, no morning news blasting from the TV. All the clocks were frozen at 10:49 P.M.

Alex and I were fumbling around in the basement with a shared flashlight, trying to find our camping stove. We needed coffee—some sense of our morning ritual to start the day. I heard the screen door open, then a timid knock. Doris Lee, our closest neighbour, had somehow managed to make her way through the maze of ice, wood and downed power lines, to arrive at our door. She looked anxious.

"Have you seen Harold and Prince?"

Our property backs onto a wooded area, and every morning we would watch Doris's husband Harold with Prince, his golden Lab, ramble off down the trail. Prince trotted quietly on the lead and always brought Harold home safely. Harold had been diagnosed with Alzheimer's disease the previous summer. Doris had been adamant about maintaining their life together and trying to keep things as normal as possible. However, she hadn't reckoned on an ice storm.

"I was upstairs, looking for batteries for the radio, when I heard the door close. Harold is so used to his routine, I just couldn't stop him from taking Prince out."

Alex rushed to pull on his coat as he asked, "How long have they been gone?" Doris hesitated. "About half an hour. I didn't want to bother you, and Prince is usually so good about finding his way home."

Alex looked at me. I turned to Doris and said, "You go home. I'll be right over. I'm going to find our camping stove. I'll bring it over, and we'll make some coffee while Alex finds Harold. They'll want a warm drink when they get home."

Doris turned and headed back to her house while Alex sprinted across the yard toward the woods. I finally found the stove, and, making my way across the icy war zone, I arrived safely at Doris's home.

She and I waited in her kitchen. I made the coffee, but Doris didn't even notice. She stood by the sink staring out into the yard, her cup untouched. I sat at her table, reading all the carefully printed notes she had placed around the kitchen—beside the stove, the light switch, the electric kettle—to remind Harold to turn off or unplug things. There were also notes on the refrigerator door, mapping out a daily routine for Harold: walk the dog, eat breakfast, wash. Doris had done everything possible to make life easier for Harold. Now she turned from the sink and walked over to the table.

"Prince always brings him home, you know," she said softly.

I wanted to say something to comfort her but I felt unqualified. I was just beginning to understand the burden Doris dealt with on a daily basis. Instead, we simply waited together quietly. An eternity seemed to pass before I finally saw Alex coming across our yard. He was carrying Harold's beloved golden Lab in his arms. Harold was walking behind him, tears streaming down his cheeks.

"Prince was hit by a falling branch," Alex explained. "Get some towels or blankets. He's alive but he must be in shock. He's been bleeding from that cut over his eye."

We covered Prince with blankets, and Doris coaxed Harold into dry clothes while Alex told us his story. At first he had called for Prince, thinking it would be the easiest way to find the pair. He was almost ready to turn back and get more help when he heard Harold's voice.

"Harold was sitting on the ground comforting Prince. He'd taken off his coat and put it over the dog. It was all I could do to convince Harold to put his jacket back on."

We sat around the kitchen table, four silent people, unable to pull our thoughts away from the dog in the corner. Prince was more than just a faithful companion. He helped care for Harold. Without him, Harold would lose his independence. We anxiously watched the pile of blankets covering the injured dog, fearing the worst. Suddenly, there was a small movement.

Alex put his hand on Harold's shoulder. "Look, Harold, he's waking up."

A doggie nose popped out from under the pile of blankets. We watched Prince wiggle out and come across to the table. Harold put a trembling hand on his dog's head.

Prince gazed at him with his soft brown eyes and gave a halfhearted wag of his tail. Doris whispered a private thank-you. I looked at Alex, and the ice storm and power outage were forgotten. Until that day we hadn't appreciated how isolated Doris and Harold were, and what a struggle they had just coping day-to-day. In that moment we decided we were going to change all that. Starting then, Prince and Doris were getting two new assistants.

Susan Owen
Kingston, Ontario

The Seal

At the age of fourteen, I landed one of the most sought-after summer jobs in Vancouver—I became an attendant at the Stanley Park Children's Zoo. Few of us are fortunate enough to experience the perfect job, but for the next five summers, I did just that.

Zoo designers from around the globe asked for tours because they had heard that our children's zoo was one of, if not the, best there was. The children's zoo, an integral part of one of the world's most beautiful areas within a city, Stanley Park, was ahead of its time. Pits were used instead of cages, and zoo attendants worked hard to make each habitat different and exciting for the animal that lived there.

Orphaned members of the local native wildlife were also brought to our zoo for care. Everything from baby pigeons to owlets, fawns to porcupines were given the best possible attention.

The harbour seal pups in our care were kept in the back building, away from small fingers. Twice a day, we would bring them out to the man-made pond in the contact area and allow them to swim. The pond was at the bottom of a waterfall of fresh, cold water.

One day, as I waded in the thigh-deep, icy water with two seal pups, some people gathered to watch. The pups stayed close to me, surfacing occasionally to catch a breath and look around. I saw a boy, about ten years of age, pointing at one and calling to his mother to come and see.

As I walked around, feeling my legs turning numb, the boy yelled, "Hey! Where's the other one?"

While one of the seals was nuzzling my leg, my eyes scoured the pond for the other, Spica. The water was clear, as well as cold, and it was soon obvious Spica wasn't where he should be. My heart skipped a beat as I realized he had swum under a rock formation, which was there to hide the drain. There was a small, fist-sized hole on one end of the formation, and another hole, just large enough for a baby seal, on the other end. But I was quite certain that the inside area was too narrow for Spica to turn around in.

"Oh no!" yelled the boy. "The little seal is under the rocks and can't get out. He's going to drown!"

Everyone in the zoo came to the edge of the pond to watch the drama unfold. I was terrified and called to another attendant to take the other pup to safety. I dove under the water and felt the small hole. Sure enough, Spica was trying to get through it. I knew that the pond would take hours to drain. I also knew that seals could hold their breath for twenty minutes or longer, but I didn't know if a week-old seal in an agitated state could.

And then, just like a white knight riding to the rescue, one of the men who worked at the main zoo arrived. Ken was a good friend to all of us and often spent his breaks at the Children's Zoo. He ran over, assessed the situation, and whipped off his shirt and shoes. Jumping in, he dove under and tried to reach Spica through the larger of the openings. He couldn't even touch him.

"Okay, Diane," he said to me. "Dive under and push him back as far as you can. I'll try to grab him from this side. Ready? Go!" he commanded.

I held my breath, found Spica's muzzle still near the small opening and pushed as hard as I could. My head throbbed from the frigid water, and my lungs wanted to hyperventilate. Every ounce of my being screamed to get out of that freezing water. It took every thread of strength I had to stay put.

Finally, I could no longer feel Spica, and with my stomach in knots, I stood up. Precious time had gone by, and Spica had been motionless, offering no resistance when I had pushed. The little boy among the spectators was now providing a play-by-play account: "Oh, the poor thing! He is suffering so much! His little lungs are probably exploding. The poor little seal . . . he's dead by now."

Suddenly, after what seemed like forever, Ken burst out of the water, gasping and coughing. He was holding a very limp body. I looked at Ken, and he lowered his eyes as he shook his head. The crowd, even the little boy, was silent.

And then, Spica raised his head, and in the way of infant seals, cooed at me.

The audience let out a cheer and applauded loudly, generously patting Ken, my new hero, on the back. He handed me the pup and I snuggled the wet, slick fur, revelling in the intense relief.

I glanced around, searching for the boy. I found him, standing perfectly still and absolutely quiet, while tears ran down his face and dripped into the pond.

Diane C. Nicholson
Falkland, British Columbia

Guests Who Dropped in from the Sky

Shirley Brooks-Jones relaxed in her seat. She and her friend Jo were returning from a satisfying trip to Denmark, where they attended a board meeting of People to People International, an organization created by President Dwight Eisenhower to foster international understanding and friendship.

On the way home to Atlanta, they stopped overnight in Frankfurt to dine with Jo's granddaughter. The next day was September 11, 2001.

Delta Flight 15 was four hours out of Frankfurt when suddenly the pilot announced that an indicator light was giving cause for concern. They had received approval from Canadian air traffic control to land in Gander, Newfoundland, the nearest airport.

Fortunately Gander was created as a military airfield and a transatlantic refuelling point in the 1930s and so has a long runway. Shirley knew of the Canadian town and its strategic significance during World War II, but little else. She wondered how long they would be there, but when the plane touched down, she realized there was something more going on than just concern over an indicator light. Already on the tarmac sat planes from many of the world's major airlines. As the Delta passengers watched, a steady stream of aircraft continued to land.

Upon landing, over the intercom the captain apologized to his passengers and explained there was no equipment problem. He calmly told them that because of a national emergency, U.S. air space had been closed and was controlled by the military. There were loud gasps and stares of disbelief. Local time in Gander was 12:30 P.M. (11:00 A.M. New York time).

No one was allowed to leave the plane. For the next few hours the captain updated the passengers every fifteen minutes, slowly detailing the horrific events that had unfolded in New York City, Washington and Pennsylvania that morning. Although naturally upset and anxious, the 218 passengers remained calm. The crew carried on their duties as if they were still in the air, and all was normal. People spent their time talking, or trying to call home on their cell phones. Shirley began to jot down notes of the experience.

Delta Flight 15 was one of the first American airliners to land in Gander on September 11. Eventually, there would be thirty-nine aircraft parked on the airport's tarmac and runways. Once darkness began to fall, Shirley realized this was not a mere twilight stopover. In the wee hours of the morning, when she spotted passengers disembarking from a neighbouring aircraft, she knew they weren't flying anywhere soon.

By the time all the people were off all the planes, approximately 6,500 people had converged on Gander, a town of just more than 10,000. With no word of when the planes would be able to leave, the community found itself in an emergency situation. However, in this region that lives with rough seas, harsh weather and an uncertain economy, helping others is part of the way of life.

Volunteers, community agencies and many other organizations all went into action to receive the passengers from all over the world, and provide them with hospitality, accommodation and welcome. The town's half dozen hotels and motels were instantly full. Schools, clubs, lodges and other large gathering places were converted into temporary hostels with mats, cots and sleeping bags. Many people opened their homes, and the oldest passengers were taken there. No passenger was left without a bed.

But the response went well beyond Gander. As the word went out, towns and hamlets nearly an hour's drive east and west also welcomed unexpected guests, bussed in by school board drivers who came off picket lines to assist. Those communities too far away to receive visitors sent whatever they could—blankets, clothing, toiletries and food. The passengers of Delta Flight 15 were taken to Lewisporte, a town much smaller than Gander but just as big in generosity.

Shirley and Jo, along with a few others from their flight, went to the Lewisporte Lions Club. Their hosts realized that after sitting for so many hours on a plane, cut off from the media, the weary travellers would be anxious to see the historic events with their own eyes, so they set up cable TV.

When the passengers walked in, they dropped their bags, stood there and said nothing as they watched what seemed like Hollywood special effects. Some went into silent shock. Others broke down crying. All experienced an emotional catharsis that helped to purge some of the pent up horror and grief and create a special bond amongst everyone there.

The Newfoundlanders responded to the passengers' needs with extraordinary generosity. The people in this region of Canada are so often in a "have-not" situation.

Still, local volunteers worked tirelessly to meet every need they could anticipate. They cooked meals, provided all the basic necessities, and even made sure medical prescriptions were refilled. Special needs for clothing came from the local's own wardrobes.

In Lewisporte, Shirley learned that the man tirelessly running around with a clipboard was the mayor, Bill Hooper. She told him how impressed she was with the way Lewisporte was handling the emergency. She was surprised when he explained that like any small community, they had never even dreamed of such an eventuality, let alone practised for it!

To keep the passengers occupied and distracted from their anxieties, excursions such as boat cruises were arranged during the day. Soon, passengers and hosts began to feel as if they had known each other for years, almost forgetting the terrible tragedy that had brought them together in the first place. Magically, people who might have never spoken to each other were drawn together, finding amazing connections.

The local Red Cross tracked every passenger in every group, making sure everyone was back at the airport at the right time. When the time came to leave, no one missed their flight.

Shirley and her new friends were happy to be going home, but the people of Lewisporte had shown them so much love, there was a real sense of regret in leaving. In a way, the town reminded her of the small community in Ohio where she grew up. It was raining the day they left, and Shirley was glad—for it hid many tears.

Four days after the travellers dropped out of the sky on the Canadian coast, Delta Flight 15 took off for home. Once in the air, people walked about the aisle, sharing experiences and hundreds of stories. Everyone knew everyone else by name as they exchanged phone numbers and

e-mail addresses. Shirley spotted a man that she remembered seeing on September 11, but hadn't seen since.
Dr. Robert Ferguson was one of the fortunate ones to find
comfort in a hotel room, and Shirley teased him in a
friendly way about missing an enriching and humbling
experience.

As they chatted, another magical connection emerged.
In spite of the good fortune of a hotel room, Dr. Ferguson
told Shirley he had experienced the pure beauty of the
Newfoundlanders in their response to the crisis. But
Canadian warmth was nothing new to him. While he now
lives in Winston-Salem, North Carolina, he was born in
Ottawa. He then spoke about Newfoundlanders; how the
province has so little, yet the people are so giving. They
both noted how no one would accept any compensation
or payment for what they had done for the visitors. When
they began to discuss what they could do to show their
appreciation, Dr. Ferguson told her he had already started.

His idea was to start a scholarship fund for the young
people of this community, where opportunities are not as
abundant as in other parts of Canada. Earlier, he had
quietly put together a statement and makeshift donation
form for passengers to pledge money toward the cause.
The form was already circulating through the first-class
passengers. When she heard this, Shirley offered to lend
her talents as an experienced fund-raiser in whatever way
she could.

The effort was going well, but Atlanta was getting
closer and closer. Shirley couldn't wait to be back on U.S.
soil, but suddenly it was coming too fast. There was no
longer enough time for all the passengers to see the form
and make a pledge before they descended into Georgia.

There was another option they had not yet considered.
It was unheard of for a passenger to speak on the public
address system in an aircraft—it's stringent airline policy.

But surely these were unusual circumstances. Why not ask?

Dr. Ferguson was uncomfortable asking such a thing of a flight crew, especially in light of recent events. Shirley felt the crew, let alone the captain, would never go for it. Even so, she asked a flight attendant if she would look over the statement and read it to the passengers. After reading it, with tears in her eyes she went to ask the captain. Perhaps it was because of the way he had treated his charges during the crisis, Shirley was sure he would say yes.

And he did! The captain thought it was wonderful, but suggested one of the passengers should read it! As Dr. Ferguson was reluctant, and so was everyone else, it fell to Shirley to address the 218 passengers. She was nervous and hesitant, but with so many other people doing such extraordinary things, it seemed the least she could do.

Before Delta Flight 15 touched down in Atlanta, those aboard had pledged $15,000 U.S. to the people of Lewisporte for a scholarship fund. An anonymous donor later matched that, and the fund grew to roughly $35,000. It is now overseen by the Columbus Foundation in Ohio, and the first scholarship was awarded June 21, 2002.

The opportunity to be of real service during the tragedy of September 11 has given everyone involved an incalculable lift and a new sense of self worth and appreciation. E-mail messages, gifts, photos and invitations continued to pour in to the folks in this area from their former guests. And all because Newfoundlanders, with small-town good neighbour values, were kind to some strangers who just happened to drop in from the sky.

Paul Banks
editor, The Beacon Newspaper
Gander, Newfoundland

Reprinted by permission of Québec City Convention Centre. ©2001.

6

ON FAMILY

I like family life. I like it when I get home at night and the kids shout, "Dad!" and trip over my feet and hug me and smell sweaty because they've been playing all day. That's love, brother.

Gary Lautens

The Legacy of Mary

*One sword can rarely overcome a score, though
one heart may be braver than a hundred.*

Samuel James Watson

It was November 1984. I had picked up a copy of
Equinox magazine from a table in my daughter's home and
gasped—there before me, in an article entitled "Ghost
Towns of Alberta," was a picture of a man named
Lawrence Stewart. Lying in front of him was a pile of
books that he called his "Memories of Etzikom." It had
been forty-seven years since I had been taken from my
home in Etzikom, Alberta, at the age of five.

I sat there in a state of shock as a little voice in my head
said, *This is it, Maree.*

In 1938 I'd been sent to live in the Kiwanis Home for
Children after my mother suffered a nervous breakdown.
My father was ill equipped to raise seven children alone,
during the Depression, and still look after his farm.

It wasn't long before I was adopted by a fine family who
was well-off enough to give me everything I could have
asked for. My other brothers and sisters were either

adopted or put into foster homes. I never saw or heard from any of them again. Over the years, when anyone would ask me if I wanted to find my family, I would say, "I will when I can never be hurt again."

I grew up and worked out a successful career for myself in early childhood education; married my husband, Leo, who loved me very much and encouraged me in everything I did; and became the mother of five wonderful children who thought a great deal of me.

If ever there was a time to find my birth family, it was now—almost fifty years later!

As I sat there in shock, staring at Lawrence Stewart's article, Leo and I began talking about my memories of my own family. I remembered the names of my brothers and sisters. There was John, Coulter, Mable, Nancy, me (Mary), May and a little brother who had been born just before we were taken away from our father.

"It wouldn't hurt to write to this Lawrence Stewart and ask what he knows," suggested Leo. I took the magazine home, and the next day, that's what I did.

Three weeks later, I received a letter from Mr. Stewart, telling me he'd been in the area for about sixteen years and knew many of the families' histories. He thought he'd be able to help me. He remembered only one family that had been broken up back then, and their name was Robinson. The father's name was Dave, and he recalled there was a son named Coulter.

I wrote back to him enclosing a copy of the birth certificate that had been issued to me when I was adopted. My husband and I were leaving the country for six weeks, but I said I'd contact him upon our return. Everyone was excited about the fact that I was finally going to find my birth family.

Upon my return, a letter from Mr. Stewart was waiting for me.

"You are indeed Mary Robinson," he wrote, "and I have located the rest of your brothers and sisters!" He told me that someone would contact me in the near future, as the family had been trying to find me for many years.

The first to call was Myrtle Keene, the daughter of the family who had raised my little brother, Seymour. I asked her to please let my family members know my where-abouts because I wanted to meet them.

A couple of nights later the phone rang and a voice that sounded like an echo of my own said, "Are you sitting down? Because if you're not, you'd better do it now. I am your sister May!" A tingle came over my whole body—it was so wonderful to hear her voice after so many years. Her name was now Gail Turner. She told me how she had been reunited with the family some years before and had even lived close to our father in Vancouver before he died. I began to learn more about my family, and we arranged to visit as soon as possible. I was walking on air, and could only think of all the questions I wanted to ask.

A few minutes later the phone rang again, and it was my sister Nancy. I was in tears by now—her voice sounded just as I remembered. Nancy was two years older than me, and she was able to tell me details that I was too young to remember. She had lived in the Kiwanis home in Edmonton until she was about ten years old, and then she had gone to live with a family by the name of Jones. We made plans to meet as well.

As if by magic, the phone rang once more. After forty-seven years, I heard the voice of my little brother Seymour. He told me he had been trying to find me for many years. Seymour had grown up in Etzikom with the Keenes, who had named him Derwood. He told me how, over the years, he had seen our father from a distance, but had been too afraid to approach him. He had also known our mother for a short time, while she lived in The

Michener Centre in Red Deer. Seymour has a wonderful sense of humour, and I felt as if I had known him all my life. It turned out that he is the one that my own son, Steven, looks like—and even acts like. We arranged to meet in July so I could hear his whole story.

About a week later, Myrtle phoned from Regina. This was the sister I'd known as Mable. When she learned I'd been found she was so happy she cried for a week! Because she was the oldest, she had somehow thought she should have kept us all together. For all these years she had searched through faces on the street, trying to find a resemblance, but no one looked like Mary. Now that she had talked to me, she wanted to see me right away.

About a month later she came out by bus, and I met her in Cache Creek. I had told her I had glasses and grey hair, but wouldn't you know—there were three other women at the bus station who answered that description! The bus pulled in and there were many faces looking out the bus window when I heard a voice cry out, "That's her, that's my sister!"

Myrtle stepped off the bus, gathered me in her arms and began to sob. She had told everyone on the bus the story of our family and about her long search for her sister Mary. Now, as the happy crowd watched our joyous reunion, we stood there holding each other and crying for a very long time.

After forty-seven years, our long search was over—our family was united once more.

Maree Benoit
McLeese Lake, British Columbia

Love Is a Two-Way Street

Love can't be hidden. It's like light.

Celine Dion

Her ashen face stood out against the startling black-
ness of her hair. She looked much younger than her fifteen years. She was a child of the British Columbia foster
care system. We weren't supposed to take a child for
another couple of months, but an emergency call came
through that morning. A home was needed for a young
girl immediately.

The whole family pitched in to get her room ready. The
kids were great. They changed linens, cleared out closets
and helped with the cleaning. My heart felt like a drum
pounding in my chest. I was excited, but scared at the
same time. This was such a new experience for me. The
children kept asking questions: "What is she like?" and
"How long will she stay?"

"We'll just have to wait and see," was all I could answer.

In our home in Surrey, British Columbia, we had four
children of our own. Margaret and Joanne were seventeen
and fifteen, and Rob and Jeff were twelve and nine. Our

friends thought we were mad to take on another child, especially a teenager. "You'll be sorry," they told us. "A foster child can give you a lot of grief."

That afternoon, Trudy arrived with the social worker Mrs. Kline. She stepped into the front hall and clung to the walls. I will never forget the look in her eyes. The first thing that came to my mind was that she looked like a hunted animal. The children moved towards her, and Jeff grabbed her hand and said proudly: "Come and see your room. I helped make your bed." Trudy pulled back, but didn't let go of his hand.

At this point, I stepped towards her and said, "Welcome to our home, Trudy." She looked at me with such blank, vacant eyes. The kids were all talking at once: "Do you want a pop?" "Do you want a cookie?" But with her head bowed, she simply said, "No thank you."

"Kids, can you go downstairs to the family room, so your dad and I can talk to Mrs. Kline?" There was a chorus of voices saying, "Bye, Trudy. See you later."

We sat at the kitchen table, and Trudy was very quiet. Her eyes darted back and forth like a creature looking for a way out. This had been her fifth foster home since she was eleven. No wonder she was afraid. I wanted to put my arms around her and tell her she would be safe with us.

For the first two weeks, Trudy was very quiet. She would come into the kitchen while I was working, and we would discuss school and what she would like to do in the future. Mrs. Kline had given us all the information about her history, but I never mentioned the terrible things that had happened to her.

I wondered if in trying to help Trudy I had taken on too much. Her life had been one crisis after another. Would she be able to put the pain behind her and get on with her life? Would I fail? Self-doubt would then flood in and overwhelm me.

It was a Friday night, and Trudy had been with us for only one week. Margaret and Joanne were getting ready to go out and meet their friends, and Trudy was watching television. "Are you going out with the girls?" I asked.

"You mean I'm allowed to go with them?" she said in amazement. Her question took me by surprise, and I didn't answer right away.

"I was never allowed to go out at night at the other house," she continued.

"Well," I finally responded, "it's different here. Friday and Saturday you can go out, but the curfew is eleven o'clock." When she heard my words, she jumped up and hugged me! I was so surprised, I almost fell backwards.

As the days went by, Trudy became a delight to have around. Very quickly, it seemed like she had always been with us. The girls would sit in each other's rooms and giggle like typical teenagers. It was a sound that warmed my soul.

One day, when Trudy had been with us for about a month, I took Joanne shopping for a new winter coat, and Trudy came too. She was not used to shopping in stores other than discount ones. The process of shopping involved filling out receipts and sending them to the ministry, and she found it all very embarrassing.

Joanne was trying on a green suede jacket with a fur collar. It was expensive, but she pleaded, promising to give up her allowance, do extra chores—anything to have the jacket.

Trudy had picked out a jacket that she liked and was promenading in front of the mirror. As I watched her, I realized it was not the same girl that had entered our home only four weeks ago. She stood taller and held her head higher. The tightness in her face had softened. She was able to look me in the eye when she spoke to me.

She walked up to Joanne, modelling the jacket, and

sighed, "Isn't it beautiful?" Joanne agreed as they both preened in the mirror. Replacing the jacket on the rack, she rejoined Joanne.

"The jacket looks so nice on you," Trudy said. "Can I borrow it sometime? Daniel will love you in it!" she teased. I hadn't seen her face so animated before.

While they were busy, I quietly asked the salesperson to wrap up the jacket that Trudy had tried on. "Please don't let her see you do it—it's a surprise," I explained. For the next few minutes, I kept Trudy busy while the salesperson rang up the jacket and wrapped it.

We bought the coat that Joanne had loved, and Trudy was still babbling on and complimenting her on her choice. The salesperson had placed the parcel containing Trudy's coat where the girls couldn't see it, and I managed to sneak it out to the car without being caught.

When we arrived home, Joanne proudly modelled her new coat for Margaret. Trudy was still talking about it, and how Joanne was going to lend it to her. I chose that moment to say, "Trudy, would you please go out to the car and bring in the parcel from the trunk?"

She happily complied, and when she returned, laid it on the table. "Would you please open the parcel for me, while I put on the kettle?" I could hear the sound of ripping paper, and then I turned and saw her reaching out to touch the jacket. Her hand recoiled as if she had touched something hostile. I walked over to her and put my arms around her. Trudy looked directly into my eyes, unable to speak. Joanne looked at me, anxiety and concern for this newly acquired sister showing in her face.

I took Trudy's face in my hands, and asked, "Isn't this the jacket you were trying on?" At that, Trudy started sobbing.

"In all my life, no one has ever bought me a beautiful jacket like this. Why did you do this?" She held the jacket and stared at it with disbelief.

On the brink of tears myself now, my voice shook as I managed to say, "Because you deserve it."

I left the kitchen and went to my room so she would not see me crying. My heart ached for this child who didn't feel she was worthy of a coat. As I was sitting there deep in thought, a knock came at the door. "Come in," I called.

There in the doorway stood my four children. The look on their faces told me they badly needed to say something. Margaret stepped forward and spoke for them: "Mom, thank you for bringing Trudy into our home. We hope we can keep her forever." The rest of the heads bobbed up and down in agreement.

My eyes welled up with tears. As I gathered my children to me, they began to say, "We love you, Mom." I looked at the faces of my treasures and whispered, "I love you too. Guess who's the luckiest mother in the world."

Carol Sharpe
Surrey, British Columbia

New Kids on the Block

After Brad and Nancy were married a few years they moved to their dream home in the country. An essential part of their shared vision of a life together was having a family. They could just see their young children running and playing on the lawn. But time went by and there were no babies. No reason could be found, and the doctors encouraged them to keep trying. More time passed, however, and still there were no babies.

For the next few years, Brad and Nancy explored many options, trying to have a child together. But after several years and a great deal of money, they agreed they were ready to consider adoption.

They decided upon international adoption, and finally Costa Rica specifically. They filled out forms, asked lots of questions and attended many seminars.

Then, on Christmas Eve, a neighbour came to the door. He handed Nancy a flyer from an adoption agency that had gone to his house in error. On the cover was a picture of three small children—two sisters and their baby brother. They were born in Costa Rica and available for adoption as a family. Nancy caught her breath, thinking, *These could be our kids!* Not wanting to influence Brad, she left it on the table, saying nothing. A short while later, he picked it up. Time—and Brad's heart—stopped for a few moments as he gazed at the picture of the three children. In an instant he recognized them as the children that he and Nancy were going to adopt and raise as their own. There was no question in his mind. It was a miracle.

Although it was Christmas Eve, on a whim Brad called the adoption agency in a small town two hours away. A recorded message announced a general information meeting on December 27. They figured it would be like all the other meetings—reams of forms to fill out and process before they would even be considered. But they changed their plans and fit in a trip to attend the meeting.

The couple that owned the agency had just returned from Costa Rica and had personally photographed the children Brad and Nancy wanted to adopt.

"Yes, those children are still available. Do you want them?" inquired the agent.

Nancy and Brad were totally stunned! It was all happening so fast! Brad said, "Yes! Let's go for it!"

Nancy was a little frightened. Three children all at once! Could she do it? But the story of how the mother's circumstances had changed, and how she had had to give up her babies broke Nancy's heart. She and Brad decided that between them they had enough love to share with these abandoned children. Before they left that day, agreements were signed, a lawyer was contacted and the financial commitment was made. Nancy joked that it took longer to decide on their new car! But they were sure and made immediate plans to go to Costa Rica to meet their kids!

Excitement and anxiety began to build. Would they all like each other? How would six-year-old Maria react to her new mother? How would three-year-old Katrine react to the tall man with the yellow beard and blue eyes?

Would tiny one-year-old Emilio find comfort in a new set of arms? How would they all communicate? Brad and Nancy enrolled in Spanish lessons right away.

A host of concerns from well-meaning friends and family followed their impulsive decision. But, undeterred and with love filling their hearts, they moved steadily forward toward their goal.

In February, Brad and Nancy travelled to Costa Rica. They had just settled into their hotel room when there was a knock on the door, and the three children entered to meet their new mama and papa. Baby Emilio was carried by the foster mother, and along for the ride was the Costa Rican lawyer, a doctor, a translator and the director of the Canadian adoption agency who just happened to be in Costa Rica! Here was an entire team committed to successfully bringing this family together. Another miracle!

At first shy, the naturally happy and trusting children were soon giggling, laughing and chasing each other around. Baby Emilio, thin and tiny for his age, quickly attached himself to Brad. To their surprise and great pleasure, it did not take long for the two girls to connect with Nancy. Soon, they heard themselves addressed for the very first time as "Mama" and "Papa." Overwhelmed, Brad and Nancy's eyes filled with tears. This was their family. There was no going back now.

They were told it would take another four months for the paperwork to navigate both the Canadian and Costa Rican bureaucracies, but if all went well, they'd be able to return in June for their children. Nancy and Brad left with reluctance—Who knew how long it would really take? Either government might decide to block the adoption for some reason. Or the birth mother, when confronted with signing the papers, might reconsider.

Weeks passed. Brad and Nancy reorganized the house, bought clothing and assembled backyard toys. Months passed. Their Spanish improved and a school was chosen. Finally, it was June. The adoption had made it through the Canadian bureaucracy, but was now stuck in some department in Costa Rica. Then it was mid-July. Dubious friends and relatives suggested it might be several months more. But waiting for months was not part of their vision. Anxious and eager for their new life to start, the couple made a quick decision. They wanted their kids!

With great urgency, Brad booked two round-trip tickets to Costa Rica and three one-way tickets back to Canada. They were determined to return in ten days with their children. Brad told the Canadian agent of their plans, and the agent informed the Costa Rican team that they were coming for their kids and would not consider returning to Canada without them. The couple flew to Costa Rica, and everyone at home held their breath.

The three children had an ecstatic reunion with their new mama and papa. Baby Emilio had gained a little weight and reattached himself to Brad immediately. Everyone was healthy, and communication was a little easier after six months of Spanish classes.

Then another miracle occurred. Instead of the resistance the couple were expecting toward their "gringo" attempts to expedite the process, everyone bent over backwards to help. The lawyer put all her cases on hold and walked papers from one government office to the next. Documents were signed, stamped and passed on to the next department. Entire lines of waiting people were bypassed as miracle after miracle continued to follow this family's coming together. One by one the hurdles fell, and then the grandparents waiting at home got a phone call. Brad and Nancy were coming home, as planned, on time—with the kids! They had done it!

Now they had to fly home to Canada, passing through

first U.S. and then Canadian immigration. Would they be hassled?

Airline agents greeted them with open arms and amazing assistance as they began their journey. They were escorted through all the checkpoints with ease, smiles and best wishes. More miracles! They arrived in Canada to the waiting arms of two sets of grandparents, seven new aunts and uncles, and many new cousins.

The fiesta held to celebrate the arrival of the children was a huge success. Brad and Nancy saw the most important part of their vision for their life together unfold that day—their own children, laughing and playing on the lawn, winning everyone's hearts. With love, patience and endless support, the new family began to form.

The love story of Brad and Nancy is now twenty-five years old, but the love story that is their children continues to unfold with each passing day. When Nancy and Brad think of how their family miraculously came together, in their hearts they believe something like this may have occurred:

At another time, in another place, two women sat quietly talking. The first woman said, "I will not be able to conceive children next time, and I very much want to be a mother. Can you help me?"

The other woman said, "I will bear three children next time, but my role is not to live out that life as a mother. Will you love and take care of my babies?"

And the first woman replied: "How will I find you, how will I recognize the children?"

And the man standing quietly nearby said: "Don't worry, I will know."

Janet Matthews
Richmond Hill, Ontario

With a Little Help from Your Friends

True friendship hath a thousand eyes, no tongue; 'tis like the watchful stars and just as silent.

Samuel James Watson, 1876

In 1994, Julie and Michael adopted a little girl named Veronika from a Russian orphanage and brought her home to Canada. My daughter Leah met Veronika in second grade and have been inseparable ever since. Leah loved Veronika's high energy and happy, optimistic attitude toward life. She also loved how Veronika could always make her laugh.

As the years passed, the girls moved back and forth between our two homes. It was as if each had the benefit of two families, not just one. My wife Krys and I loved having Veronika in our home, and we watched with pleasure how she greeted each day as an adventure. She truly became a part of our family and often travelled with us on our family vacations.

When they both turned thirteen years old, Leah and Veronika decided to have their bat mitzvahs together—a ceremony and celebration in Judaism when children reach this age. The hall was full of members from both families who had gathered together to celebrate this special day.

After the ceremony, Veronika's mom, Julie, delivered a toast to our daughter Leah and shared with the room the story of how they first met.

"Leah, this is something I should have thanked you for years ago. As most of you know, Veronika was adopted when she was in second grade. At the time, Michael and I were trying to get Veronika out of Russia, and it was a very difficult process.

"We were hoping she would be with us before summer began. Michael went to Russia for a couple of weeks, but unfortunately, he was not able to get her. So we anxiously waited throughout the summer. At the beginning of August, we were told it was time to come and do the paperwork and bring Veronika home. It would take about a week.

"This time, I went to Russia. But instead of a week, it turned out to be over a month. It was a heart-wrenching time for all of us, not knowing whether we would get Veronika out or not. But we were very determined that we would not leave Russia without her. Finally, on the September long weekend, we landed back on Canadian soil. I was home to my family and Veronika was home to her new family. As you may imagine, we were thrilled!

"The unfortunate part of this, though, was that Veronika had just three days with us before she had to start school. Needless to say, this was a very disturbing and upsetting time for her. So the first day of school I went with her and sat with her at the back of the room, and she was so scared she left bruises gripping my arm. The next day was basically the same. Eventually, she actually had the courage to go and join the rest of the class.

"I realized it would have to come to a point where I couldn't keep going to school with her, and I would have to leave her. But this wasn't so easily done, for Veronika had never had someone who would go with her and come back for her. So on Thursday, I was about to leave her there, but I couldn't do it. I couldn't find the courage to leave her. But Friday was the day I said she was going to stay at school and learn that I could leave and that I would come back for her.

"We went to the lunchroom. She ate her lunch and I was about to leave and again she started to cry. I bent down to her and she was holding on to my arm. I let go of her hand and I said, 'Veronika, you have to stay and I'll be back.' Of course, with our language barrier this was hard to do and she was crying. I was ready to start to cry again.

"As she went to grab my hand again, instead of her having a chance to put her hand in mine, this beautiful girl came up to me and she slipped her hand in Veronika's. She looked me straight in the eye and said, 'You can go. I'll take care of her. I promise, I won't leave her side.'

"Leah, you have kept your word. You have never left my daughter's side. This was such a difficult time for Veronika and me, and I don't think you ever realized the important role you played for us that day in helping the two of us out. For me, being able to leave, to show Veronika I would come back. And for Veronika, to realize she wasn't alone.

"I lay with Veronika one night in bed, and I asked her, what did she think of the school? She told me she thought it was another orphanage—a big building with lots of kids and few adults. Leah, you helped her through that time. You did this unselfishly, without even realizing how you were helping me and how you were helping Veronika.

"I have seen you with Veronika and with (Veronika's sister and brother) Jade and Ryan and with your other friends. You are a remarkable young woman. And if I could have one wish for you, it would be to always have that open heart, to see when people need help, and not just to see it, but to do something about it. That is a true gift, Leah, because not everyone possesses that quality.

"So I want you to know that you hold a most special place in my, and Michael's, heart. Family are relatives that you are born into. Friends are family that you choose. We are so honoured to have you as a part of our family."

When Julie sat down, there wasn't a dry eye in the place.

As any parent knows, there are moments in life when you are so proud of your kids your heart just about bursts. For Krys and I, this was one of them. For Leah, it was the greatest gift of all.

Lorrie Goldstein,
editor, The Toronto Sun
Toronto, Ontario

Four-Legged Guardian Angels

*If you talk to the animals they will talk with you
and you will know each other. If you do not talk
to them you will not know them, and what you
do not know, you will fear. What one fears, one
destroys.*

Chief Dan George

Snow had just melted off the ground that April day at
our house in Regina Beach, Saskatchewan. My husband,
Doug, had just cleaned up the pool in preparation for selling our house. The year before, Doug had lost his job with
the provincial government, and now our financial situation was grim. In despair, we had finally put our home on
the market, and a real estate agent was due to show up
later that day. Even worse, we would have to give up our
two beloved Great Danes, Bambi and Brigitte, because we
could no longer afford the cost of feeding them. The
thought of losing our dogs and our beautiful home was
almost more than I could bear.

Deep in despair, I sat typing up resumes and cover letters for Doug. Out of the corner of my eye I could see our

thirteen-month-old son, Forrest, as he lay on the carpet, playing near our big, gentle nanny-dog, Brigitte. I hadn't typed more than two sentences when our other dog, Bambi, began barking furiously and running back and forth to the sliding glass door overlooking our pool.

I raced to see what was happening and noticed that the sliding door was slightly open. Suddenly, I realized Forrest was nowhere to be seen. In a panic, I opened the door and ran outside. There I was surprised to see Brigitte, who was terrified of water, splashing around in the pool. Then to my horror, my eyes caught sight of Forrest's yellow sleeper. Brigitte was bravely doing her best to keep him afloat by holding on to his sleeper with her mouth. At the same time, she was desperately trying to swim to the shallow end. I realized that Forrest had somehow opened the door, wandered out and fallen into the pool.

In a split second, I dove in, lifted my precious baby out and carried him inside. But when I realized Forrest wasn't breathing, I began to go into shock. I was trained in CPR, but my mind went completely blank. When I called 911, all I could do was scream. On the other end, a paramedic tried to calm me down so that I could follow his CPR instructions, but in my hysteria I was unable to carry it out successfully. Thankfully, Doug, who was a former Canadian Forces officer and was trained in CPR, arrived and took over. I stood by with my heart in my throat, and after about three minutes, Forrest began to breathe again.

When the ambulance arrived, I rode with Forrest to the hospital. Along the way he stopped breathing a couple of times, but each time the paramedics managed to revive him.

Once at the hospital, it wasn't long before a doctor told us that Forrest would be all right. Doug and I were overwhelmed with gratitude. They kept him for observation for a total of four days, and I stayed by his side the whole time.

While Forrest was in the hospital, Doug was often at home. When he went into Forrest's bedroom, he discovered that both Brigitte and Bambi had crammed themselves under the crib. For the entire time that Forrest was in the hospital, they ate little, coming out only to drink water. Otherwise, they remained under the crib, keeping a vigil until we brought Forrest home. Once they saw he was back, Brigitte and Bambi began to bark with apparent joy and wouldn't let Forrest out of their sight. Our two wonderful dogs remained concerned about our baby's safety, and even my first attempts to bathe Forrest were traumatic. Brigitte and Bambi stood watch, whimpering the whole time.

In time they settled down, but both remained dedicated to Forrest and followed him everywhere. When Forrest finally learned to walk, he did it by holding on to the dogs' collars.

The press discovered the story and soon Purina dog food called. They offered the dogs an award and gave us tickets to fly to Toronto for a ceremony where Brigitte and Bambi were awarded medals for their bravery. We were also given a beautiful framed picture of our dogs, which we now display proudly above our mantle. Perhaps best of all, Purina gave us a lifetime supply of dog food so the problem of keeping our beloved dogs was solved.

Those gentle giants helped raise our other two children as well. Things in our lives are much better now. Most importantly, almost losing Forrest—and then getting him back—erased any despair I might have had about losing our home. A house can always be replaced, but knowing we have each other is the greatest blessing of all.

Our two dogs are both angels now and probably guarding other children up in heaven. We miss them both, but we are eternally grateful they were part of our lives.

Karin Bjerke-Lisle
White Rock, British Columbia

Christmas Lights

Before my dad died, Christmas was a bright, enchanted time in the long, dark winters of Bathurst, New Brunswick. The cold, blizzardy days would sometimes start as early as late September. Finally, the lights of Christmas would start to go up, and the anticipation would build. By Christmas Eve the ordinary evergreen tree that my father dragged in the door ten days earlier took on a magical, sparkling life of its own. With its marvellous brilliance, it single-handedly pushed back the darkness of winter.

Late on Christmas Eve, we would bundle up and go to midnight mass. The sound of the choir sent chills through my body, and when my older sister, a soloist, sang "Silent Night," my cheeks flushed with pride.

On Christmas morning I was always the first one up. I'd stumble out of bed and walk down the hall toward the glow from the living room. My eyes filled with sleep, I'd softly bounce off the walls a couple of times trying to keep a straight line. I'd round the corner and come face-to-face with the brilliance of Christmas. My unfocused, sleep-filled eyes created a halo around each light, amplifying and warming it. After a moment or two I'd rub my eyes and an endless expanse of ribbons and bows and a free-for-all of bright presents would come into focus.

I'll never forget the feeling of that first glimpse on Christmas morning. After a few minutes alone with the magic, I'd get my younger brother and sister, and we'd wake my parents.

One November night, about a month before Christmas, I was sitting at the dining room table playing solitaire. My mother was busy in the kitchen, but was drawn from time to time into the living room by one of her favourite radio shows. It was dark and cold outside, but warm inside. My father had promised that tonight we would play crazy eight's, but he had not yet returned from work and it was getting near my bedtime.

When I heard him at the kitchen door, I jumped up and brushed past my mother to meet him. He looked oddly preoccupied, staring past me at my mother. Still, when I ran up to him, he enfolded me in his arms. Hugging my father on a winter night was great. His cold winter coat pressed against my cheek and the smell of frost mingled with the smell of wool.

But this time was different. After the first few seconds of the familiar hug, his grip tightened. One arm pressed my shoulder while the hand on my head gripped my hair so tightly it was starting to hurt. I was a little frightened at the strangeness of this and relieved when my mother pried me out of his arms. I didn't know it at the time, but my dad was suffering a fatal heart attack.

Someone told me to take my younger brother and sister to play down in the recreation room. From the foot of the stairs, I saw the doctor and the priest arrive. I saw an ambulance crew enter and then leave with someone on a stretcher, covered in a red blanket. I didn't cry the night my father died, or even at his funeral. I wasn't holding back the tears; they just weren't there.

On Christmas morning, as usual, I was the first one up.

But this year, something was different. Already, there was a hint of dawn in the sky. More rested and awake than usual, I walked down the hall toward the living room. There was definitely something wrong, but I didn't know what until I rounded the corner. Then, instead of being blinded by the warm lights, I could see everything in the dull room. Without my dad to make sure the lights on the tree were glowing, I could see the tree. I could see the presents. I could even see a little bit of the outside world through the window. The magic of my childhood Christmas dream was shattered.

The years passed. As a young man, I always volunteered to work the Christmas shifts. Christmas Day wasn't good, it wasn't bad; it was just another grey day in winter, and I could always get great overtime pay for working.

Eventually, I fell in love and married, and our son's first Christmas was the best one I'd had in twenty years. As he got older, Christmas got even better. By the time his sister arrived, we had a few family traditions of our own. With two kids, Christmas became a great time of year. It was fun getting ready for it, fun watching the children's excitement and most especially, fun spending Christmas day with my family.

On Christmas Eve I continued the tradition started by my dad and left the tree lights on for that one night, so that in the morning, my kids could have that wonderful experience.

When my son was nine years old, the same age I was when my father died, I fell asleep Christmas Eve in the recliner watching midnight mass on TV. The choir was singing beautifully, and the last thing I remember was wishing to hear my sister sing "Silent Night" again. I awoke in the early morning to the sound of my son bouncing off the walls as he came down the hallway toward the living room. He stopped and stared at the tree, his jaw slack.

Seeing him like that reminded me of myself so many years ago, and I knew. I knew how much my father must have loved me in exactly the same complete way I loved my son. I knew he had felt the same mixture of pride, joy and limitless love for me. And in that moment, I knew how angry I had been with my father for dying, and I knew how much love I had withheld throughout my life because of that anger.

In every way I felt like a little boy. Tears threatened to spill out and no words could express my immense sorrow and irrepressible joy. I rubbed my eyes with the back of my hands to clear them. Eyes moist and vision blurred, I looked at my son, who was now standing by the tree. Oh my, the glorious tree! It was the Christmas tree of my childhood!

Through my tears the tree lights radiated a brilliant, warm glow. Soft, shimmering yellows, greens, reds and blues enveloped my son and me. My father's death had stolen the lights and life out of Christmas. By loving my own son as much as my father had loved me, I could once more see the lights of Christmas. From that day forward, all the magic and joy of Christmas was mine again.

Michael Hogan
Victoria, British Columbia

For Better or For Worse®

by Lynn Johnston

7

SURVIVING LOSS

And as we look toward the dawn,
our spirit rises high on wings of certainty.
We will share eternity.
This is how it's meant to be—
For life goes on, and we must be strong.

Bob Quinn

Ryan's Hope

. . . Weeping may remain for a night, but rejoicing comes in the morning.

Psalm 30:5

The day started out normally enough. It was May 1, 1997. Ryan was upstairs preparing to leave for school, while his six-year-old sister, Jamie, waited for him at the front door. Suddenly Ryan started to tell us all about Albert Einstein with such enthusiasm and excitement, it was as if a light had gone on in this head. He said, "$E=mc^2$—I understand what Einstein was saying: the theory of relativity. I understand now!"

I said, "That's wonderful," but thought, *How odd.* It wasn't his thinking about Einstein—Ryan was so intelligent—but rather the timing that seemed peculiar.

At ten years old, Ryan loved knowledge and seemed to have an abundance of it, far beyond his years. The possibilities of the universe were boundless to him. When he was in first grade, the children in his class were asked to draw a picture and answer the question, "If you could be anyone, who would you be?" Ryan wrote: "If I could be anyone, I'd want to be God." At age seven, while sitting in church one day, he wrote:

The tree of Life, O, the tree of Glory,
The tree of God of the World, O, the tree of me.

Somehow I think Ryan just "got it."

In the midst of his strange outburst about Einstein, Ryan suddenly called out that he had a headache. I went upstairs and found him lying on his bed. He looked at me and said, "Oh, Mommy, my head hurts so bad. I don't know what's happening to me. You've got to get me to the hospital."

By the time we arrived at the hospital in Newmarket he was unconscious. We stood by helplessly as the doctors fought to save his life, and then they transferred him by ambulance to Toronto's Hospital for Sick Children.

A couple of hours later we were finally allowed to see him. He was hooked up to a life support system. When the doctor told us our son had suffered a massive cerebral haemorrhage and was "legally and clinically brain dead," it felt like a terrible nightmare. We went into shock. Nothing more could be done, the doctor said, and asked if would we consider organ donation. Astonishingly, we had discussed this with Ryan only recently. We looked at each other and simultaneously replied, "Oh yes, Ryan would have wanted that."

In April, Ryan had seen his dad filling out the organ donor card on the back of his driver's license. His dad had explained to him about organ donation and how you could help save another's life by agreeing to donate your organs when you die. When Ryan wondered if you needed a driver's license to do this, his dad replied that anyone could donate their organs.

Organ donation made such perfect sense to Ryan, he went on his own campaign persuading the entire family to sign donor cards. We had no doubt that donating Ryan's organs was the right thing to do.

After a small bedside service, we said our good-byes to our son. When we left the hospital, we left a part of ourselves behind. Driving home, I could feel a thick fog roll in and surround me, crushing me. We were in total disbelief. My husband, Dale, and I cried in each other's arms all that night and for many nights after. It was as if part of me had died with my son.

Grief consumed me for a long time. We kept waiting for Ryan to walk in the door. We grieved for the loss of today, and also for the loss of our hopes and dreams. I realize now you never get over the death of your child. With time you heal, but you are forever changed. It was our daughter Jamie who gave us a reason to get up in the morning and carry on.

Then, on a beautiful morning four months after Ryan's death, the first letter arrived, addressed to my husband and me. As we read it, we both began to weep. It was from a twenty-year-old university student thanking us for our "gift of sight." He had received one of Ryan's corneas and could now see again. It is difficult to describe our emotions—we wept, but at the same time, we felt wonderful.

Sometime later we received a second letter from a young woman of thirty who had received one of Ryan's kidneys and his pancreas. She'd had diabetes since she was five, spending much of her recent years hooked up to a dialysis machine. She told us that because of Ryan, she was now free from insulin and dialysis, able to work again and return to a normal life.

Early May brought the painful first anniversary of our son's death. Then we received our third letter. A young boy of sixteen, born with cystic fibrosis, had received Ryan's lungs. Without the double lung transplant he received, he would have died. Besides being able to return to school, he was now doing things he had never done before—running, playing hockey and roller blading with his friends. Knowing this boy's life had been renewed lifted our spirits immensely. Due to confidentiality laws, organ donation is completely anonymous in Canada. However, organ recipients and their donor families can communicate through the organ transplant organization. Although we didn't know the identities of the individuals who had received Ryan's organs, we were given updates about their health.

We learned about a six-year-old girl who had received Ryan's other kidney and was now healthy, free from dialysis and attending school full time. We also learned that the forty-two-year-old woman who had received Ryan's liver was doing well and was able to again spend time with her young family.

Such joy seemed to come from our sorrow, so much happiness from our loss.

Although nothing could take away our pain, we took great comfort and peace in knowing that Ryan had done something most of us will never do—he had saved lives!

That summer, while on vacation in Haliburton, we met a young man—by sheer coincidence—who had had a kidney and pancreas transplant at the same hospital where some of Ryan's organs had been transplanted. He knew the young woman who had received her kidney and pancreas on May 2 from a ten-year-old boy he believed to be our son. Her name was Lisa, and she was doing great. Afraid to ask her last name, I later wondered if I might have passed up my only chance to meet one of Ryan's organ recipients.

This chance meeting inspired me, and the following spring I decided to share our experiences with others. I'm not a writer, so it was a challenge to write a story and send it to the newspapers for National Organ Donor Week. I faxed my article to three papers, and to my astonishment, all three wanted to feature it! A flurry of interviews and photo sessions followed, and we experienced an excitement we thought we were no longer capable of.

When the first article appeared, Dale and I were totally overwhelmed when we opened the paper to find that Ryan's story of hope was the banner story—right on the front page! Included in the article was the poem Ryan had written when he was seven, just as we had it inscribed on his tombstone. We wept tears of joy and sadness as we read it over and over. In his brief ten years on this earth, our son Ryan had made a difference.

A few days later, the article appeared in the other two papers, and for a few weeks we received calls from people all across Canada. Surprised but delighted, we hoped the story would help raise awareness about organ donation and perhaps inspire others to donate.

Apparently Lisa also read the article. When she saw Ryan's poem, she recognized it from a letter we had sent her and realized he was her organ donor. The article said we would be at the Gift of Life medal presentation in Toronto two weeks later, so she decided to attend. Once there, she was unsure about introducing herself. We all wore name tags, and when Lisa found herself standing next to my husband Dale she just couldn't hold back. You can imagine the emotional scene of hugs and tears that followed! It was truly a miraculous, unforgettable moment! It felt so wonderful to see her standing there alive and healthy, knowing that our son had helped make that possible. Ryan's kidney and pancreas had apparently been a perfect match. And part of him now lives on in her.

Moments later, a woman approached us with her eight-year-old daughter. "I think my daughter has your son's kidney," she said. Kasia was just four when both of her kidneys had shut down and she had gone on dialysis. The details of her transplant matched, and we all felt certain it must have been Ryan's kidney that had given this lovely girl a new life. A few weeks later when we visited Ryan's grave, we wept tears of joy when we found a beautiful drawing left there, signed "Kasia."

Due to the Canadian confidentiality laws, meetings such as these are very rare, and it is impossible to describe the intense emotions that result. When Ryan died I thought I would never again feel joy. But meeting Lisa and Kasia was a kind of miracle, opening my heart to those feelings I thought had been forever buried with my son.

Today, I now know I will always be the mother of two children. Ryan is, and always will be, part of our family and our lives. Although the pain of losing him will never completely leave me, I have begun putting the pieces of my life back together, though it now takes a different shape. Part of our healing came from our experience of donating Ryan's organs. I am so grateful that God allowed me to meet Lisa and Kasia so my heart and soul could reopen. Meeting them allowed me to experience that "once in a lifetime" kind of feeling again, the one I thought was gone forever.

Nancy Lee Doige
Aurora, Ontario

The Red Sweater

In search of my mother's garden, I found my own.

Alice Walker

Time didn't ease the pain of losing my mother. Each day brought new sorrow since her death over a year ago; often I found myself fighting back unexpected tears.

Mom died just before the Christmas season the year before, after a short battle with cancer. At the age of seventy-two, she had been well prepared for her death, but I was not.

All her life, Mom was there for me; although now a grown woman, I still needed my senior parent for advice and comfort. We were the best of friends, and over the years, we shared, laughed and cried together.

I often found myself wearing her red sweater, holding it to my cheeks, drinking in its aroma. It had been Mom's favourite, and it was faded and worn from years of use. I claimed the sweater after her death. It held so many memories, and now I drew comfort from them.

Mom came from West Arichat, a tiny Acadian fishing village on Cape Breton Island, Nova Scotia. Of both French and Indian background, she had a gentle, soft touch. To cope with my grief, I began imagining my aged parent reaching out to comfort me. Her tanned hands, worn and shrivelled from age and work, had cradled babies, cared for a large family, and brought life to plants and flowers. I would imagine her wearing the red sweater, her hand reaching out and covering mine, and then she would whisper a memory in my ear.

I'd smile, remembering.

Mom lost both her cultures when she married my father, a white man, and moved from her island to live on his. When she arrived in isolated and rural Cardigan on Prince Edward Island at the age of eighteen, she began to learn English. Sadly, her knowledge of both French and her native Chinook began to fade away.

One of my favourite memories are the native pow-wows we attended on Panmure Island. Part of Prince Edward Island, Panmure Island is an old Mi'kmaq gathering place. First Nations people from all over North America travelled there to participate in the powwows. It was an opportunity for Mom to mingle with the First Nations people, wear her native shirt, dance in the sacred circle and socialize. She loved going to those powwows and proudly identified with her ancient roots, which had been silenced for so many years. I remember her telling an elder once, "I'm Indian, too." Although she had moved into the white man's world when she married, she never lost her Chinook heritage of strong native spirituality, deep respect for the land, and love for the outdoors—all of which she passed on to me and my eight brothers and sisters.

During the last powwow we attended, a few months before she became ill, I heard the Great Spirit whisper in my ear that it would be the last time we would travel to the powwows together. It was.

Now, her image travels with me in the car or visits when I feel grief and pain. She always wears the red sweater and for an instant, our hands join. Death has not separated us.

Sometimes the momentary images are so strong I find myself reaching out my hand to her imaginary one. It is as if she is always there, always with me, watching over me.

One day I sat waiting for my turn to have my hair done in the beauty parlour. I was exhausted from working, and I became frustrated with the wait. Then I noticed a small child watching me. She and her mom were holding hands while they stood at the counter. They moved to the area where I was sitting, so I moved over one chair to give them room to sit down.

The little girl looked around, then said to me, "Where did the woman go that was sitting beside you?" Surprised at her question, because no one had been sitting next to me, I asked her who she was asking about. "The woman wearing the red sweater," she quipped. "She was holding your hand, just like my mommy and me."

My fatigue and frustration were suddenly gone as a warm glow washed over me. Smiling, I realized my mom never left me. She really is only a shadow away.

Stella Shepard
Morell, Prince Edward Island

Tommy's Tangerine Tree

Seek not to calm my grief, to stay the falling tear; Have pity on me, ye my friends, the hand of God is here.

Nora Pembroke

When Tommy, our youngest son, was a little boy, he loved tangerines. At Christmas, when they came on the market, I always kept a plentiful supply especially for him. He ate them for breakfast and supper, and there were always lots of them in his lunch box. As well, he loved to snack on them while he read or watched television.

One day I caught him flipping the seeds on the carpet. I scolded him, telling him to put them in an ashtray or a flowerpot. The result was that come spring, four little orange trees sprang up in a pot of geraniums in the kitchen window. I selected the tallest and sturdiest and replanted it in its own little pot. Tommy was intrigued.

"Do you think I can have my own tangerines?" he asked. I told him that it might take a very long time.

Time passed. Tommy grew up and became a petroleum geologist on the east coast, searching for oil and gas off

Newfoundland. He loved the Atlantic Ocean with a fervor which I attributed to the fact that he had seagoing ancestors on both sides of the family. He married and built a house in Nova Scotia in sight of the Atlantic.

But he always came to visit us on his birthday, which was on New Year's Eve, and each time he would ask to see his tangerine tree.

In the twenty years that had passed since the little tree sprang up, it had grown amazingly. Each year I would put it into a bigger pot and place it in a warm, sunny spot in the garden, then bring it inside for the winter. But by the fall of 1981, I had no receptacle large enough to hold it, as it was now six feet tall.

Our daughter, who lived near us, offered to look after it as she had a very large urn, which she placed in a sunny window. When Tom came that New Year's Eve, he wanted to see his tangerine tree in his sister's home.

"Do you think it will ever bear fruit?" he asked.

I told him not to hold his breath—that although it would bear both male and female flowers if it ever bloomed, it was a Japanese tree and probably our climate was too cold for the flowers to set. He decided that he would take it down to his home in Nova Scotia the following summer. The foliage was beautiful anyway, he thought.

At that time he was working as a geologist on the *Ocean Ranger* oil rig off the coast of Newfoundland, and he was very proud to be doing exploration on what was probably the largest and most modern oil rig in the world. It was like a huge man-made island—indeed, the crew called it "Fantasy Island." They had to go out to it by helicopter, the only time, Tom said, that he was actually nervous. "It's a long, long way down there, Mum!"

I said, "I do wish you didn't have to go out in this bitter winter weather."

"I'm safer than you are, driving out of your driveway between ten-foot snowbanks," he assured me. "Besides, the rig's unsinkable!"

"So was the *Titanic!*" I said.

"You're mixing apples and oranges," he replied.

So when he telephoned us after he had returned to Nova Scotia and said he would be going out on the next shift change in a few days' time, I said, as I always did, "Be careful!"

Early on the morning of February 15, my husband turned on the radio and woke me.

"Tommy's in trouble," he said. "The *Ocean Ranger* is listing!" We did not know it then, but it had already gone under the waves around one o'clock that morning.

There followed grief mixed with desperate fear, until we finally realized the unthinkable had occurred. Our dear, kindhearted, life-loving son had been taken from us. Amidst the wild despair and unbearable sorrow, we were borne by the belief that a spirit such as our beloved son's could not possibly disappear completely—that he was still with us and loving us.

But I longed for some kind of assurance. And how I dreaded the coming of Easter that year! How could I join in the celebration of eternal life when I was not sure of it myself?

Then, on Good Friday, I got an answer. When our daughter telephoned, she said excitedly, "Mum, you won't believe this, but Tom's tangerine tree is full of blossoms!"

It was true. On Easter Sunday they opened fully, and their fragrance filled the house. Surely no flowers had ever been so beautiful! Someone had responded to my doubt and hopelessness with this little miracle.

Since the tree was inside, with no honeybees to pollinate it, we did not expect the blossoms to set. But again a miracle happened! Four tiny tangerines appeared. A short time later, two of them dropped off. Over the next few months, however, two more beautiful tangerines grew and eventually ripened. On the following Christmas Day we ceremoniously divided and ate Tom's tangerines. We felt that he knew it, and we were comforted.

A horticulturist has said that perhaps people had spread the pollen when they smelled the fragrant blooms. But I believe "someone" sent those blossoms to comfort us when we most needed a miracle—the miracle of Tom's tangerine tree.

Now, five years later, another little tangerine tree, a child of Tommy's tree, is growing on my windowsill. We had planted the seeds of the tangerines we ate on Christmas Day, 1982. I shall not live to see it blossom, but I shall nurture it as a symbol of life everlasting.

Ruth Hilton Hatfield
Rosemere, Québec
Submitted by her daughter, Margaret Herman

[MARGARET'S NOTE: *My mother died peacefully in my arms in 1998 at the age of ninety. I have three "children" of Tommy's tree now growing in a single pot on my windowsill, but to date, they have not blossomed. The original tree stands beside the smaller pot for comfort. Tommy's tree took over twenty years to blossom, so I have not yet given up hope.*]

The Littlest Angel

Come, O wind, from the dreaming west,
Sweeping over the water's breast;
Bring my unquiet spirit rest.

Norah Halland

It was the winter that I taught in a small country school on the West Coast of Vancouver Island. I had three grades of little people in my class, all beaming with the desire to learn all they could. One little boy named David from my grade one class wanted to learn more than all the others. His round puffy face would smile up at me, reminding me over and over that perhaps one day he would leave us. His frail, six-year-old body harboured a dreadful disease—leukemia. More often than not, he would be missing from our classroom because when he was subjected to another round of treatments, he would take his schooling in Vancouver.

All of us were so pleased, then, to have that happy little boy with us for Christmas. We decorated our classroom, practised for the concert, and coloured many pictures of Santa, snowmen and angels. We read Christmas stories, and some of the older children wrote very good ones of their own.

Two days before school let out for the three-week Christmas holiday, I read a new story to the class. It was the story of "The Littlest Angel." This little angel had an awful time in heaven. He could not adjust to the routine. He was always in trouble, bumping into other angels, tripping over clouds or dropping his halo. Nothing seemed to make his time easier until one celestial day an archangel suggested that the little angel return to earth and retrieve some items from his home. Just a few things to remind him of his past time on earth.

As I read the story, a heavenly silence fell over the class as each child became more involved in the plight of the angel. In hushed voices we discussed the story as the end of the school day drew to a close.

The following day during our regular show-and-tell time, David asked if he could share something with the class.

He sat in front of us on the old worn carpet holding a small wooden box.

"This is my first tooth," he explained. "This is a ribbon from my sister's hair, and this is my puppy's collar. My dad gave me this old key. My mom says this big coin is for good luck."

Even before he told us the purpose of the box, we all seemed to know. Shiny tears went dot-to-dot down the faces of the other children—we were all thinking of the story of "The Littlest Angel."

"I have all these things so when I go to heaven I won't be too scared. Maybe you guys could make a picture for me to take so I will always remember you?"

The rest of the day was spent doing just that. Each of us prepared a picture, folded it carefully and placed it in David's wooden box.

The day ended with all of us saying good-bye to each other. Everyone gave David a special hug and received a beautiful smile in return. I went home that day with the memory of a little boy who fought his disease bravely and would one day accept his destiny.

When the holidays came to a close, we all returned to our class—all except David. He had died over Christmas in a hospital, clutching the wooden box that held his hopes and memories, and ours.

I have never forgotten him. I am sure many of the students from that class, who are now grown with youngsters of their own, also remember "The Littlest Angel"— and the gifts of love he gave to us all.

Brenda Mallory
Telkwa, British Columbia

8

A MATTER OF PERSPECTIVE

If we had no winter, the spring would not be so pleasant. If we did not sometimes taste of adversity, prosperity would not be so welcome.

Anne Bradstreet

Motherly Advice

A man, to see far, must climb to some height.

Ralph Connor, 1900

I had the kind of mom who was never in a hurry. This would sometimes drive my dad crazy, as he prides himself in being always on time and totally organized. I sure know where I get my relaxed attitude from, and it's not my dad!

During all those years of early morning skating practices, mom would wake me up at 4:50 A.M. with a gentle nudge and a soothing voice. She followed this up five minutes later with another wake-up call. My dad had a different style altogether. He would call from the door of my room and then again only ten seconds later. He had no sympathy!

Mom would have breakfast for me in the car, and truthfully, I think we really savoured that thirty-minute drive from our home in Caroline, Alberta, to the rink in Rocky Mountain House. She would think nothing of stopping to look at some deer at the side of the road, or to sit on the hood of the car and wonder about the northern lights. Sometimes it seemed like we had the whole country to ourselves. Sure we would be a little late, but she knew that sometimes there were just more important things to experience. Well, the years went by, and eventually more important things did come along.

My coach, Louis, and I were on the bus on the way to the arena when we heard the news. It seemed most of my toughest competitors, including Brian Boitano and Victor Petrenko, had already finished skating, and the results were not what we had expected. Since I pulled last to skate, I had a perfect opportunity to see most of the event unfold before I even stepped on the ice—and so far it was looking good. The event just happened to be the 1994 Olympics in Lillihamer, Norway, and I just happened to be the reigning Men's World Figure Skating Champion.

Jogging around the arena, I felt optimistic. A clean skate without even a triple-triple combo would leave me in the necessary top three spots; heck, it might even leave me first! The path to Olympic gold had been cleared for me, and now I just needed to get out there and do it. But the Olympics sometimes have a way of twisting destiny. They had already put a bend in the road for Brian and Victor a few hours earlier. Little did I know they would do the same for me.

The Olympics had been good to both of those guys in Calgary '88, and then in Albertville, France, in '92, and then they had turned pro. By the rules, neither of them should even have been allowed into these games—but these games were different. Only two years had passed since Victor had won his Olympic gold, and Brian, one of the toughest competitors ever, had played a big role in getting professionals into these Olympics. It would be the toughest Olympic Games ever with these names back in the pot, and now, here I was set up to take the gold.

The Albertville Olympics two years earlier had not been so good for me. Then, as now, I was coming in as

World Champion, but I was recovering from a slipped disk and was not even close to being the skater I could be. I had always dreamed that when the Olympic experience came to an athlete, everything would be perfect and you performed to the best of your ability. But why should the Olympics be different than any other aspect of life? You have to play the cards you are dealt. Now, like Brian and Victor, I was being handed a second chance. It was starting to look like this time it might just be my turn.

The warm-up before the short program was going well. With only one minute left, I had already run through everything I needed. And then I started to think. That was my mistake.

Anybody who knows me well would have chuckled a bit there. You see, there are only two really big moments in a short program: the necessary combination of jumps, and the necessary triple jump out of footwork. Once these two are out of the way, you are flying. I had a triple axel planned with a double toe for the combo, and a triple flip out of footwork. I was a little worried about the flip, so I decided in that moment of "thinking" to practice the take-off for that jump. I did this by trying a double flip. This is a very easy jump, and I never practice it. I simply warm up and then just do the triple flip.

Well, I fell. Not a normal fall but a hard one. The kind that jars you, and not only that—I was embarrassed. I looked up at my coach, and he had the strangest look on his face. Then, instead of just going and skating it off, I tried it again. I landed it, but not well, and then the announcement came to clear the ice. I did—but I left my confidence behind. Doubt had crept in, and for the next fifteen minutes, I guess I let it grow.

My program was going well. My triple-axel combination was perfect, and I was on my way. I really don't remember what I was thinking going into that triple flip, but I do remember being in the air, and feeling a lean. But instead of doing something about it in the .7 seconds I was up in the jump, I froze. If it had been a practice, I would have just fought for it, but I think I lost it—just for a second. I dropped my right hand, slipped off the edge and all was gone . . . just like that. Did I say I lost it for a second? It wasn't even a full second, but like so many Olympic stories, within that moment, somewhere, I gave away the gold medal.

Right after the marks—and, oh, they were awful—I did an interview with Rod Black. It was tough, but what can you do, you can't hide. I held up through it, but I was not expecting to see my parents at that moment. Somebody had got them through security and there they were, right down at ice level. When I looked up and saw them, well, I just lost it. And then, as I blubbered away like a child, my mom hugged me and said something only she could have pulled off.

"Kurt, if you had won that gold medal you would have been so busy. I know you. You never wanted to be that busy in your life anyway."

I wasn't sure I had heard her right, but deep inside I knew two things. First, that a smile had already snuck across my face. Second, that as usual, she was right.

My mom passed away during the summer of 2000, and losing her makes me hold onto moments like these even more. She was one of the most loving people I have ever known. Sure, I sometimes miss the fact that I never won that medal, but when you really think about priorities, I miss my mom a lifetime more.

Kurt Browning
Edmonton, Alberta

A Christmas to Remember

Oh child! Never allow your heart to harden.
Welcome the unicorn into your garden.

Phyllis Gottlieb

"Ruth! Are you up?"

"Yes, Momma!"

I slipped from bed and closed my window, shivering from the chill November air. Cold weather would mean a hot breakfast! And Momma had this wonderful way of simmering oatmeal in a double boiler at the back of the stove for the whole night. In a mood of happy anticipation, I quickly washed, dressed and ran downstairs.

I opened the kitchen door and was hit by a blast of cold air. The woodshed door was open, and there was no fire in the stove—something was terribly wrong.

Momma rushed in with a handful of kindling. "You're up," she said, and plopped a box of Shredded Wheat on the table. "Here, look after yourself."

"Where's Daddy?"

"Daddy's sick." She grasped a chair, as if for support. "I've sent for Dr. McLay. Eat your breakfast now."

I picked up my spoon and tried to eat while Momma busied herself at the stove.

Typical of a 1930s rural Ontario home, our wood-fired range was a massive cast-iron and nickel-plated contrivance. It had seven lids in its top and a brick-lined oven that could hold a half-dozen loaves of bread. But Momma had never developed Daddy's skill with just how to place the slivers of pine kindling or which damper to open. Fifteen exasperating minutes went by before flames crackled in the firebox and the water in the big brass kettle began to simmer.

A knock came at the side door and our neighbour Mr. Fenn stepped inside. "Doc'll be here as soon as he can," he said.

"Oh, thank you, Mr. Fenn!" Momma answered. "George warned me that having our phone taken out would be a foolish economy."

"Would you like me to look after the stock?" Mr. Fenn asked quietly.

Momma's face registered dismay. "Oh, my goodness, those poor animals!" In her concern over Daddy, she'd forgotten about his "livestock," as he jokingly called them: Daisy, the jersey; the pigs; the barn cat; and the steers we were raising for meat that Momma refused to give names to because it would be like sending one of our pets off to the butcher. Daddy took care of all these creatures before breakfast and after supper each day. "Oh, yes, please!" Momma exclaimed.

The old man nodded and headed for the barn. He often visited with Daddy at chore time and would know just how much feed to put out and which animal should be let into what enclosure. Besides, when Mr. Fenn had been laid up with gout last winter, Daddy had looked after his homing pigeons, so turnabout was fair play.

When I arrived home from school Momma met me at the door.

"What's up?" My heart was thumping a mile a minute.

"Daddy has bronchial pneumonia."

I didn't know what pneumonia was, but Momma's fear was evident.

"He's not going to die, is he?" I asked. "We can do something, can't we?"

"Doctor says we must keep him warm, see that he gets lots of rest and takes his medicine. After that we can only hope and pray for the best."

"Oh, Momma!" We enfolded each other in comforting arms.

Aylmer, Ontario, was a small, closely knit farming community a hundred and fifty miles west of Toronto, and when word of Daddy's illness spread, the men began dropping by to split firewood or do barn chores, and the women took over the housework. Mrs. Peters from up the road scooped our laundry into a butcher's basket and took it home with her. Mrs. Randall finished Momma's batch of bread and started yeast for another, and Mrs. Chute marshalled the churchwomen to look after our meals. Momma was left free to care for Daddy.

I was barred from the sickroom altogether. People came and went, but whenever I offered to help, some adult would tell me that I was "too young" or "too little." I felt isolated, useless. These were the pre-penicillin years, and two weeks passed before something called "the crisis" was over and my father was up to seeing me.

By mid-December Momma had learned how to bank the wood stove to keep the kitchen warm, and Daddy finally began to spend his days sitting up.

One night, when Momma had returned from helping Daddy back upstairs, I kissed her cheek. "Goodnight, Momma."

"Ruth, wait . . ."

"What is it? You look so solemn!"

"I know Christmas is next week, but . . . between the doctor's bills and no money coming in, our savings are almost gone. And Daddy won't be able to work until spring."

I felt a chill of fear. "Are we gonna lose our house, like Mr. Meeks?"

"Good heavens, no! This place is paid for and we have lots of food in the cellar. It's just that cash will be short for awhile." She flushed. "Which means there won't be any money to buy Christmas presents."

I hugged her as tightly as I could. "Momma, I don't care about any old Christmas presents!"

But once alone, I snuggled into my feather tick and tears filled my eyes. I'd lied to Momma. I did care. I cared a whole lot! For months I'd been praying for white figure skates like Sonja Henie's. Being told I was not going to get them was a terrible disappointment.

Then I felt a rush of shame. Wasn't I better off than lots of kids my age? One girl in my third-grade class had to wear dresses made from bleached-out flour sacks, and I knew of two boys so fearful of scuffing their only shoes that they walked barefoot to within sight of school.

But I sure had wanted those white skates!

I awoke Christmas morning to see my breath in the air. Momma had started hanging quilts over doorways to direct heat up the back stairs into the room she shared with Daddy, and my room had been getting progressively colder.

I wriggled into my goose feathers and felt sorry for myself. A room with no heat, Christmas with no presents—gee whiz!

Then I thought of Momma. Red-faced with guilt, I dressed and hurried downstairs. A fire crackled in the stove, the big brass kettle was boiling and Daddy was seated in his rocking chair.

"Merry Christmas, punkin'!"

"Merry Christmas, Daddy!" I shifted the kettle to a back lid. "Where's Momma?"

"Out doing chores."

Then I turned and saw the tree . . . a lopsided, sparse-limbed little spruce—even the scrawny trunk nailed to crossed boards was slightly askew. But in the eyes of an eight-year-old who had taken a parent's warning literally and not expected a Christmas tree at all, this tree was extravagantly, unbelievably beautiful! It was decorated with tinsel salvaged from Christmas trees past, along with strings of popcorn, cranberries, crocheted snowflakes of sugar-stiffened lace and gingerbread cookies shaped like tiny stars and elves.

And—although Momma had said there was no money—there were presents, in profusion!

There was a doll, purchased with months of hoarded soap coupons, with a wardrobe that almost took my breath away—an evening gown, a skating outfit, a cape, a kimono, dresses both long and short—each piece hand-sewn, knitted or crocheted with materials from the scrap basket. I recognized the fine silk of Momma's old blouse and a cotton print that had been a dress of my own. Later I would learn that the shirred velvet of the skating costume came from a muff belonging to my father's mother, who had died years before I was born.

Speechless with wonder, I turned to my father.

"Your mother did all that by herself." His voice was soft, reverential. "Sawed that tree herself, hauled it out of the woods, wading hip deep through snowdrifts. And she made those doll clothes after you were in bed asleep." He brushed a hand across moist eyes. "Child, your mother was bent, bound and determined you would have a proper Christmas, and that's all there was to it!"

The woodshed door slammed and Momma stood in the doorway.

I rushed to hug her. "Oh, Momma, thank you!" I felt the coldness of her cheek and smelled the delicious odour of soap and wood smoke in her hair.

"You're welcome, sweetheart." She hugged me back, but only for a moment, and as she backed away her cheeks were flushed. Like many women of her generation, Momma was not comfortable with praise or with overt displays of emotion.

"I just wanted you to have a little something for Christmas," she continued. "But it's mostly homemade. Nothing really."

Then my father made a comment I've never forgotten.

"Mable, I think maybe you've taught Ruth something—there are times in life when one person's nothing can be somebody else's everything!"

He was right.

Ruth Robins-Jeffery
Hampton, Prince Edward Island

A Change of Heart

As an additional safeguard against self-pity in our home, Mama kept several charity boxes that were marked "For the poor." We gave regularly. It made us feel rich.

Sam Levenson, Humorist

It was a cold December, at the tail end of the Great Depression, and things were tough. Mum had a hard time raising us kids on her own in our small community of New Westminster, British Columbia. My father had drowned in Pitt Lake five years earlier—I still remember it like it was yesterday. Because Dad had no pension or benefits, there was not much money; we went on relief, now called social assistance. We relied on the Salvation Army to keep us clothed, and although our clothes were secondhand, we thought they were beautiful.

Looking back, I realize what Mum went through sending us kids to school. Every morning she would tuck a new piece of cardboard in our shoes because our soles were worn out. When we got home, Mum would have French toast ready for us. This was bread deep-fried in lard. Constant moving was typical for my family in those days, and it didn't look like we'd be in our current house much longer. Rent was $25 a month, but Mum couldn't pay it, and we knew we would be evicted right after Christmas on the first of January.

The holidays were fast approaching, and we were entitled to $25 for Christmas from social services. An inspector came to our house and searched it from top to bottom to be sure we didn't have any food hidden away. When he didn't find any, he issued the cheque to Mum. It was four days before Christmas. Mum said that instead of buying food, she was going to use the money to pay our back rent. That way we'd have a roof over our heads for a little while longer. Then she told us that there would be no Christmas gifts.

Unknown to Mum, I had been selling Christmas trees, shovelling snow and doing odd jobs to earn enough money to buy a new pair of boots—boots that weren't patched; boots with no cardboard in the soles. I knew exactly which boots I wanted. They were ten-inch, Top-Genuine, Pierre Paris boots, and they cost $23.

The big day for getting my boots came on Christmas Eve afternoon. I was very excited as I hurried up the road to catch the bus into town. It was only a half-mile walk, but on the way I noticed a house with Christmas lights and decorations. It was then I realized that at our house, we had no lights, no decorations and no money for Christmas goodies. I also knew we would have no turkey or ham for Christmas dinner. But at least there would be French toast.

As I continued walking, I began to feel bewildered. I was eleven years old, and I was feeling a strange sense of guilt. Here I was going to buy a new pair of boots, while Mum was probably home in tears, thinking of ways to explain why there were no presents. As I arrived at the bus stop, the driver opened the big manual-hinged door. I stood there for what seemed an eternity, until eventually the driver asked, "Son, are you getting on this bus or not?" I finally blurted out, "No thanks, sir. I've changed my mind."

The bus drove off without me, and I stood alone in a daze, feeling as if a weight had been lifted off my shoulders. My mind was made up, and I realized what I had to do.

Across the street from the bus stop was a big grocery store called the Piggly Wiggly. Into the store I went, brimming with happiness and excitement. I realized that the twenty-five dollars I had worked so hard for went a long way toward groceries. I bought a turkey, ham, oranges and all the Christmas trimmings. I spent every dime of my hard-earned money.

The owner of the grocery store said, "Son, you can't pack all those groceries and carry them home yourself." So I asked two boys with carriers on their bicycles to run them the half-mile down to our house. As I walked behind the delivery boys, I whispered to them to quietly unload the groceries on the porch and pile them against the door. Once they had done this, I knocked on the door. I could hardly wait to see my mother's face! When Mum opened the door, some of the groceries fell inside onto the floor, and she just stood there, dumbfounded. Holding back the tears, I hollered, "Merry Christmas, Mother! There really is a Santa Claus!"

I had a lot of explaining to do as we unpacked all the food and put it away. That day I got enough hugs and kisses from Mum to last two lifetimes. To see my mother's prayers answered more than made up for the boots I never got. It was a Merry Christmas for us after all!

George Mapson
Burnaby, British Columbia
Submitted by his niece, Diane Pitts

Monsieur Gaton

When I was a young girl, I spent several weeks each summer with my grandparents in Callander, Ontario. Those were wonderful times. Besides being doted on by Grandma and Poppa, I was quickly included in the activities of the neighbourhood kids, and, of course, adopted their brand of devilment. One of the objects of our attention was a local character everyone called Bozo. His real name was Raoul Gaton, but I would not discover this for some time.

When I first became aware of Bozo, I was almost eight years old; he might have been in his late teens or early twenties. People said he was retarded. He seldom spoke, and he wore a vacant expression below puppy dog eyes that belied the unintentionally cruel remarks we directed his way. His appearance seldom varied: green work pants, peaked green cap, plaid flannel shirt and sneakers. He rode an ancient girl's bicycle with a basket carrier in front, and that bike was as much a part of him as his clothes. Bozo and his bike were a familiar sight in town as he carried out odd jobs for local shopkeepers and the church. He was considered too slow for anything more challenging.

We kids offered up our own brand of harassment each time he rattled down the dirt road past my grandparents' home. His approach would be relayed down the street by the hoots of neighbourhood kids. We'd hurl ourselves into position at the edge of my grandparents' property and wait—but well back from the road, fearful in the knowledge that he was "different." As he passed, we would taunt him with yells of "Bozo! Hey, Bozo." He would look our way, smile and wave, oblivious to our cruelty. With this acknowledgment we would tumble on the grass in fits of laughter, crossing our eyes, belting out nonsensical words in throaty voices, amusing ourselves with our Bozo performances.

His brief appearances did not hold our attention for long. As children on summer holiday, we'd soon look for amusement elsewhere. Hanging out at my grandfather's barbershop was a favourite haunt of mine, despite the fact that it was the only place I had to wear shoes and remain quiet while customers were present.

A red and white pole outside the shop flagged down local gentlemen for haircuts, shaves or just conversation. The front window displayed models of local logging boats—either defunct or soon-to-be—and sailing ships with rigging that defied imagination. Inside, I would watch my grandfather wield scissors and razor as he trimmed a month's growth of hair from the head of the boy or man in the chair. Often, haircutting was secondary to the flow of conversation that slipped easily into French to hide adult secrets from my young ears.

I can't remember what the conversation was about the afternoon that Bozo showed up, but I do recall that my grandfather was preparing to close for the day when he came through the door. I was sitting on the long oak bench that ran the length of the shop, leafing through a comic book, when my grandfather greeted him with, *"Bonjour Monsieur, comment ça va?"* and waved him to the chair that grandfather used while doing his paperwork.

My cheeks began to burn as grandfather and Bozo huddled over something the young man had put on the desk. Although my grandfather did most of the talking and the conversation was in French, I was certain that the gist of it was a complaint by Bozo that I was one of the children who was being cruel to him. I hunched deeper on the oak bench, wishing that the hardness of the wood would give way to a secret doorway through which I might escape.

After what seemed an eternity, Bozo rose from his seat, shook my grandfather's hand and left. My grandfather waved me to the chair where Bozo had been sitting, and my fear of being reprimanded increased. Instead, my grandfather showed me a piece of paper on which the name "Raoul Gaton" had been repeatedly printed in clear but painfully drawn letters. The humble document was the first inkling I had that my grandfather was teaching this unteachable young man how to write his own name. "Without knowing how to sign your own name," he told me solemnly, "you can go nowhere."

I learned sometime later that my grandfather had helped arrange for Raoul to receive a government grant in lieu of his disabilities. Raoul had signed his first disability cheque with an "X" and cashed it at the credit union my grandfather ran from the barbershop. From that moment on, my grandfather was determined to teach the young man to write his name.

Many years later, my grandfather passed away. At the funeral home in the nearby city of North Bay, the crowds of mourners who had made their last farewells left, and only the family remained by the casket. My grandmother felt a presence in the room and glanced back through the shadows to the small pool of light that illuminated the visitor's book. There, with green hat in hand, stood Raoul Gaton.

As we left the room, my grandmother placed a comforting hand on Raoul's shoulder, and her heart welled at the depth of sadness in his eyes. With a slight turn of her head and a nod toward the casket, she acknowledged his desire for a moment alone with the man who had been his friend.

I found I could not move as I watched Raoul walk hesitatingly through the dim light to the casket. After a moment he stretched out his hand and rested it on my grandfather's chest. "*Bon homme*—good man," he said in little more than a whisper, then he slowly turned my way.

As he walked towards me, I glanced at the visitor book. There, written boldly in neat and legible script, was the final entry on the page: "Raoul Gaton." For a brief second, as he passed me, our eyes met. I hoped that he could detect the respect that I felt for him. I had been allowed to glimpse into the window of his being, and I had discovered a dignity there that humbled me.

As I accompanied the other family members from the funeral home, I noticed a battered girl's bicycle, with a basket up front, leaning against the wall. I remembered my grandfather's words: "Without knowing how to sign your own name, you can go nowhere." Monsieur Gaton and his battered bicycle had indeed gone many places, and one of them was into my heart.

Jayne Harvey
Keswick, Ontario

Finding Your Own Medicine

Being oneself . . . is really the essence of all wisdom!

Roland Goodchild

Those who analyze such things say children who lack parental love don't thrive. It was true for me—I didn't thrive, I didn't want to thrive. Specifically, I lacked the will to live. So, when in my early thirties, I found myself faced with death within a year, I chose not to take radiation and chemotherapy. Instead, I embraced death.

I didn't have any close friends and had severed family ties long ago. It was easy to slip away from my urban life. I had enough money on hand to last a year—six months more than I figured I needed. I chose Quadra Island for my retreat, just across an inlet from Campbell River in British Columbia. I found and rented a small cabin by the Pacific shore at Cape Mudge near an old Indian village. Then I settled in with booze, smokes, music, books and death on my mind. I walked and contemplated, cried and laughed. I met people here and there, and when they got curious about me, I would make up a story. Whatever came to mind was the theme for the day.

Some days I was sick and scared. On most days, however, I had a surprisingly uncommon feeling of security, of being held and nurtured. My days were filled with wandering the shore and tidal pools and the high meadows.

I first saw the woman in a high meadow—a native woman gathering plants. "Medicine," she later told me. I watched as she gathered leaves, flowers and roots— stooping low to bury tobacco offerings in Mother Earth. Her connection with the plants made me conscious of the tall graceful shaggy-headed plants circling my cabin. My landlord had told me to get rid of them.

"They take over," he said. "They're just weeds."

I'd put it off. I just couldn't do it. The plants seemed to be there for me—guarding me, looking after me in some way. I came to think of them as "my standing people."

The next time I saw the woman she was digging up the root of the very same plants that circled my cabin. Surprised by this synchronicity, I asked her to tell me about them.

"You've found your medicine," she said. "This root is good for the blood and good for tumours. This is your medicine." She handed me a small shovel and we dug maybe twenty roots together. For every root she dug up, she dropped tobacco in the hole, making an offering of thanks to the plant. She gave me some tobacco so I could do the same. It made me feel connected to the earth, and part of something. I began to feel the power of earth medicine.

I learned her name was Standing Woman, and she was Kwakiutl. Words weren't needed between us; she seemed to know everything she needed to know about me. That day she invited me for tea at her summerhouse—a tent beside a creek at the edge of the tree line. The tent was large, airy and filled with earthy smells. It was furnished with a cot, table and chairs. As we sipped our tea she told me she had known about me even before we met, and knew she could help me. The grandmothers had told her this. It was simply understood between us that I would stay with her and use her medicines to get well.

I stayed with her for three months. She took me with her to gather plants for my daily needs, telling me their story and how to prepare them. We would make the medicine together. Some days I wasn't well enough to venture out, and on those days she sat with me and cared for my needs with more love and tenderness than I had ever known. As the days passed I became stronger, more confident, and more deeply connected to the earth—the same earth I had wanted to leave just a short time before. One morning, I awoke and simply knew my disease was gone. I also knew my apprenticeship with nature had just begun.

Now, some twenty-five years later, I walk close to the earth, and like her, I listen to the stories the plants have to tell. They teach me their medicine, and I pass it on to those who want to learn. Before she died, Standing Woman asked me to carry on her work. I cannot replace her, but I can walk with people to help them find the medicine they are seeking.

Some want to walk this way and some do not. For those who do, I am here in the meadow.

Kahlee Keane, Root Woman
Saskatoon, Saskatchewan

Three Words

The only limits are, as always, those of vision.

James Broughton

As I stood outside the arena on that bitter February day, I had no idea of the warmth that I would find inside. Before entering the building to join 5,000 people, I slipped a three-word sign on my baby's stroller. I very much wanted to connect with the people inside. I hoped that someone would read my sign and welcome us into their community.

Nine months earlier, I had given birth to my third child, Jimmy. He was a beautiful baby in every way. On his second day of life, I was told he had Down syndrome. I read everything I could get my hands on about Down syndrome and received encouragement from other parents. Jimmy was nine months old when I read that Toronto and Collingwood, Ontario, were hosting the Special Olympic World Winter Games. I wanted to go with my baby and get a peek into our future. Before leaving the house, I raced down to the basement and made a three-word sign out of white felt and red marker.

When Jimmy and I entered the arena, we took a seat

alongside the boards. Within minutes, my sign was being noticed. Parents squeezed my hand and told me of the challenges and unbelievable joys I would know. Athletes came over to meet my baby and wish him luck. Volunteers who travelled thousands of miles to be a part of the games attached their country's pins to the little square of felt. It was also noticed by a crewmember from The Sports Network (TSN), and by Frank Hayden, the founder of the Special Olympics movement worldwide.

It was Frank Hayden who put my little, three-word sign into a context I never imagined. He told the Canadian Parliament and the news media that it was the "defining moment" of the games and of his thirty-year career as a sports scientist. He said, "Thirty years ago, even ten years ago, would a mother have walked into a public place and proudly announced that her child had a mental disability? She was looking toward the future, not with fear and trepidation, but with great expectations."

Last July I received a beautiful letter from an artist in Ottawa. He had been commissioned to create a logo for the ninth Special Olympic Canadian Summer Games in Sudbury, Ontario. Bernard Poulin wrote, "You and your child have been my creative muses. The 'challenge sign' on your baby's chest said it all." Poulin created a circular logo that he says "reminds us of the hearts and souls of the parents who fuel the dreams of the athletes, who are supported and encouraged by the organisation." Poulin added, "It exists because in a crowd at the Centennial Arena in North York, Ontario, a proud mother and a beautiful child challenged the world with their daring."

The impact of the three words on that makeshift sign continues to amaze me. It said only, "Future Special Olympian."

Jo-Ann Hartford Jaques
Etobicoke, Ontario

The Orange Tabletop

Who needs a gag writer? Life itself is funny enough!

Honest Ed Mirvish

Brent's Hill was without doubt the best sledding hill imaginable—incredibly high at the top, a long, steep run in the middle and a flat stretch at the bottom. Today the conditions were perfect for sledding. We had watched all day from the windows of our Presteign Heights Public School classrooms. Good, outdoorsy, Canadian kids, we knew our snow and what weather conditions were needed to create the fastest runs: bitter cold; enough sun to melt the top layer so it would freeze over as the sun dropped; and no wind to set the snow drifting.

The thought of our tobogganing plans was almost too much. I couldn't keep my mind on my studies at all. The fluorescent orange tabletop consumed my thoughts. It was ready to go!

It was an idea that had hit us just yesterday. We had been playing hide-and-seek when we noticed the round patio tabletop leaning against the wall of our house. The rest of the table had long since rusted out and disappeared; who knows why my dad had kept the top. It was about four feet across, weighed an unbelievable number of pounds, and more importantly, it was fluorescent orange. My father had sprayed it the previous summer with orange surveying paint in the hopes of preserving it for one more year. Who came up with the idea to use the tabletop as a toboggan? I can't remember, but we all knew it was brilliant.

History would be made. I could see it now: we would fly down the hill, easily passing everyone else. Whether we would take the safer route to the left, or the narrow, more challenging one to the right was the decision we pondered. There were, of course, advantages and disadvantages to both.

"Billy, you're daydreaming again," chided Mr. Kenniger. "You are never going to get through grade six if you continue like this."

I put my head back down and pretended to be studying. I could not afford to get a detention that night! Eventually it was 3:30 and the class was dismissed. I was free! The plan was set. We would race home and meet in my backyard to get the tabletop.

It was 1960. We lived on Northdale Boulevard in East York, Toronto. It was a dead-end street on the edge of the Don Valley, but the slopes there were thickly wooded, so we had to go elsewhere to toboggan. Several blocks into the neighbourhood took us to Brent's Hill. We called it that because you had to walk through Brent's backyard to get there.

The tabletop was way too heavy to carry, so we took turns rolling it to Brent's. On the way, we discussed which route we would take, how we would steer it, and most importantly, who would have the first turn. Would it be my younger brother, Tom, my next door neighbour,

Janet Patterson, also several years younger, or me? We all wanted to be first. At the hill, conditions were excellent—a thin veneer of ice over a thick base of snow, no noticeable wind and no drifts. The snow looked flat, smooth and incredibly fast. We stood at the top looking down, digging in our boots to keep our balance and holding fiercely onto the tabletop.

A change came over us as we stared down the hill. It seemed steeper than usual—and for some strange reason, there was no one else there. Perhaps it was the freezing temperatures or the late-afternoon hour, but whatever the reason, the total absence of other kids created a dark, eerie feeling. Suddenly, the urge to be the first one down the hill lost its appeal—but someone had to go.

"Janet, you're a girl, I guess it's only fair that you go first," I said gallantly.

"What about you being the oldest and the most experienced, and what about the fact that it's your tabletop from your backyard?" she inquired innocently.

"That's alright," I said, "I'll have lots of turns after you. Go ahead."

"But what about Tom, shouldn't he go first? He loves sledding more than anyone and he's the best at steering."

"No, I really think we should stick to the 'girls first' rule here," I said.

"Well, if you really think so. Thanks."

Tom and I held onto the tabletop, while Janet settled into the middle of it. She suddenly looked very small—and not very confident. I had a funny feeling in my stomach, a feeling I couldn't identify at the time but I now recognize as guilt. We planned her descent. The hill split into a kind of broad Y near the bottom, and Janet would stay to the left, which was the longer, but safer, route. If the sled went so fast that it reached the Don River, Janet would bail out. Separating the route on the left from the one on the right was a ridge that rose and dropped off over a cliff. The cliff was steep and covered with tall evergreen trees, fallen branches and bushes. This did not concern us because, even without steering, you automatically veered to the left or right of the ridge. We knew there was no sledding device fast enough to carry you up and over the top of the ridge.

"One! Two! Three!" we hollered, and released the tabletop. The thing took off like a rocket, and we knew immediately it was going way too fast—faster than anything we had ever seen. The heavy metal against the icy surface was a lethal combination: Janet was heading straight for the ridge at breakneck speed. But then, you always headed straight for the ridge at first. The veering-off point was coming up soon. We held our breath. *To the left! To the left!* We said repeatedly to ourselves, willing it to happen. She reached the critical veering-off point, but her direction did not alter one iota. She was a goner.

"Bail! Bail!" we screamed.

Janet was clutching the rim of the tabletop for dear life; there would be no bailing. Up the ridge she raced, and then—she took flight. The scraping sound of the table against the ice vanished and there was silence. For several seconds, Tom and I just stood there stunned. We were stuck. We were as much a part of the landscape as the trees, the boulders or the ice sculptures formed by the rushing waters of the Don River.

Then we were all arms and legs as we raced down the hill, tripping over our own feet, sliding on our hands and knees, gripped with absolute terror. We had killed our next-door neighbour. We as good as threw her over the cliff. What would our parents say? What would Janet's parents say? Life would never be the same on our quiet little street in Parkview Hills. We would be the despised Gorman brothers, boys with no moral fibre, boys without souls.

"Please, God," I remember saying over and over again, "badly injured maybe, broken limbs and battle scars to show her friends, but please—not dead!"

We reached the ridge, gasping for air, shaking with fear.

"Janet, Janet!" we screamed.

Nothing.

"Janet, are you alright?" we wailed wishfully.

Nothing.

Then, on the very edge of collapsing from anguish, we heard a sound, almost a squeak, come from above.

"I'm up here, up in the trees. I'm okay! It was great!" She began to ramble on about the speed, the sensation, the excitement.

We looked up in disbelief. Janet was wedged in a tree, between two branches. She had flown up into a tree and was not only unhurt, she was exuberant. Then, as though released from a spell, Tom and I started screaming and laughing. We laughed so hard we fell on the ground, rolling around, holding our stomachs. When we finally caught our breath, we stared up at the night sky and felt that incredible sense of peace you feel not often enough in life. Janet clambered down the tree and joined us, totally oblivious to our anxiety and her near death.

Our reputations were intact. Our lives would be allowed to return to normal. We might even give the orange tabletop another try—but not today, not today.

Bill Gorman
Toronto, Ontario

For Better or For Worse®

by Lynn Johnston

Peacekeeper's Coffee

It is one of the most beautiful compensations of life, that no man can sincerely try to help another without helping himself.

Ralph Waldo Emerson

It was a long drive to Okachani. Over two-and-a-half hours in a convoy of the Canadian M113 APCs (armoured personnel carriers), which rattled and shook as they kicked up clouds of dust along the dirt roads of the former Yugoslavia.

The 4:30 A.M. start was no big deal. Neither was the long drive and diet of road dust. Those came with the job. No, it was the attitude of the locals that was starting to wear on our sense of humour.

When we got to Okachani, we passed by the usual war-torn, roofless brick houses with their weed-infested yards. Some of the intact houses had Serbian villagers still living in them, determined to stay. As our carriers rumbled past, they would either give us a curious look, a scowl, or simply ignore us altogether while they tended their gardens and eked out their existence. We would wave or just act like they weren't there, both sides engaging in mutual tolerance.

Today our job was maintenance patrol—a nice name for cleaning up after someone else. It was a never-ending routine of repairing damages or replacing materials stolen by the desperate local population. The men kept grumbling about the constant cleanup. I kept hearing, "Just let the two sides go at it and sort it out. Isn't that what they want?"

I was a sergeant in charge of an eight-man section responsible for a defensive area in the corner of the village. This defensive area was a couple of houses that we had previously cleared of glass and other debris born of conflict. We had then fortified the buildings with sandbags, chicken wire and lumber. We would routinely check on its sturdiness, then grudgingly clean up more debris and replace stolen corrugated iron, wire, plywood and sandbags.

"Look at the bloody mess," someone cursed. "Let's just . . ."

I cut him off.

"Let's just get the job done," I snapped. "The day's not getting any cooler."

I had left Canada months ago, full of high ideals about helping Second- or Third-World countries, protecting the downtrodden and saving all the homeless children. We were going to set everything right and make the world a better place. Now, I was not so sure. I was no longer the noble liberator I had first envisioned myself. Every report I heard of torture, infanticide or execution was starting to wear on me. Every time some drunken villager pointed an assault rifle or pistol at us, or told us to "Get out of my country," I thought how pointless this was getting to be. To top it off, our own Canadian media back home was relentlessly criticising us every step of the way. I wondered if there was anyone benefiting from this misery.

I was numb to the loud griping I was hearing today as the soldiers hauled the sheets of corrugated iron. Other days I would tell them to keep it down. But today, between the constant cleanups, restacking sandbags and make-work projects from headquarters (such as making flowerbeds), I really no longer cared.

I turned my attention back to the unloading of the APC. The men were starting to get careless and were flinging off the supplies. There was so much flying metal, dust, spit and swearing, I was about to shout something. Then suddenly this young woman appeared. I had never seen her before, and I had no clue from which shell-ridden house she had come. But there she was, carrying a tray of small ceramic cups.

Right here, amongst the crumbling buildings, bullet-holed walls and broken glass, was this young Serbian villager with a tray of what smelled like coffee. She approached us just like she was serving up some friends at a tea party.

She was a slim woman with well-kept dark hair, but the lines on her worry-etched face, along with her missing teeth, made her look older than her probable late twenties. Despite the sadness in her dark eyes, she spoke cheerfully, in Serbo-Croatian, as she offered the tray to me, hostess-style. It was a curious sight. Well, my mother had always taught me that it was rude to refuse hospitality. The "show no favouritism" rule could bend some.

"Over here," I hollered at my section. "C'mon for a coffee break."

"*Hvallah* (thank you)," I said, gratefully accepting one of the small cups full of floating coffee grounds. I sipped it carefully as, one by one, the soldiers in my section each grabbed a cup, like kids after candy. The stuff was warm and bitter, and I don't even like coffee, but I drank it just the same.

I replaced my cup on the tray with another *hvallah,* followed by some theatrics to describe "delicious." Some of the guys gave a humourous performance of "mmmmmm, coffeeeee" that rivalled Homer Simpson with a doughnut.

She cheerfully said something, flashing that sweet, missing-tooth grin, and then she walked away, amongst the rubble. Her head was held high and her walk was proud. I wondered how she could be like that when she had likely lost everything.

For all we knew, that might have been the last of her coffee—something that she normally reserved for her own family's meagre meals. And there we were, six healthy, fit Canadian soldiers, with food in our bellies, money in the bank and a few thousand dollars of dentistry in our mouths. Back home in Canada we had our homes and our families—safe and waiting for our return.

We all must have been thinking the same thing. For the next few hours, sweat poured off us like running water as we worked hard into the late afternoon. Only now, there wasn't a single gripe coming from anyone.

Doug Setter
Winnipeg, Manitoba

9

SPECIAL
CONNECTIONS

*Any relationship of love and respect is to
be cherished in a dark world where only
such things give meaning and warmth,
understanding and hope.*

*The Right Honourable Adrienne Clarkson
Governor-General of Canada*

Granny's Rosary

Miracles do not happen in contradiction with nature, but in contradiction with what we know about nature.

Saint Augustine

When I was a young boy back in Italy, I used to love to sit on my granny's lap while she recited her nightly rosary. I would snuggle up in her arms as she sat rocking in an old wicker chair by the fireplace counting beads and whispering prayers in a soothing foreign language (Latin, I later learned). Sometimes she'd let me hold the rosary and keep count for her until I fell asleep. And although by age eight I felt a little silly about this awkward nightly routine, I continued because I knew how much it meant to her. She was old and frail, and so it was that in 1966, when my father, brother and sister immigrated to Canada, my mother and I stayed behind in Italy to care for Granny, who was too old to make the trip.

Two months before my twelfth birthday, Granny shattered her hip in a nasty fall and became bedridden, never to sit in her rocking chair again. She passed away ten months later.

The afternoon before her departure, when I returned from school, she called me to her bedside. The long months in bed had not been kind to her. In the dimness of the room, she looked so incredibly small in that big bed, her face drawn, her long white hair wispy and dull.

Extending one of her long, bony hands she beckoned me to her side. "Come," she said in a voice that seemed to travel miles before reaching me. And when her hand closed around mine, I noticed that it was cold and waxy— almost lifeless. "Oh, you're such a wonderful boy," she whispered as she stroked my face. "And you're going to be a handsome . . . handsome man one day soon!"

When I knelt down to hear her better, I noticed her eyes were swimming in tears, her thin bloodless lips quivering. She sniffled, drew a laboured sigh and then continued, "The time has come for Granny to move on." Understanding well what she meant, I immediately protested.

Putting a finger to my lips she hushed me. "Nothing to be afraid of, my child, it's just part of life," she explained, "merely the completion of a wonderful cycle. When the angels come for me, miss me not, because I will always be here by your side." She then reached under her pillow and brought out the rosary. "Here," she said, handing it to me. "I want you to have this. Keep it close to your heart and remember me by it." Oh, how she loved me.

Again, when I tried to interject she sealed my lips with her cold fingers.

"Go and play with your friends now," she said. "Granny is tired and would really like to get some sleep." Then she turned over as much as her broken hip would allow. I kissed the back of her head and left the room clutching her rosary. That was the last time I saw her alive.

After Granny died, my mother and I made the trip to Canada and joined my father, brother and sister in Toronto. It was 1969, and I was fifteen years old.

I never did use the rosary the way Granny had perhaps intended me to, as I wasn't totally sure how the whole thing worked. Instead, I strung it between two nails on the wall behind my headboard. It hung for many years where I could look at it every day. In times of turmoil, I even took it down and held it in my hands for comfort.

At the end of my senior high school year, my class organized a trip to Heart Lake in Brampton, just outside Toronto. Here we felt five years of camaraderie could be brought to adequate closure; in other words . . . party time!

It was an overcast cool June morning and the beach area was mostly deserted. One of the girls hop-skipped up to the water and gingerly dipped one foot in. "It's freezing!" she announced, running back.

The biggest and baddest dude of the class, known simply as Ox, shook his head. "Women, ha!" he said, looking at me. "What say we show these skirtsies and the rest of these pansies what real men are made of! Race you to the raft . . . loser moons the principal!"

"You're on." I replied, stripping down to my swimming trunks and racing for the water. I plunged in just before Ox. The water wasn't merely freezing, it was downright galvanizing! As I came up gasping and began stroking, I heard whooping and cheers from our classmates and Ox blowing air like a whale beside me. Ahead, fifty yards or so, the raft awaited the victor. As I halved the distance, a whole body length ahead of my bovine friend, a sudden cramp seized my abdomen, and a moment later both my legs went numb . . . dragging behind me, weighing me down. Ox passed me; someone on shore yahooed . . . I went momentarily under. Using only my arms, fighting cramps that were quickly spreading to every muscle in my body, I managed to regain the surface. The raft now seemed at least fifty miles away. Ox was almost there. I was too proud to scream for help.

As I went under again, it suddenly became clear that I was going to drown, right here, in front of all my friends. When I finally decided to forgo my pride and yell for help, I no longer had breath to do it with. As I slipped under, it was not my life that I saw flashing before my eyes, but my granny's rosary. If only I could touch it just one last time, I thought as I watched it dangling in the shimmering light just below the surface of the water. I reached for it. I touched it. It broke; beads slipped through my numb fingers and went floating down past me. As my lungs compressed, begging for oxygen, rising from the depth of the lake I thought I heard those foreign whispers from my childhood. With one last desperate lunge, fighting a spreading torpor, I reached for the rosary again, and managed to get a grip of its tiny silver crucifix. This time it was as strong as a rope, and I felt it pulling me up.

I don't know how, but moments later I was hoisting myself up onto the raft to join my already gloating friend. After a brief rest, without saying a word of what had happened, we swam back to shore without further incident.

When I got home later that day, the first thing I did was run up to my room to check on the rosary. As I threw the door open, I noticed it was gone; one of the nails had fallen out and the other hung askew downwards, as if someone had pulled it down in haste. Then, I stepped on what felt like a couple of tiny pebbles. With my heart knocking in my chest, I knelt down for a closer look and saw in amazement a scattering of loose beads . . . my granny's rosary.

Vince Fantauzzi
Brampton, Ontario

When I Met My Hero!

When I was a child, I loved the work of Charles Schulz, creator of the famous *Peanuts* comic strip. I read it because it spoke to us as children. It attributed to us common sense and personalities, and the ability to think cerebral thoughts. To me it spoke to real kids, it wasn't "just a comic strip." I collected his books, and when I was in my twenties, I had illustrations of his characters all over my bedroom wall. He really was one of my heroes!

I had always known that comics were more than just drawings. They're a wonderful way of communicating and of telling the truth. Charles Schulz kept me aware of that. Somehow, he accompanied me through my life. Wherever I went, he was there, because no matter where I was, I could open a newspaper and find his work.

I certainly never expected to meet him. So, when the phone rang one day, and I heard the words, "Hi, this is Charles Schulz," I was so stunned I said, "Who?" And he said, very apologetically, "I do *Peanuts*."

He called me simply to say, "I like your work." I was so blown away, I had to sit down. He called me several times after that and we talked about our work. I just couldn't wait to meet him!

About a year after that first phone call, we finally met in Washington at the Reuben Awards, which is sort of the Oscars of the comics' industry. I was nominated that year for my own comic strip, *For Better or For Worse*. In fact, I actually won! Charles Schulz came up to me at the meeting and whispered in my ear, "I voted for you!"

We got along so well that he and his wife said, "If you're ever in California, please drop by and visit." How often do you get an invitation like that from one of your heroes? When my husband and I did go out to California, we called, and to my total amazement, they invited us to stay at their home.

It was a lovely, quiet place on a hillside, with a beautiful view of meadows and rolling hills. Charles Schulz wanted to take us for a walk around his property, but I had arrived with only good clothes, and didn't have any shoes suitable for hiking around the woods and trails.

He said, "Your feet aren't very big, let me give you a pair of my shoes." He looked through his closet, pulled out a pair of his own running shoes and stuffed some tissue in the toes. When I put them on, they fit just fine! We then went for a walk around his property, and had a great visit. Later it occurred to me that something truly amazing had happened. "Good grief," I said with a laugh. "I've just walked a mile in your shoes!" From then on, we had a "running gag" between us. He's someone I'll never, ever forget.

Lynn Johnston, creator of For Better or For Worse
North Bay, Ontario

A Street Kid Named Mike

The greatest good we can do for others is not to share our riches, but to assist in revealing their own.

Benjamin Disraeli

Mike was a street kid. He never knew his father, his mother was a "lady of the night" and he lived with a feeble and indifferent grandmother. His clothing was in constant need of repair, as ripped pants were not yet the thing. He was ten years old, undernourished and unkempt. Compared to the other kids around him, he was at a distinct disadvantage.

It was September 1966, and I was twenty years old, facing my first class of kids as a new teacher. Like most new, young teachers, I was full of enthusiasm and determined to make a difference. My grade 4/5 class in an elementary school in downtown Toronto was made up of thirty-eight angels, and one street kid named Mike. Being so young, I knew very little about parenting. I did however recognize a child in need, and decided that this was as good a place as any to reach out and see if I could make a difference.

And so it was that early in September, my special "foster father" relationship with Mike began. Astonishing as it may seem, I became the only parent figure he ever had. Each day as I arrived at school around 7:30 A.M., Mike would already be in the parking lot waiting for me. Because he was usually hungry, I'd take him out for breakfast. I showed him how to sew, and together we began mending his ripped and torn clothes.

Each noon hour as I shared my lunch with him, I taught him a host of new skills—for a while we worked on the proper method of using a microscope. On another day we constructed a pinhole camera, then we classified rocks and minerals. Still later, we did some archaeology. Mike would then "help" me teach these skills to the rest of the class. We all had a lot of fun, and a kind of unspoken trust began to build up between us. Surprisingly, he appeared eager, perhaps even hungry, to participate in this new father-son relationship.

One day near the end of September, on a Monday, I taught Mike to play chess. By Friday of that same week, he was giving me a really good game. That year, and for several years thereafter, Mike was the chess champion of the Toronto Board of Education.

Early in our special relationship, Mike told me of his dream. Most of the kids in the class wanted to be doctors, musicians, teachers or some such thing, but not Mike! His ultimate desire in life was to be a gangster! This was no joke—this was his wish, and he was most serious about it.

I believed then, and after thirty-four years of teaching I still believe, that all children have a gift. Everyone has the same opportunity to be the best person they can be. I realized this boy was brilliant, and that with a little love, attention, understanding, guidance and encouragement, he could probably accomplish whatever he put his mind to. I figured if he wanted to be a gangster, I would do all I could to help him become the very best gangster he could be.

I got permission from his grandmother to call on him every Saturday morning. You see, I had a plan. First, I took him for breakfast. Afterwards (after making special arrangements through a friend), I took him to the Osgoode Law Library, attached to the University of Toronto.

He was awed by its impressiveness. I explained to him that a good gangster had to know something about criminal law, and reading up on law was the only way to learn. His young mind was eager and interested, and he dove right in.

That was how we spent each Saturday morning that year. I'd drop him off at the law library, and three hours later, I would return and pick him up and we'd go get a burger at Harvey's. After lunch together, and a recap of his morning's work, I'd take him home. He wasn't my son, but I sure felt like a father. There were numerous Saturdays I felt like sleeping in, but a commitment had been forged between us, and I was not going to let him, or myself, down.

The following year I was transferred to another school some distance away. Sadly, this prevented me from continuing to participate physically with him on those Saturday mornings. But I was determined to follow through with what I had begun, so I continued to provide him with public transportation tickets so he could keep up his regular study at the law library. Every so often I'd get together with him and take him out for lunch, so I was able to keep up with his life.

Some time after that, I met a wonderful young woman named Carol. Soon afterwards we were married, and we started a new life together in London—about two hours west of Toronto. The unfortunate part of this love story is that somehow, sadly and to my great regret, I lost contact with Mike.

The years passed, and I often thought of him, wondering how his life turned out and what had become of him. Then, one day in 1995, I was in Toronto on business and decided to look up the number of a former colleague. I flipped open the telephone directory, and there on the page, as if it were in twinkling neon lights and lit up just for me, I saw Mike's surname as part of a title of "Barristers and Solicitors!"

I wondered, *Could it be? Naw!—What are the odds?*

On a whim, I dialed the number, gave my name to a secretary and was put on hold. A very long fifteen seconds later, I was talking with a husky voiced gentleman. His opening statement was, "Mr. Kowalchuk, I've really . . . missed you." Then there was silence.

Somehow I managed to answer. "Mike, I'm really proud of you. I only wish that I had managed to keep in touch with you all these years." My eyes welled up with tears, and I blurted out again (between sobs), "Mike, I'm really proud of you."

In a quivering voice on the other side, Mike answered, "I wouldn't be here now if it weren't for you."

I was so very proud of him! If he had been my own son, I couldn't have been more proud of him.

When we were able to get together, I learned that Mike had risen to be one of the most successful criminal lawyers in Canada! A far cry from the street kid I once knew, who dreamed of becoming a gangster. He repeated that I was the only parent figure he had ever had, and that he owed it all to me. Had it not been for me, he said, he wouldn't be where he was today.

Ernest Kowalchuk
Ailsa Craig, Ontario

War, in Peace

One of the most valuable things we can do to heal another is to listen to other's stories.

Rebecca Falls

I first met Percy Hopkins of Calgary in April 1977, as he was getting off an Air Canada jet in Paris's Orly Airport. He was tired, as were the other twenty-four Canadian veterans of the Battle of Vimy Ridge who were setting foot, once more, on French soil. This return visit to France was a federal government–sponsored pilgrimage to commemorate the sixtieth anniversary of that famous World War I engagement.

I felt lucky to be chosen by the Department of Veterans Affairs to accompany this group of "reluctant heroes," since they did indeed require assistance throughout this visit. Their average age was eighty-two.

Once safely aboard a hired tour bus, Percy Hopkins and I shared the front seat. Our group of bemedaled Canadians was transported north from Paris to our hotel in the town of Arras, some ten to twelve kilometres from the site of the famous Canadian battle at Vimy Ridge.

Percy Hopkins was using crutches. He had only one leg.

It didn't take too long before curiosity got the best of me and I asked him if this was the result of "his" war. It was.

Percy insisted I call him Hoppy, the nickname all his friends used; the name he had worn ever since his wartime service.

It wasn't long before Hoppy told me the whole story about the day in which he gave so much and lost so much. He vividly described how the infantry tactic employed by the British Army using three waves of attack was taught to the Canadians. This included his unit—the Tenth Battalion of the Second Canadian Infantry Brigade.

"Which wave were you assigned to Hoppy?" I asked.

"The first," he replied.

As he continued his recollections, I felt I was becoming privy to a part of his life that even his own family was not aware of.

"One of the nurses in the field hospital where I was treated," he said, "told me I lost my leg in a battle that took place in a valley outside a village which she called, of all things, 'Peace.'"

Hoppy asked me if I knew where this village was, but I didn't. He really wanted to go back there. He thought his final pilgrimage to France would be complete if, one more time, he could see the spot where he had lost his leg and his war had ended.

As he talked, Hoppy recalled the sleepless night before the engagement, the early issue of the rum tot and the last-minute instructions from platoon corporals and company sergeants.

He recalled how when the whistles blew at 5:05 A.M., he went "over the top" with his Lee Enfield rifle, firing in the general direction of the enemy. He told me he was crying, laughing, praying and firing his gun all at the same time. The world was exploding around him, and heavy artillery barrages took out many of his friends. Machine gun bullets whistled past close to his ears. Hoppy continued running forward, closer and closer to the centre of a narrow valley where there was no cover and in which he and his comrades were exposed to a horrendous bombardment from an unseen enemy. This was the first wave.

Then it happened. He was hit.

Momentum caused him to fall forward, face down in the weeds and mud. He tried to get up and continue. But he couldn't.

He soon realized his leg had been blown off between the knee and the hip. As he slowly drifted into merciful unconsciousness, Hoppy Hopkins's last vision was that of an odd-shaped steeple of a village church just over the top of the sloping hill in front of him.

The sounds of war, the flashes of artillery fire and the pungent smell of cordite all disappeared from the senses of young Hoppy Hopkins.

Some long hours later, he awoke in a field hospital, tended by a surgeon and a nurse. It was then that the nurse told him she thought the location of the battle was just outside the French village of Peace.

Three days after our long chat, the entire Canadian delegation breakfasted together. While preparing to board the bus for a scheduled visit to Beaumont Hamel, the memorial to the Royal Newfoundland Regiment, Hoppy felt a bit under the weather. After examining him, our doctor suggested he remain behind and not participate in the scheduled events for that day. As a conducting officer, I was detailed to stay with Hoppy in case he needed help— or, if he later felt better, to drive him to rejoin the tour.

Within a couple of hours, Hoppy felt better—and guilty about missing the day's events. At his insistence, we climbed into our rented car, and with a Michelin map of Northern France set off like a pair of Canadian tourists in an attempt to catch up to the rest of the group.

No sooner had we agreed upon the best route to the memorial at Beaumont Hamel than we arrived at a construction detour in the highway. Not knowing which alternate route our tour bus had taken earlier, we made our choice and headed east. The numbers of sheep, cows and livestock we encountered along the way attested to the fact that this was definitely not a major highway.

As we travelled through the picturesque countryside of France, we were silent as we enjoyed the sights. Besides, driving this twisting, winding highway was taking all of my attention.

As we topped a small hill, Hoppy yelled, "Stop! This is it!"

"This is what?" I asked, as I pulled over and stopped.

"This is where I lost my leg," said Hoppy. Taking his crutches from the back seat, he exited the car, crossed the ditch and ducked under a snake fence surrounding an overgrown hay field. When I caught up to him, we proceeded to a point some 100 metres from the road, down a hill and into a small valley.

Then he stopped.

"This is it," he said. "This is the spot where I caught it."

There was nothing else he needed to say. He became silent.

I felt like an intruder in this private pilgrimage to a hallowed spot, so I retreated the short distance to the car. Before too very long, his solitary vigil completed, Hoppy returned, and still in silence, we both took our last look over this small, tranquil valley with so much history.

It was then that Hoppy gasped, "Look! Look up there on the horizon, just over that hill!"

Sure enough, there was the odd-shaped steeple of the village church, the last visual memory of Hoppy Hopkins before he lost consciousness that day, some sixty years ago—the very steeple he had described to me on the day of his arrival in France.

Back in the car, we proceeded down the hill, across the valley and up the rise leading into the village. As we reached the top of the hill opposite us, Hoppy and I both gasped at once. There on the side of the road was a sign announcing our entry into the village of "PYS."

The nurse in the field hospital had indeed been correct. And Hoppy's years had not betrayed him. His aging memory had served him well.

Call it coincidence, or call it fate. It had taken sixty years, but Hoppy Hopkins had finally completed his pilgrimage and returned to his village called Peace.

Vern Murphy
Charlottetown, Prince Edward Island

The Other Language

My Aunt Imogen Spark didn't speak a word of French. Her neighbour, Mrs. Letourneau, didn't speak a word of English. They had lived next door to each other for thirty-six years, and neither had learned to say so much as hello in the other's language. They were two of the stubbornest old geese I had ever seen.

If you had your eyes half open, you wouldn't miss much in the Ontario-Québec border town I grew up in. Especially if you were a little spy-bug snooper like me: at fourteen, that's what my mother called me. I guess I was curious, and it was easy to keep track of the goings-on in our little town.

The trees never caught on very well; they were rather stunted, with skinny trunks and big spaces between the branches. People in our neighbourhood didn't go in for hedges or fences much, either. The nearest thing to a fence was the picket one between Aunt Imogen and Mrs. Letourneau's front yards. It didn't come up past their knees. One of the few things the town did manage to agree on was well-lit streets. So I had an unobstructed view of our neighbours' yards and houses. For example, because we lived right across the road, I knew exactly how many times my cousin, Mavis Spark, sneaked in through the side porch window late at night, while young Mike Letourneau sneaked in his.

In summer, I'd sit on our front steps and simply watch what was going on. Across the street, Mrs. Letourneau would be leaning over the fence into Aunt Imogen's yard, examining a quilt pattern. She would be talking fast in French, and I could catch phrases like, "*C'est très beau, très beau!*" She would point out unique features of the design using grand gestures. Aunt Imogen would have no idea what she was saying, but would look satisfied.

Other times, they had long "conversations" about gardening across the fence. Aunt Imogen would point from a special concoction of fertiliser in a bucket to the base of her delphiniums and back to the bucket. Often she made a whipping motion with her hands. Mrs. Letourneau would smile and nod, glancing over at her own perennials. Sometimes, while hanging out wash, one or the other would point to the sky as if something unusual might fall from it into their yards. In winter, they used a type of sign language to demonstrate the more subtle points of snow removal. Raising imaginary shovels, they looked like they were in a game of charades. But neither one ever crossed over the fence to the other's yard. And this had been going on as long as I could remember.

Almost anyone else in town was more bilingually adept, if you could call it that. Garage operators mastered the basic linguistic tools for fill-ups and oil-changes in the other language. French waitresses could carry on polite, even jocular, exchanges in English and vice versa.

It was hockey where you noticed it most. The town's English team had an alarming array of francophone curses, which splintered the icy air when they heaved themselves at their opponents. The French team had their artillery of curses, too, the meanings of which were all too obvious to the Anglo players. Add to this the fans from both sides heckling each other and the noise was deafening. As a result, my mother didn't let me go to games very often. But I went a couple of times, and saw Mavis Spark sitting all alone on the French side. Every time Mike Letourneau scored a goal, she'd jump up and cheer, shaking her long red scarf.

One spring day, around dusk, we heard sirens. Ambulances and police cars were seen driving down our street. Everyone came out of their houses: *Qu'est-ce qui se passe?* What happened? We stood on our porch and watched the red lights throb in the distance.

Mrs. Letourneau and Aunt Imogen must have received the phone calls at the same time. Mike and Mavis's car had hit black ice. It was over in seconds, the police said later. Aunt Imogen came out of her house first, groped her way down the front steps, fell on her knees in her frozen yard and wept. Mrs. Letourneau came out of her house then. Long strands of gray hair had pulled away from her face and she was wiping her hands on her apron. Mrs. Letourneau hoisted up the layers of skirts she always wore, and lifting first one leg then the other, carried on right over the picket fence. Then she did a surprising thing. She turned around, looked back at the fence and kicked it hard. It buckled, sending up a spray of big white slivers. Then she knelt down on the ground with Aunt Imogen. The two women held each other, sending up a wail of agony only they understood.

The fence was never replaced. They planted delphiniums where it stood, blue spires that spilled over into each other's yards, like grace.

Jeanette Lynes
Antigonish, Nova Scotia

10

THIS GREAT LAND

I *have vaulted over an immense land*
which is both forbidding and beautiful
and it took my breath away.
There are no people more fortunate
than we Canadians.
We have received far more than our share.

Marc Garneau, astronaut

Ogemah

We are all creatures of the wilderness, children of the frontier, even though the frontier has been pushed back into the mists of the North, even though the wilderness has given way to concrete. Wild and mysterious, savage and forbidding, this is the cyclorama against which the drama of our past has been staged; for better and for worse it has helped to fashion us into our distinctive Canadian mould.

Pierre Burton

It had been the best year of my life. I had signed on with the mighty Hudson's Bay Company (HBC), which still reigned in Canada's north after three hundred years. An adventurous soul, I had fled the stifling poverty of Cabbagetown, in Toronto's inner city. Before this, I had taken a year off after graduating high school and enjoyed an exciting career working swing shift in a hockey puck factory. It was grimy and sweaty work and I was sure there had to be a better life out there, somewhere. Having spent my summers as a ranger in Algonquin Park, I had a secret ambition to be a bush guy and impress female tourists with my uniform and outdoorsy ways.

One day I saw an ad in *The Toronto Star.* "Join the HBC, See the North!" the ad cried out. It was illustrated with a handsome young native family, waving to a departing floatplane. I sent in my resume, carefully leaving off my puck-making credentials. The thought of escaping to the north kept me going through a long, hot Toronto summer, during which I saw more hockey pucks than Gordie Howe. At some point, I suddenly became aware of the monotonous, soul-draining torment that factory workers face every day. It clearly explained the despair and pre-mature aging I had seen in my parents. And I knew my own soul was withering.

In early November of 1975, a letter from HBC head-quarters in Winnipeg arrived. It contained a job offer, a hotel reservation and a plane ticket to Winnipeg. A short time later, I woke up in the Hotel Fort Garry, right across the street from Hudson Bay House in downtown Winnipeg. I had thirty bucks in my pocket and a whole new life ahead of me.

At the HBC office, I was greeted by a guy named Len from the Garden Hill Reserve in northern Manitoba. He showed me the ropes and gave me a ticket to board the Polar Bear Express, a train from Manitoba, up to James Bay. I would be trained to purchase fur from the native trappers and to run the little general stores the bay still had scattered about the north. My destination was a little reserve called Ogoki, on the Albany River.

The people of Ogoki were Cree, like Len. He told me that both the Cree and Ojibway words for my position was *"ogemasis,"* which loosely translated meant "little manager." If I played my cards right, I would make man-ager within a couple of years. In days gone by, the HBC called their manager the "Factor," but the natives called

him "Ogemah." Well, from that moment on, I was determined to make Ogemah, and nothing was going to get in
my way.

I spent the following year in the single-minded pursuit
of "Ogemahness." I moved from northern Ontario to
northern Saskatchewan and then on to Baker Lake in the
Northwest Territories. Sadly, I soon discovered that
because of my extreme youth, I would not soon be
accepted as an Ogemah. An Ogemah had to be older and
much wiser than I could possibly be, even with my newly
forming downy whiskers.

It was in Baker Lake that I got the call—I had been promoted to manager, and the remote Lac Seul Post would
be mine. Elated beyond measure, I flew out on the next
DC-3, and made my way to Sioux Lookout, Ontario, and
then by boat to my new post on an isolated island. The
HBC outpost there had been in continuous operation for
over a hundred years, and there I was—the newest
Ogemah! Five miles across the lake was the Kejick Bay
Reserve: log houses, no water, no sewage, no power, no
phones and some of the best trappers in Canada.

The post had a World War I–vintage, 32-volt generator
and a single sideband radio. At 5:30 P.M. each day, I powered up the generator and allowed the vacuum tubes to
warm to the orange glow that meant it was ready. If the
conditions were right, I could contact the HBC posts at
Webequie, Grassy Narrows, Landsdowne House and
Sioux Lookout. On a good day, I could reach the radio
operator in Thunder Bay and actually make a radio-
phone call.

Although the people were kind and understanding as I
learned their ways and tried hard to fit in, no one actually
called me Ogemah. I referred to myself as Ogemah a few
times, just to see, and was greeted with puzzled looks and
occasional laughter.

Isolation led me to read a lot, and I enjoyed the abundance of Hudson Bay Company legends and memoirs I found at the post. I learned that in days gone by the Hudson Bay Factor often enjoyed a lofty position in native communities, and was frequently called upon to be a counsellor, doctor, lawyer, clergy, police officer or undertaker. In a pinch, one would seek out the Factor for help or advice. A respected Ogemah enjoyed the prestige accorded a chief, elder or medicine man.

Unfortunately, those days were almost over. It seemed that Ogemah prestige was fading along with the fur trade itself. I felt I was living through the end of a significant era, to which there would be no return. I began to despair when I realized what I had missed. Still, I enjoyed getting to know the trappers, and slowly grew fond of the people of Lac Seul and they of me.

The end had come to a long, hot summer. I had learned much from the Cree of Kejick Bay, including how to read the weather and when to stay off the lake, which could be whipped into a maelstrom with the howling north winds. Not even the most experienced trappers would brave the waters of Lac Seul when she was angry.

It was on such a day that I was surprised to see a small boat carrying four people picking its way towards the post through the unforgiving rough waters. Something had to be very wrong for anyone to attempt crossing in this weather.

It was Philip and his wife, with their young son Andy and his wife, Sarah. Sarah had just arrived home the previous week with their newborn child, named Mequin, which meant "feather" in the local dialect. The baby, born several weeks early, was very tiny.

I got soaked dragging the boat up onto the beach as the breakers crashed over its transom. The four grim-looking soaked figures scrambled ashore, and Andy turned to me, without emotion, and said, "Our baby is sick. Can you help?" Sarah pressed a bundle into my arms, and then all four stepped back, looking into my eyes.

In my arms lay a tiny baby, soaked to the skin, with blue lips, struggling to breathe.

"What do you want me to do?" I asked. My heart raced as I realized there was no medical help available. And with the lake raging, there was no hope of a plane or boat getting in.

Philip looked at his wife and then at me, "But you are the bay manager, there must be something you can do . . ." Philip's voice trailed off as he looked at the panic in my face. The baby was by now quite blue, and although I was trained in CPR, there was no getting any air into her lungs. She obviously had pneumonia, and all of her tiny air passages were blocked.

"I'll try the radio," I shouted as I passed Mequin back to Philip. With pounding heart I sprinted to the post, knowing there was slim chance of making contact. The weather was bad, my batteries almost exhausted, and it took at least twenty minutes for the tubes in the old radio to warm up.

The tubes were still quite dim when I impatiently began sending my distress call, but there was only silence. After repeating the distress call several more times, in desperation I flipped the switch and tried Thunder Bay and then watched helplessly as the radio died. With no radio, there would be no calling for help.

I raced back to the beach to find that Andy had built a small fire and the family was seated in a circle, their faces calm, their voices soft. "No radio," I almost choked on the words. Philip quietly motioned to me to join their circle, then each of us took a turn holding Mequin, rocking her, her family saying a silent prayer.

As I held Mequin close to my face, I felt a soft warm breath on my cheek, almost a sigh, and then she was gone. It was the most beautiful and peaceful journey I had ever witnessed. All the parts of my soul that hurt me softened and were released. All the pain and despair I had pushed down deep inside of me long ago left me. All that had happened in my life before this moment became pure and clear.

In that gentle moment, my life was saved. Sitting in that circle of love under the cloudy sky, warmed by the fire, this small family and a tiny girl had created a circle of peace—and there was room for me in it. The family sang several traditional songs, which I did not understand but could feel. When we stood and walked back to the boat, we found the lake had calmed. Philip's family quietly boarded, and I leaned into the bow to help push them off. As Philip leaped into the boat, he turned and called out, "Ogemah, thank-you."

The breath caught in my throat at his words as the boat moved away and they took Mequin home. I walked around the shoreline of the island until dark, seeing it all for the first time, my heart bursting.

I stopped and sat by the dying embers of Mequin's fire and watched the sun dip behind Kejick Bay. I put my hand to my face, where Mequin had touched me with her last breath. I closed my eyes, and it was there I waited for the sun to return. I wanted to be sure, that without Mequin, there would be another day. But I knew that there would be; I was Ogemah.

John J. Seagrave
Yellowknife, Northwest Territories

The McRae Lake Shrine

My people's memory reaches into the beginning of all things.

Chief Dan George

On the edge of beautiful Georgian Bay lies an exquisitely private and majestically wild lake. As old as the rocks that surround it, the lake has witnessed and reflected the birth of our nation and the human struggle that accompanied it. Particularly special because it is pinched off at both ends and accessible only by canoe or a good hike, McRae Lake has held its secrets fiercely, beneath its cool, deep waters. Back in the 1960s, it was my good fortune to enter McRae Lake by canoe from the Georgian Bay side. As I looked up, I noticed a dash of unusual colour on the southern cliff face as I paddled by.

Leaving my canoe on the rocks below, I climbed up the cliff to discover a tiny statue of the Virgin Mary perched on a ledge amongst a grove of cedar trees. The elements had taken their toll; the statue had obviously been there for many, many years. As I looked at the shrine, I wondered what its story was.

A year later, while canoeing in the same area, I came across a magnificent yellow tepee sitting on the bank of the Musquash River. Curious about its solitary, elderly male occupant, I couldn't resist stopping. I'm glad I did. What I learned that day changed my life forever.

The gentleman, a retired ambulance driver from Toronto, had visited the area every summer since the Great Depression. Originally sent to camp nearby as a child, he, like so many others, had fallen in love with the beautiful land and with McRae Lake. Over the years, by patiently watching, listening and researching, he had managed to discover some of the lake's secrets. He shared with me many wonderful stories that day. The one I am most grateful for, however, was the story of the little Virgin Mary statue resting on the ledge at the entrance to McRae Lake.

The entrance into McRae Lake is an island of rock on the edge of Georgian Bay. The tiny island is constantly exposed to the westerly breezes, which steadily stir the waves against its primeval rocky shore. In the early part of the last century, a trapper and his wife and young daughter lived in a cabin on a large island in the middle of the lake. Early one morning they were startled awake by grunts and woofs and breaking wood. The trapper and his family were in sudden and great danger—a hungry bear was trying to break into their cabin. While trying to chase it away, the trapper was seriously mauled by the bear and left near death.

Frightened and alone, with only an old rowboat for transportation, the woman and her young daughter dragged the barely alive body of her husband out to the edge of the lake and managed to lift and roll him into the boat. Then they desperately began to row their precious cargo towards the Georgian Bay entrance, the only possible source of help. The boat was difficult to row and the cargo heavy. When they arrived at the rocky narrows separating the lake from open Georgian Bay, they were completely exhausted and unable to continue. Not knowing what else to do, they walked between the cliffs of the narrows to the end of the long rock island separating the two bodies of water. Out of ideas and out of hope, the woman sat down and prayed for a miracle. She promised to build a shrine there if help should come and her husband lived.

Soon, to their great joy and amazement, a Georgian Bay taxi, powered by a converted gasoline auto engine— somewhat rare in those days—was passing by the entrance. Seeing them waving, the driver came to their rescue. He was only too happy to take the family to the town of Penatanguishine, where the injured man received the medical help he needed—and his life was saved.

Grateful beyond words, the unnamed woman returned to the lake and, good to her word, built her shrine of thanksgiving high up on a ledge, on the wild shore of Georgian Bay.

As a biologist, I noticed years ago that the shrine was perched in amongst a grove of cedar trees, Eastern white cedars to be precise. But as I looked around at the vast expanse of shoreline and forest, I realized there was not one single Eastern white cedar tree anywhere to be seen— except right at the site of the shrine. Curiously enough, the Latin name for The Eastern white cedar is "arbor vitae"—which means "the tree of life!"

Steve Magee
Brookville, Ontario

Swamped by a Thunderbird

With camping, there's that first morning splash
of dappled sunlight on the tent walls that releases
that unforgettable fragrance-to-sigh-for of pine,
canvas and earth. And you know with every
breath that Canada is the best place to be in the
entire world.

Dianne Rinehart

When I was twenty-one, I landed the best summer job in the world working up north in the bush with Lloyd Walton. He was producer, director and cinematographer for Ontario Provincial Parks, and I was his all-around assistant.

That summer, we had to shoot footage for six commercial spots promoting the parks, so along with another Parks' ranger named Felix, we headed up to Quetico, a large wilderness park just east of Manitoba. At Quetico we met Shan Walsh, the Parks' naturalist, who had decided to take us to Mackenzie Lake. Everything was arranged, including extra help from his sixteen-year-old daughter, Bridget.

After a full day of paddling and portaging—that is, carrying our boats and supplies on our heads and backs for those parts of the trip we couldn't navigate on water—we arrived exhausted at our campsite at Trousers Lake. That first night, Shan told us of an old coffin lying on a tiny windswept island in the middle of Mackenzie Lake where an Ojibway chief was laid to rest years ago. Only a skeleton remained in what was now a sacred place. And further up the lake, on a rock not far from the burial site, was a pictograph of a thunderbird.

Lloyd and I were captivated. Pictographs are paintings of animals, people, canoes and mythological beings painted long ago on rock faces rising out of the water. They are sacred places where novice archaeologists sometimes encounter supernatural experiences. A pictograph of a thunderbird is of special significance. The thunderbird embodies the power of nature itself. It is a very potent symbol: neither good nor bad—just powerful.

Between Mackenzie Lake and us were two long gruelling portages, with Cache Lake lying in between. Travelling light, we'd leave most of our camp behind, stay at the old ranger cabin for one night and then head back.

It was a long, muggy and buggy day of portaging and paddling, and towards the end of the second portage, large storm clouds appeared and the sky began to darken. The wind picked up, and thunder and lightening flashed all around us. Lloyd grabbed the camera and ran ahead to shoot me walking with the canoe on my head—and bolts of lightening striking somewhere behind me!

Finally we reached Mackenzie Lake. The rain stopped and we quickly paddled the last two miles to the ranger cabin. Two Americans were already there, but there were ample bunks, so we welcomed them to stay.

That night a thunderstorm raged overhead, and while the rain pounded on the roof, I lay there listening to the show and falling asleep with the "cozies."

In the morning, the sun was shining, and a light breeze came from the west. Shan wanted to show us the island with the coffin, so we headed out for a prebreakfast paddle. After a couple of miles we wanted to go back for breakfast, but Shan insisted, "It's only another mile."

A half-hour later we approached a small, rocky islet crowned with scraggy pines. Carefully disembarking, we walked to the middle where we found a stack of rotten wood. With quiet respect, Shan lifted up what resembled an old wooden door, and there amongst the dried red pine needles lay the skeleton. Suddenly, a strong breeze came out of nowhere, lifting the hair on the back of my neck. We stared in silence, offering our respect.

The two Americans sharing our cabin were right behind us, and when they approached the island, the winds whipped up even more furiously. Shan put down the door, and out of respect for native beliefs and traditions, Lloyd quietly sprinkled some tobacco around the grave.

I was starving, but Shan was leading, so while Felix, Lloyd and I shared his Kevlar canoe, Shan and Bridget paddled ahead in the aluminium canoe. We headed up the lake a couple of miles to the pictograph sites. As we approached the first odd little pictograph on the face of a big rock, the wind picked up again. We had to paddle with all our might just to stay in one place while Lloyd filmed the rock.

Now we approached the thunderbird pictograph. Located on a small rock outcropping on a point, it resembled a rust-coloured stick figure reaching out with its wings. We tied up, disembarked and Lloyd set up the camera. As if on cue, the strong gust of wind blew through again. The camera's battery cable got finicky, and I had to hold it together with my hands so Lloyd could get the shot. The wind blew even stronger. Waves lapped furiously and banged the aluminum canoe against the rocks, causing rivets to pop out. Eerily, as soon as we stopped the camera, the wind immediately subsided. By now it was almost noon, and Lloyd had the shot, so we started back to the cabin for a late breakfast.

We strung up our rain ponchos as sails and let the warm breeze push our canoes down Mackenzie Lake. Racing along at a good pace, we passed Coffin Island, but as we rounded the point, we headed directly into the wind. The ranger cabin was still two miles away, so we dropped our makeshift sails. Large waves were rolling behind the point like a set of big, wide rapids. Shan and Bridget started into them, and feeling a little uneasy, Felix, Lloyd and I followed. The water was warm and the canoe would always float, but we had unprotected camera gear and extra weight. Paddling with all our might, we went for it.

As the waves began splashing over the gunwales, and we bounced up and down, Lloyd began bailing. I just kept paddling like crazy. Then it happened. It seemed as if the lake just swallowed the canoe all around me, and suddenly we were in the water. We grabbed for the cameras, shoved them back into the canoe and began kicking our feet. Suddenly I started to smile. It wasn't funny, but there was nothing else to do. We knew we would all be okay. Shan and Bridget came back, threw us a line and towed us to shore.

We lost all of our still pictures and film footage that day, including the lightening storm, our swim in Cache Lake, and . . . the thunderbird! A sudden awareness came upon me. That's it! The thunderbird did not want to be filmed. Whatever spirit world existed, it was present today and not happy with what we had done. It was willing to spare us, but not our film.

After a few hours, the wind lost its power, so we piled into our canoes and finally headed back. It was very late, so we spent another night at the cabin. It was some time later when we learned that we should have found a native elder before our visit, and asked permission to film the sacred places. Then, in accordance with Ojibway tradition, we should have left a small offering at the site of the thunderbird. Apparently, if we had done this, all our difficulties could have been avoided.

The return trip is always much easier, and I can't even recall our journey back. After a wonderful dinner, we explored an archaeological site on a beach just across from our tents. It was an ancient native campsite, and it was there I found a broken arrowhead.

There was no one else on the lake; but that evening everyone heard voices coming from that beach, voices speaking an unknown language. I didn't need to hear them; I already had proof enough.

The hollow winds arrived again while I lay in my tent that night. I could hear the nighthawks hunting and the lonely loon call in the distance. I thought of the long portages, the sacred site of Coffin Island, the thunderbird and the swamping of our canoe. Mackenzie Lake is one of those places where one comes face-to-face with the power of nature. Neither good nor bad—just powerful. Although I was sad to return to the city the next day, I felt alive and revitalised. I knew I would be able to survive until my next adventure to a magical place, when I would be reminded again that we live in a spiritual world.

Peter Elliott
Toronto, Ontario

My Heart Soars

The beauty of the trees,
the softness of the air,
the fragrance of the grass,
speaks to me.

The summit of the mountain,
the thunder of the sky,
the rhythm of the sea,
speaks to me.

The faintness of the stars,
the freshness of the morning,
the dewdrop on the flower,
speaks to me.

The strength of fire,
the taste of salmon,
the trail of the sun,
and the life that never goes away,
they speak to me.

And my heart soars.

Chief Dan George, 1899–1981
Chief of the Salish Band
Burrard Inlet, British Columbia

The Birth of Nunavut

To some Inuit, with a deeper knowledge of the language, when the word "nunavut" is spoken, the silent understanding means, "we share in this together, unconditionally," and there is intense gratitude.

Ann Meekitjuk Hanson

After years of negotiation and struggle, the Northwest Territories were formally divided. Nunavut was created, and a new territory in Canada was born! To the Inuit, the word "nunavut" means simply, "our land." The more emotional, spiritual, deeper meaning of nunavut is "our homeland."

In February 1999, the people of Nunavut held their first election. And on April 1, 1999, the governor general of Canada, The Right Honourable Romeo LeBlanc presented the new territory with a brand new flag and a new coat of arms. With the design process being guided at every stage by input from Inuit elders and leaders, the result was a unique set of beautiful symbols designed especially for them.

His Excellency travelled to Iqaluit, the capital of the new territory, and the following is his moving presentation to the people of Nunavut.

Today I have the honour and privilege of presenting a flag and coat of arms to Nunavut. These symbols will recognize not only a new territory, but also an ancient heritage.

Inuit have lived here for thousands of years. You have respected the spirit of the land and the wisdom of your elders. But let me add that, in a sense, all the First Peoples in our country are elders. You were here first, long before the rest of us. You first understood the lessons of our northland. You know that here we need cooperation to survive, compassion to help one another and cheerfulness to endure.

Through courage, sharing and ingenuity, the Inuit have prevailed in the harshest land on earth. And your new coat of arms reflects your history. It shows the caribou and the narwhal to remind us how you gained food, clothing and shelter from the creatures of land and sea. It shows the igloo and the stone lamp to remind us how you turned a frozen land into a home full of music, art and love. Your own spirit was always your main resource. But today your history is entering a new stage.

You have now gained the powers of a territory. You control many resources. And you have the tools to govern everyday life. Every new venture presents challenges. You must create jobs, safeguard communities, educate the young to take over. But you have always faced challenges. You have always prevailed. And you will win again.

The new flag of Nunavut shows an inuksuk and the North Star. Through the centuries, they have guided you across the snow to your homes. You are the closest people on earth to the North Star. And your courage and your values are a light and a lesson to others.

Tonight when Canadians look up to the North Star, we will remember your long history of courage, compassion and endurance. We will look forward with hope to your promising future.

And we will ask that all blessings descend on Nunavut.

Speech given by The Right Honourable Romeo LeBlanc,
former Governor General of Canada,
April 1999

Up from the Farm

There is a profound attachment to the land rooted in the Canadian character. Farming is the single most important factor in the Canadian experience.

Allan Anderson, broadcaster

The tractors started going by early—about 7 A.M. One by one they roared past, a majestic parade of sound and colour. Blue ones, red and white ones, green and yellow ones. All with signs anchored to their fronts, backs or doors. Signs that read: "Don't criticise farmers with your mouth full," and "If you ate today, thank a farmer." From where I stood at the window, I could actually feel the vibrations all the way from the highway. The goose bumps rose on my arms.

When the last tractor passed I returned to my easy chair, but I felt far from easy. Restless, I switched on the radio to see if I could learn more. ". . . The biggest farm demonstration this country's seen since the dirty thirties, maybe bigger," the announcer was saying. "They're on the move, and they're coming into the city from every direction. Traffic will be backed up on most major routes. Let's go live to Cindy, who's in the procession coming in from Winchester."

I listened, enthralled. How could I settle into my morning routine when I couldn't erase from my mind the image of hundreds of huge tractors invading Ottawa? This wasn't another demonstration; this was a piece of living history—something that once witnessed would never be forgotten. Most unusual was the fact that the demonstration involved a segment of the population who rarely even spoke, never mind shouted. Indeed, they were virtually an invisible group, at least from some perspectives. That they left their farms unattended even for one day spoke volumes about the troubles they were facing. Their message was, "If the government doesn't help us now, God help us all later."

But would the support they needed be forthcoming? Would the public rally around them? Who was the public? Wasn't I part of that public? And didn't I have a personal stake in the matter, having been raised on a farm myself, and having come from a fourth-generation Ontario farming family?

Galvanised, I sprang into action. I searched my attic for a sheet of construction paper and some coloured markers. I laid the paper on the kitchen table and wrote out my message. Then I found some wire and heavy tape and raced out into the biting March wind to secure the sign to the front of my car. Despite the wind trying to lift me, the sign and the car into the air, I was finally ready to roll.

As I sped down the highway, praying that my sign wouldn't fly off into someone's field, I noticed other drivers waving at me. I beamed back at them. Halfway to the city I passed an older tractor stranded by the roadside, its front-end loader raised as if in supplication. The sign on its side read, "Headed for Ottawa—Went Broke." I didn't know whether to laugh or cry, but it did make me more determined than ever to lend my support.

I caught up to the procession just as it was entering Landsdowne Park at the heart of the city. Hundreds of tractors filed by, interspersed with farm trucks of every description. The streets were snarled and horns blared— some in support, some in obvious anger—as city dwellers were trapped within the dramatic web being spun around them. People poured out of apartments and stores, shop- keepers and customers alike lined the streets, all curious, all awestruck, most waving and smiling.

One woman pointed at my sign and spoke to the man beside her. They both smiled and waved at me. I nodded with the dignity befitting the occasion. As I approached an intersection, a police officer started to wave me aside until he spotted my sign. With a small grin, he signalled me to continue.

I may have looked tiny and insignificant in my little Mazda, but I was riding as high as any of those in the big machines.

As we crawled along the Queen Elizabeth Driveway, and my clutch foot began to ache, I had plenty of time to pause and reflect upon the moment. Other than the obvi- ous pride I felt, I also harboured a deep regret about the fate of my own family farm. None of us were in a position to take it over, and even if we did, it wasn't large enough to be financially viable.

Hand in hand with the regret came the memories: my father struggling in the burning sun to fix the baler for the twentieth time . . . my father stooped in the dusk, picking stones with bleeding hands . . . my father shouting and waving his arms at an errant cow in a predawn, rain- soaked field . . . my mother's straw hat glistening in the sun as she drove the tractor while I loaded the hay . . . my mother allowing a sick baby piglet to be brought in the house to "warm up" . . . my mother's tears when farm life seemed a little too hard to bear . . . my parent's delight when their hard work paid off and the money came in.

I also remembered my own rosy dawns when I slipped and slid over silvery-dewed grass to pick up the latest crop of duchess apples that had fallen the night before. I remembered the heartbreakingly sweet smell of fresh cut hay as I drifted off to sleep beneath a fluttering curtain that flirted with a full moon. I remembered delicious evening swims in a sun-warmed lake after hours of struggling with heavy bales in a boiling hayloft.

No, I don't have a farm, and technically, I'm not a farmer. But I've lived the life, and it will never leave me. Even the arthritis that dampens my body and spirits can't extinguish those bright flames of memory.

That's why I drove with the farmers on that cold day in March, and that's why my sign read: "On Behalf of My Parents, Who Farmed all Their Lives."

Wanda James
Morewood, Ontario

11

MAKING A DIFFERENCE

I don't believe for a minute that I am going to save the world, but if we have a few hundred people saying, "I can make a difference," we will.

David Suzuki

Becoming the Man in Motion

Canadians are people who care about each other and constantly give of themselves. This generous spirit has helped me overcome adversity and chase my dreams. It continues to inspire me, every day, to be determined to make a difference.

Rick Hansen

I thought my life was over. I was alone in a stuffy hospital room hanging face down and strapped to a bed that was flipped over every few hours to relieve the pressure on my spine. I was fifteen years old.

A friend and I had skipped volleyball camp and gone fishing. It was such a perfect summer day; we couldn't resist the chance to celebrate our freedom exploring the wilderness around Williams Lake. I loved to explore, I loved sports, and I loved fishing.

We hitched a ride home in the back of a pickup truck. It was 1973, and riding without seatbelts in the back of a pickup, or having a few beers—which we later discovered the driver had done, was no big deal. Until the truck swerved and flipped over, catapulting us out the back. I landed against a metal toolbox. Although I realized I couldn't feel my legs, it didn't occur to me anything serious had happened.

Later, I learned my spine was shattered, and I would never walk again. After four months in a Vancouver hospital and another three in rehabilitation, reality slowly set in. Then anger. I couldn't believe this had happened to me, that it wasn't possible to recover, that I wouldn't become a famous athlete, that my life as I had known it, was over. I lashed out at my family and friends, at the nurses, doctors and therapists.

Back home in Williams Lake, I learned how hard it was going to be to get around in a wheelchair. One day, I went with my brother and our friends to our favourite swimming hole, but I ended up staying alone in the sweltering truck. Unable to make it down the steep riverbank alone, I was too proud to ask for help. When I finally realized my pride would keep me away from people and experiences I loved, I let my brother piggyback me to the river's edge. The rushing water soothed my aching heart, and for the first time since the accident, I enjoyed myself.

Allowing others to help was a turning point. I realized my attitude was the biggest barrier I had to face. How could I expect others to see my potential if I didn't see it myself? What was my potential if couldn't realize my dream of being an athlete? I couldn't yet see myself anywhere but on the sidelines, watching.

Then, my high school coach, Bob Redford, asked me to coach the girl's volleyball team. As I worked with them I became faster and more agile in the chair. Then, Stan Stronge arrived. Stan had been assigned by the BC Paraplegic Association to help me adjust, but when he learned I was an athlete, he encouraged me to move to Vancouver and compete in wheelchair sports. I was already accomplished at table tennis—enough to compete in the 1975 Wheelchair Games in Montreal. The level of competition and the toughness of the players blew me away.

As high school ended, I wondered what to do. My goal of being a phys ed teacher seemed no longer possible. Bob urged me to apply to the University of British Columbia, anyway. When I was rejected, he asked me to choose between defeat and challenge. I convinced the faculty to let me try, and, four years later, was the first person with a disability to graduate with a degree in physical education.

While at UBC, I met Tim Frick, who coached me in wheelchair track and marathon. With his help and friendship, I began marathon training, and resultantly won nineteen international wheelchair marathons, many track medals and competed for Canada in the 1984 Olympics.

Shortly before the Olympics, I crashed, dislocating my left shoulder. But Amanda, my physiotherapist, took such good care of me, I managed to qualify, and was able to compete. That injury was a wake-up call, as I tried to picture my life without being an athlete. I knew I wanted to travel, and do something to make a difference in the world.

Once I was late for class at UBC. I was speeding up a hill and noticed a girl jogging behind me. She sped to catch up and was gasping when she reached me. "Can I help push you up the hill?" she sputtered. "Well, actually, you're the one who's out of breath," I laughed. "Maybe you'd like to sit on my lap, and I'll give you a ride." This is just one small example of what people with disabilities faced, every day. Whenever I encountered a limiting attitude I thought, "I'll show them . . . somehow."

When I was first in rehab, I daydreamed about wheeling around the world, but I didn't think it was actually possible. But as I became stronger, the idea took hold. Then I met Terry Fox. Someone told me about this kid who had just lost a leg to cancer. So I called him and invited him to come out and play wheelchair basketball. We became roommates, good friends, and trained together. When Terry ran across Canada, I was in awe of how people responded to his courage—and how public perception changed as a result.

I realized my dream of wheeling around the world could make a difference for others. And so the Man in Motion Tour was born.

On March 21, 1985, I left Vancouver accompanied by my friend Don Alder, Tim Frick and my cousin Lee Gibson. Wheeling south across the border to Washington, the world lay ahead. We had romantic notions of the adventures we'd have and no idea of the enormous challenges in store. It took everything I had every day just to keep going . . . over mountains, through scorching deserts, freezing snow, and torrential rains. After two years, two months and two days, we had crossed thirty-four countries, four continents and I had wheeled 40,000 kilometres, doing the equivalent of two marathons a day, seven days a week.

Mostly, people either thought we were crazy or they were apathetic. During one difficult phase, Amanda came out to assist with her skills as a physiotherapist. When I felt like quitting, she pulled me through with her grit and strength, and her love.

When we landed back in Canada at Cape Spear, Newfoundland, Canadians rallied. As we made our way back home to British Columbia, the whole country became ignited. We were overwhelmed by the support and enthusiasm of the people who came out, by the thousands, to cheer us on, to give money and to volunteer in countless ways.

Our arrival in Vancouver was beyond anything I had ever dreamed possible. I thought my heart would burst.

The streets were lined with wildly cheering people, all reaching out to me. BC Place Stadium was filled to capacity with people welcoming me home. As I wheeled onto the podium, I saw a banner proclaiming: *"The End is Just the Beginning"*. My heart lurched, as I realized, despite the unspeakable hardships we had just overcome to reach the end of this journey, it was true.

When we began, we hoped to raise $1 million. By the time we arrived back in Canada, we set a new goal of $10 million. The total was a stunning $24 million, enabling me to start a foundation. We'd been tremendously successful in raising awareness of the potential of people with disabilities, to show that anything was possible if you put your mind to it.

To date, we have provided more than $130 million to spinal cord injury research, rehabilitation, injury prevention and wheelchair sport programs. Now we're about to embark on a new journey . . . to accelerate the discovery of a cure for spinal cord injury. Research has advanced so rapidly in the last ten years scientists believe, for the first time in history, a cure is possible. It's an amazing thought.

When I think back to when I was first injured, I remember my despair, and how I mourned the loss of all life's possibilities. But, today, I truly feel it was meant to happen. I wouldn't trade the life I have created, for the use of my legs. I feel so lucky. That accident began a journey to accomplishments beyond my dreams—as an athlete, a husband (yes, Amanda and I married), a father to three beautiful daughters, a business leader and an ambassador for what happens when you dream big dreams. My life was far from over . . . it had actually just begun. And, I believe, my best work is yet to come.

Rick Hansen
Vancouver, British Columbia

An Unlikely Hero

You see things and you say, "Why?"
But I dream things that never were;
And I say, "Why not?"

George Bernard Shaw

Fred hated school. Having grown up on a farm near Alliston, Ontario, Fred was a good worker but felt uncomfortable and unaccepted in a town school. Although he tried hard, he was not a good student. In order to graduate, he had to repeat some of his exams. An academic career just did not seem to be in the cards for Fred, but he had a persistent streak.

After graduation, he began studies to become a minister. When that did not go well, he changed his goal to medicine, working strenuously to become an orthopaedic surgeon. World War I arrived, and the great need for field medics facilitated the early graduation of many doctors, including Fred.

After the war, the young Canadian doctor returned home to set up his practice. To his dismay, business was slow to nonexistent. He waited a whole month before treating his first patient, and his payment was the grand sum of four dollars! Fred had so much time on his hands as he waited for patients to materialize that he whiled away the hours reading medical journals. He began to focus on articles on diabetes, a disease that had claimed the life of a neighbour's child.

Realizing that research might solve the problem of this disease, Fred decided he needed a laboratory. He approached Dr. J. J. R. Macleod at the University of Toronto. Dr. Macleod was initially uninterested—he believed Fred knew nothing about research and refused to waste laboratory facilities on him. But Fred stubbornly persisted and eventually convinced Dr. Macleod to support him. In 1920, Fred happily entered a poorly equipped laboratory and was given a young assistant named Charles Best.

In those days, there was no support in the medical and scientific communities for an unknown surgeon's research. Fred and his assistant were given lab animals left over from other scientists' studies. But they dedicated themselves to working long hours without pay, and Fred even sold his car to finance the needed experiments. Dr. Macleod soon grew more interested in the team's work, and he eventually became involved in the research.

Fred and Charles worked day and night, but early results in producing the hormone preparation they called insulin were discouraging. Many of the animals they treated died, but finally one animal survived for several weeks. The team appeared to be finally getting somewhere, and it was time to move on to human subjects. Before treating human patients, however, Fred and Charles tested the safety of their insulin on each other. Their tests were a resounding success.

The first patient to be treated with Fred and Charles's insulin formulation was a fourteen-year-old boy named Leonard. The year was 1921. For two years, Leonard had been on the "Allen diet"—a starvation diet for diabetics that allowed only 450 calories a day. The poor boy weighed only seventy-five pounds, and he was barely alive. But the new insulin treatment administered by Fred and Charles was a great success. Leonard gained weight, and his health dramatically improved. History shows that Leonard, the very first insulin patient, actually lived to adulthood.

By now, interest in insulin was growing rapidly. Charles Best developed methods for quick, large-scale production, and by the end of 1922, diabetics from all over the world were coming to Toronto for treatment. It had been only two short years from the first, rudimentary insulin experiments with animals to the successful widespread treatment of diabetics.

In 1923, the Nobel Prize in medicine was awarded jointly to Canadian doctors Frederick Banting and J. J. R. Macleod. In keeping with his character, Fred gave half of his $20,000 prize money to his assistant and friend, Charles Best. Fred then put his share of the money right back into research, establishing the Banting Research Foundation and the Banting Institute at the University of Toronto.

Fred could have made himself a millionaire with his discovery. Instead, he sold his patent for the production of insulin to the University of Toronto—for one dollar—so that the drug could be marketed cheaply and thousands of lives could be saved and improved.

Since 1922, millions of lives worldwide have been saved by insulin, and because of Fred, diabetics are able to live normal lives where before it was impossible.

Fred—Dr. Frederick Banting—was just an ordinary man in many respects, but he was a man with a vision and the stubborn will to pursue his goal. He had the heart of a true Canadian hero.

Mary Turner
Victoria, British Columbia

The Will to Survive

Hope is ever ready to arise.

James De Mille, 1888

Joe Spring was packing his car. His parents, Tim and Teresa, as well as his siblings, had tried their best to persuade him to take the bus for the 700-hundred-mile trip from their home in Aldergrove, near Vancouver, to Prince Rupert. Joe, however, wanted to drive. He was planning a stopover with friends in Quesnel before going on to Prince Rupert for a long-time friend's graduation party.

"The bus would probably be cheaper," his parents said. "It's a long trip, and you might have car troubles." In the back of their minds, Tim and Teresa tried to push away the very real fear that was starting to develop. "At least wait until tomorrow morning, after you've had a good night's sleep," they pleaded.

Joe loved driving his bright red sporty car, however, and he was convinced that he would be fine. At 11:00 that Monday evening, he walked into his parents' room with a broad grin and said, "Well, this is the last time you might see me!"

Unimpressed by his bravado, Teresa declared, "You had better make sure I see you again!" His dad was silent, fighting back a feeling of dread. His parents knew they had given it their best shot, but they also realized that in the final analysis, it was Joe's life and Joe's decision. They hugged him good-bye, and off he went.

Several days later Tim and Teresa Spring were becoming increasingly alarmed because their son had not called home. At first the Springs thought he had simply driven a hitchhiker to his destination or decided to tour another area. But as time passed, and no one had heard from Joe, the Springs' alarm took on a desperate tone. They contacted the police, who opened a missing person's file. The local TV station, BCTV/Global, aired Joe's picture and story, and the *Vancouver Sun* ran a front-page photo and coverage. Friends uploaded Joe's image to the Internet and drove up and down highways and back roads, searching. People all across British Columbia now knew about Joe's disappearance and began to keep their eyes peeled for his red car.

In Kamloops, the Royal Canadian Mounted Police air detachment was informed about the missing nineteen-year-old. At the time, its search helicopter was in pieces, undergoing a major safety inspection; it couldn't be flown. Pilot Jodeen Cassidy was frustrated in her desire to join in the search.

Flying had always been in Jodeen's blood. Her father was an Air Canada pilot, and he had passed along to her his passion for exploring the world from above. Jodeen served for seventeen years as a RCMP officer in Vancouver before the urge to fly became too intense to ignore any longer. So she took a hiatus and trained to be a helicopter pilot. After completing the necessary flying hours, Jodeen became the only female RCMP helicopter pilot in Canada. She was posted to Kamloops, in the interior of British Columbia.

Flying almost daily had honed her observation skills. She soon memorised the many surface variables in the vast forests and rough terrain of the province.

Jodeen was growing restless. She knew it was probable that Joe's car had been in an accident, leaving it just off the highway and only visible from the air. But with the helicopter still in pieces, she remained grounded. Anxious to be out looking for him, she tried hard to be patient, knowing the engineers were working as fast as they could to safely complete the inspection.

Every day, Tim and Teresa drove and even walked sections of the highway that Joe had driven—looking for tracks, newly replaced cement barriers, skid marks—anything that might show them where Joe was. They even tried to tap into his spirit to find a clue to his whereabouts. It was an unnerving quest. As desperate as they were to find Joe, they were also aware he might not be alive. Despite all their careful searching, they found nothing.

It seemed like Joe had simply vanished.

On the following Monday morning, almost a full week since Joe was last seen, Kamloops' helicopter still wasn't ready to fly. That afternoon, Jodeen lay down for a short nap. While she slept, she dreamed that she was piloting the helicopter over the dense forest alongside the highway. And then she glimpsed the red car. . . .

When she awoke, Jodeen was even more determined to find Joe Spring.

The next morning finally found the helicopter good to go. With no one available as an observer, Jodeen jumped in and took off alone. Once up, the cockpit became filled with the smell of fuel. She decided to land near the small town of Clinton to check the situation out. An off-duty RCMP corporal, Al Ramey, drove over and Jodeen explained the situation. Al had met the Springs when they were handing out posters to all detachments along the route Joe might have travelled. When Jodeen suggested Al come along as an observer, he jumped at the chance to assist. Everything important to the helicopter's safety checked out fine so they took off with the windows open, trying to ignore the odour. They flew on, checking gullies and crevices. Then, to their dismay, both radios suddenly quit working. Landing in the small town of Williams Lake to refuel, Jodeen found an engineer who discovered the source of the smell. It was a relief to know that, although irritating, it was not dangerous.

It was late afternoon, and most people would have quit for the day. Jodeen, however, was persistent.

"Come on, Al," she said. "We have to go find that kid." By now she was sure they were looking for a car that contained a body, but she wanted to give Joe's family peace of mind. It had now been eight days since Joe had disappeared, and everyone knew a human being simply could not survive injuries along with dehydration for that length of time.

Jodeen and Al continued flying north for ten minutes, when suddenly Jodeen saw what she had been looking for—a splash of red amidst the trees, just like in her dream!

"There he is!" she called excitedly over the intercom, "I've got the car here, Al!"

"You're kidding! Where? I can't see anything!" he replied.

Jodeen circled the helicopter. "There!" she pointed. Totally amazed, Al saw it, directly beneath. Jodeen spotted a suitable field nearby and landed. "Do you mind climbing down and checking the car?" she asked.

Al jumped out, and after lowering himself down the steep embankment, he could see Joe was still in the car. After steeling himself for the worst, Al noticed that Joe's arm—held in an awkward position behind his head—was moving back and forth in a faint wave.

Joe was alive!

Al ran to the car and placed his hand on Joe's shoulder. "It's the RCMP, Joe," he said gently. "We've found you." When Joe groaned as if trying to respond, Al looked at his eyes, which were swollen shut, and his thin, severely weakened body. He realized Joe was very close to death.

"Everyone's coming, Joe. Your parents know we've found you." Al wanted to make sure Joe was at peace and not worried about his folks.

When Al ran towards her yelling, "He's alive! We need fire and ambulance!" Jodeen was stunned. Overwhelmed, she called the dispatcher on the police radio, which in this moment of extreme need miraculously started working. As she made her call for help, her first thought was, *His family will be so happy!* And then there was gratitude: *What a blessing it is to have this helicopter!*

Only an hour away from Quesnel on the first night of his trip, Joe had fallen asleep at the wheel. His car had drifted across the road to the other side of the highway, hit a tree and proceeded down the bank. The saplings by the road sprang back, hiding all traces. The crumpled dashboard pinned his legs—breaking his ankle—and held him fast. His seat belt stopped him from falling forward as the car rested at a steep angle. His head was injured, perhaps allowing him to drift in and out of consciousness.

It wasn't only Joe's family, friends, Jodeen and Al who celebrated the news of his rescue. Indeed, when the media announced that Joe Spring had been found alive, the astonished silence across British Columbia was broken only by the entire population's collective sigh of jubilant relief.

Joe remembers nothing about the nightmare. Spending eight days with untreated, serious injuries, with no water, exacted a huge toll on his body. But it was unable to touch his love and zest for life. With his injuries treated, and the love of his family supporting him, Joe recuperated beyond everyone's expectations—returning to sports, driving and living life to the fullest.

If Joe harboured any doubts about how much his family loved him, those reservations have vanished. The experience gave him a calming peace about death, but at the same time confirmed for him how much he is wanted and needed in this world.

Joe knows that his years of tae kwon do and, more recently, kickboxing, served him well. He is convinced he owes his survival to his excellent physical condition, his positive attitude and his strong will to survive. Oh yes, and the determination and vision of Jodeen Cassidy—one persistent helicopter pilot who just wouldn't quit.

Diane C. Nicholson
Falkland, British Columbia

Into the Night

To be of service IS to be happy. What else brings greater satisfaction?

Honest Ed Mrivish

As the streetcar rattled down Roncesvalles towards Queen, the scene outside was eerie. There was no one on the streets, not even a police car. When you don't even see a police car, you know it's bad out there. It was a Sunday night in February 1978. I was on my way to report for the night shift with Metro Toronto Ambulance, and the snow was really coming down.

When I got to the station at 6:25 P.M., the day crew gave me a review of their day, including how passersby had to push the ambulance out of the snow when it was stuck. *Not good,* I thought. My partner, Joe, arrived a few minutes later, and the other crew went home.

The call came in at 7:20 P.M. The dispatcher was requesting volunteers to pick up an incubator and a special transport team of a nurse and a doctor from Toronto's Hospital for Sick Children, take them to McMaster Medical Centre in Hamilton, wait, and then bring the team back with a baby. The problem was this raging blizzard. All of southern Ontario was shut down, and nothing was moving anywhere. So they were asking for volunteers; they weren't going to order anybody to go. The driving conditions were so bad that Metro Ambulance had not yet actually accepted the request from the hospital. Then I spoke to the dispatcher and listened to the story.

At Toronto's Hospital for Sick Children, there was a baby with a healthy heart but near death and on life support. In Hamilton was another very sick baby who was waiting for a heart transplant. If we could get the Hamilton baby to Sick Kids in time, the parents of the dying baby were ready to discontinue life support for their child, and the doctors would be able to use its heart to save the other baby's life. With our help that night, although one baby would die, the other one might live. That was the deal.

When I explained the situation to my partner, he just looked at me. And suddenly I said to the dispatcher, "Okay, we're going. Let's saddle up now."

The ambulance slid out of the station onto the road. The trip to Hamilton would normally take about forty minutes, but who knew how long it would take tonight. We certainly needed a full tank of fuel, so we stopped to gas up, then headed over to Sick Kids. We picked up the incubator and the special team, and slowly began our journey down University Avenue. I took the ramp up to the Gardiner Expressway at about three miles an hour, and I think it was only because of the extra weight in the back that we made it up that ramp at all.

Faced with gusting winds and whiteouts, we inched our way along the expressway. As we passed the lights of St. Joseph's Hospital, it felt like we were flying a plane in the middle of a fog—sometimes we couldn't see anything. We slowly made our way west to Hamilton under near-impossible driving conditions.

We crawled onto the Queen Elizabeth Way. After what seemed like an eternity we finally passed Oakville and approached the Burlington Skyway—a great, high bridge, almost three kilometres in length that spans the Burlington Channel. Potentially dangerous in extreme weather such as this, the Skyway is often closed. However, we knew the most direct route into Hamilton was blocked by an accident, and we were forced to use the Skyway. We were not looking forward to it.

As we approached, there was not another vehicle in sight. I called the provincial dispatcher asking for any information on conditions. To our surprise, she told us the Ontario Provincial Police (OPP) had a car on top waiting for us. Sure enough, as we made our way slowly up the steep slope of the Skyway, there was an OPP cruiser waiting for us at the top. Buffeted now by a severe crosswind as we followed our escort, I hung onto the wheel with white knuckles as we slowly crawled across the top and then back down the other side. Our OPP escort left us at the first exit, and we continued on our way to Hamilton.

After four-and-a-half hours on the road, we finally pulled into Hamilton's McMaster Centre, and I gratefully shut the ambulance down. While the special incubator team went into the hospital, Joe and I tried to relax and stretch our legs. It had been a stressful four hours and the night was only half over. Forty-five minutes later the team returned, and we loaded the incubator into the ambulance. It now contained a small baby wrapped in tiny blankets, with a little tube in its nose and an IV in its arm. Standing back in the hospital's foyer, clinging to each other, were the frightened, but hopeful, parents. The life of their precious baby was now in our hands. Once everyone was safely on board, we pulled out and headed back into the night.

With Joe now driving, I would normally sit in back. But with the medical team there, I remained up front. Driving conditions had worsened: The snow was very deep, and the highway hadn't been plowed yet. We were now travelling even slower than earlier, and the west wind driving at our back made it difficult to steer.

Again, we were the only vehicle on the Burlington Skyway. Now, however, the violent wind was causing the ambulance to fishtail back and forth. Between the fishtailing and the deep snow, Joe had to really hang on. I think if we hadn't had the extra weight in back, we might have blown right off the bridge. But Joe was a very skillful driver—determined and very steady—and he brought us through.

When we had arrived in Hamilton earlier, we had had just over half a tank of fuel left—more than enough to get back to Toronto. As we approached Oakville there should have been a quarter of a tank left, but suddenly, in what seemed like just a minute, the fuel gauge fell to just over an eighth of a tank. As we drove past Oakville and into Mississauga, I watched the needle sink even further. We were burning more fuel than usual because of our slow speed and the bad conditions.

As we approached Toronto, Joe and I were both watching the fuel level and not saying a word. We couldn't get off the highway now. We would likely use up as much fuel trying to find a gas station as we would to just go for the final destination—Sick Children's Emergency. It was not a calculated gamble: we had to go for the hospital. We set our sights on pulling the ambulance into Emergency without running out of gas a block before we got there.

By now the plows had cleared the Gardner Expressway to some extent, and once there it was pretty clear sailing. As we went down the ramp at York Street, however, I saw the needle going into empty as we rounded the curve. We were watching for the fuel warning light to come on any second. Now, on the home stretch, we put on our full emergency lights, and with everything flashing, we headed straight up University Avenue. As we passed Dundas and made that right-hand turn onto Gerrard Street, I swear I heard the engine make a little cough. I'll never forget that tiny sound as we crawled past Toronto General, took another right-hand turn into Sick Kids, kicked it up the ramp and stopped right in front of the doors.

We shut off our lights, our engine—everything. Joe and I both took a deep breath, looked at each other and with a huge grin gave each other a high five! We called the dispatcher to say we were "10-7," meaning we were out of the ambulance and had successfully completed our mission. It was now nearly five A.M. A round-trip that should have taken just over two hours had taken over nine!

A team was waiting for us at the Emergency doors, and before we even had the ambulance shut down, they had whisked the incubator with the baby through to the elevators and up to the fourth-floor cardiac ward. We later learned the surgery was a success, and one set of parents that day had cause to celebrate life. We were totally wiped, but also elated, knowing that because of our efforts, a baby had lived. When I got home later that morning, I dropped into bed exhausted—but fell asleep feeling good about myself, and my life.

Gary Robert Walsh
Toronto, Ontario

A Piece of It All

I have travelled a great deal in my life. I've been all over the world, to every city in Canada and pretty much every juke joint in the United States. I'm on the road 250 days a year. It's my job. It's what I do.

Every few days, I'm off again to another town, another show. Not quite as glamorous as I had imagined it would be oh-so-many years ago. I had thought there'd be limousines and champagne and tall handsome men carrying my bags. I really did! But no, I carry my own bags, and I have learned to pack light. Yes, I thought that I, Jann Arden, a seasoned, ripened traveller, had seen it all.

I was shamefully wrong.

In 1998, I was contacted by a humanitarian organization called World Vision. They invited me to go on a media trip to Africa, to be spokesperson in the infomercials they air to raise awareness and money for child sponsorship. I could take a friend. Was I interested?

First I said yes, and then after a bit of thought, no, then yes and then another no. I was so afraid of going. I'd seen those infomercials and felt my heart break and my hope fade, wondering what I could possibly do—me—just one person, to change anything. I was horrified at the thought of seeing that hunger and sickness and poverty with my own eyes. I didn't want to go. Why travel anywhere when I would have been so happy to just stay home during my wee bit of time off?

In my heart I knew I'd be missing the opportunity of a lifetime. So I spoke with my parents and friends, discussing the various horrible and wondrous possibilities. When I finally chose my country—Tanzania, and my travel partner, I was still frightened.

I had to get several immunizations and take malaria pills two weeks before I left. I'd heard nightmare stories about those malaria pills. That you could die from just taking them the first time. I'll never forget popping that first pill and waiting to see the Lord.

I didn't.

Two weeks later I was flying over Africa with my mouth hanging open. Twenty-seven hours on a plane, and voilà I was there—in the middle of nowhere. The most beautiful nowhere I'd ever seen. I fell in love with Africa looking out that tiny, nose-smudged window. I woke my friend Kerry and said, "Look, oh my God. . . . Kerry look at Africa!"

"I know," she said.

My mission was to tell the story of the Masai in the northern plains of Tanzania. Drought had nearly wiped them out entirely over the past several years. Killed off most of their precious livestock, starved their fields, dried their treasured water holes and left them dying. I didn't know what to expect. I surely didn't expect these poor and starving people to change my life forever. I was there to help them, not the other way around.

The first day we awoke to a glorious breakfast of eggs and tomatoes and chicken and French fries. I had to smile. Every effort was made to make us feel at home. I myself think french fries are an excellent source of . . . breakfast. We were all starved and ate well. It was a beautiful morning. I could just make out the tip of Mount Kilamanjero—"Killy" to the locals.

We piled into the Land Rover and headed off into my wildest dreams and my deepest fears. Both would pale in comparison to what came next.

We left the main road after several hours and began our bumpy journey toward the Masai. (You need a good bra in Africa). The dust and dryness, the cracked earth and the burning sun made us all thirsty just looking at it. We drank bottle after bottle of water. I've never thought the same about drinking water since. As we rounded the last bit of brush, there standing proudly in the middle of their village were fifty or so members of the Masai tribe. I felt like I was in a *National Geographic* movie. The men were wrapped in bright red cloths and had long iron spears. The woman had children on every hip and jewelry weighing heavy everywhere else. I could not believe my eyes. Time folded over me, and I became lost in it. It seemed I had travelled back to the beginning of time.

The huts, or "bowmas," were made of cow dung and straw and sticks. There were newborn goats dragging their umbilical cords beneath their little bellies, naked children covered in flies, dogs with large beetle-type things attached to their armpits and feeding off of their very lives. I couldn't move. I did not want to get out of the Land Rover. I wanted to put the movie on pause and call my mother.

They stood looking at us like we had fallen off the moon. I didn't blame them. We looked uncomfortable with our own selves. We were. My friend Kerry is a big girl, and they were so taken with her. They had seen few white women, never mind big ones, and they were fascinated. The village chief asked the translator what she ate, and Kerry told him she ate everything. We all laughed. The chief laughed, the men laughed, the women and children laughed. It was the laugh that melted the ice. We started talking as fast as the translator could go. The camera crew was shooting film the whole time, but pictures do it no justice. They cannot show with a true heart these precious, beautiful people.

How could these starving poor people without a spoon or a bowl or a chair to sit on, laugh like that? These people whose skin hung from them like a sheet.

They had nothing, but somehow they seemed to me to have everything. It showed in their eyes. The peacefulness. The calm. The serenity. This was not what I thought I would find. Everything I knew I wanted, but didn't know how to get, they had. They had more joy in their hearts than I had ever known in my life. They knew who they were. Why they were. Where they were.

They didn't think of themselves as poor. They were hungry because nature had been cruel these few years, and they were thirsty and their children were dying. Everyone at some point in their life needs help. Everyone.

We began our filming, concentrating our profiles on the lives of two little girls. We would tell their stories as accurately as possible: Who they were and why they needed our help. How our helping them would benefit the entire village. How through child sponsorship we would somehow be saving ourselves. But I didn't know that yet.

Eight-year-old Nariamu had never been to school or seen a doctor or bathed in clean water. She walked up to fifteen kilometres everyday to fetch wood, and did it with one horribly disfigured clubfoot.

We began with her. As you can imagine, she was very shy, not really understanding what we were trying to do. It was hard for me. I tried to be as comforting as possible, but ironically, it was she who comforted me, making me feel welcome and safe and fine. She always wanted to hold my hand. I felt so special and honoured. I don't know how else to explain it. It's hard to find the words.

We followed Nariamu around for four days—while she gathered wood and fetched water. I've never seen a more disgusting pool of disease and sickness anywhere than the water hole where she dipped her old plastic detergent bottle. The water she collected for the family to cook with and to drink was green and thick with animal feces floating in it. I'd been drinking clear, clean, bottled water for days, and she was about to drink this slop. She was grateful to have any water at all. I was ashamed.

I can't explain how sick I felt seeing her carry that water home on her head. I was so moved at her pride and how brave and accepting of her life she was. She knew nothing else. No heroine in a book or movie ever compared with her dignity and grace. After that visit to the water hole, I never again heard the camera crew complain about carrying their gear. In fact, I never heard anyone complain again about anything.

Their laughter and generosity dumbfounded us all. I remember Kerry telling me how much my life would change by going to Africa. She said I'd never be the same, and she was right. I think I'm a much better version of me now. I'm trying to understand the circle I'm in, and that I'm that little girl in Africa, and she is me.

On our last day, the entire village gathered, shined up like new pennies in their finest, to sing us a song. I felt a tear climb up through my stomach, through my lungs, past my heart and into my eyes. I cried like I was ten years old. I wailed. I soaked the earth with my gratitude. I felt the presence of God, the universe; I felt eternity behind me and eternity before me. I was emptied out right there on the dry plains where all humanity was born. It felt like I had returned home. The song they sang said how glad they were I had come, and they hoped I would return and bring news of the world. The song said they were alive and they were together and that nothing—not famine or hatred or the modern world or death—could keep them from living out their destiny. I understood something that has no name.

I cried until an old grandmother cupped her hands over my eyes, saying one word over and over. "Poli" has a lot of meanings. One is to slow down. Another meant they knew of my sorrow. That old grandmother cared about me—this visitor with strange hair and skin and talk, and I cared about her. I cared about all of them.

One world.

One white flag.

We were the same person for a split second.

I went to Africa to help, but these people helped me more than they will ever know. When I returned home to Canada, I fired my management of eleven years, ended a horrible relationship and moved to the country to be closer to my family. I changed everything. I started again and felt wonderful about doing so.

Through World Vision I was able to get Nariamu's foot fixed in Nairobi. It's now perfect in every way and will help her live a normal and active life. I was so happy to be able to do that. The last thing her father said to me was, "Will you help fix my daughter's foot?" "Yes," I replied, "I will. No matter what it takes, I will do that for her."

I now know the meaning of what a promise is. I don't think I ever did before. That promise is the bar for me now. To be a person whose word can be counted on. That, in itself changed my life and would have been enough. I am still counting the blessings, the lessons, the wisdom given me by the richest people I will ever know.

Someday, I will go back to meet the woman who taught me how to live without fear, the little girl named Nariamu.

Jann Arden
Calgary, Alberta

A Holy Night to Remember

*Community is not built upon heroic actions,
but rather upon the love shown in the little things
of daily life.*

Jean Vanier, founder of L'Arche

As northern Canadians we share many memories of cold winters. At Christmas time, I often reflect upon one particular evening of a prairie winter in the early 1960s. Though the frost was cruel, the reminiscence is warm.

We were students at college in Prince Albert, Saskatchewan, most of us living away from home for the first time. Hanging a few strips of tinsel in our rooms didn't relieve the feeling of homesickness that had overtaken our dorm. What could we do to bring on the Christmas spirit, stave off our longing for home and maybe brighten someone else's life? One of my friends suggested going carolling. That was it! Every student at our small college was rousted out for the occasion. No auditions. No voice lessons. No excuses. Warmth of spirit was the only requirement. And our enthusiasm served as an electric soul-warmer for those who seemed lacking in spirit.

We divided into groups so our music would resound over most of our college town. The group I joined had nothing resembling four-part harmony, but we could collectively make a joyful noise. Bounding boisterously and carrying a tune in our hearts, we made our first call. "Deck the Halls," we tra-la-la-ed.

Soon we discovered that carolling brings a variety of responses. When you carol for people you know, you can be sure of open doors and open hearts; when you carol for strangers, you can't be sure what kind of reception you will get. Some folks remained in the safety and cosiness of their homes, watching and listening passively through their living room windows. Others cautiously propped the door open enough to hear us, but not enough to let in the cold—or their unknown guests. Some flung their doors wide open and sang along; others watched in silent reverie.

One of the stops on our journey was a three-story apartment building. With no intercoms or security cameras to deter us in those days, we walked right in. Starting our performance in the basement, we sang mostly to closed doors. After a couple of songs we headed for the main floor. Two doors swung open. One doorway framed a young couple, obviously expecting a child. In another doorway, two preschoolers clung to their parent's legs. What were they feeling: *Surprise? Wonder? Curiosity?* Their faces seemed to ask, *Who are these strange, bundled-up people? And why are they doing this?*

We sang "Away in a Manger" for the young ones. We continued with "O Little Town of Bethlehem" for our seemingly appreciative gathering. Mounting the stairs to the third floor, we burst into "It Came upon the Midnight Clear," a song that suited the night.

One door on the top floor creaked open. A stately gentleman, gray-haired and thin, held onto his doorknob.

He became our audience of one. As we murmured about what to sing next, the elderly fellow asked, "Would you come into our apartment and sing for my wife? She's bedridden. I know she'd love to hear you. My wife used to be an opera singer," he added proudly, "and she's always loved music."

All eight of us stepped timidly into the couple's tiny, crowded bachelor suite. Books, records, china, antique furniture and mementoes whispered stories to us. I reminded myself not to stare for fear of invading their privacy. This was their home, their sanctuary and a hallowed place where the old-timer watched over his fragile partner. Her silver, bed-mussed head made only a small dint in her pillow.

Without a word, he adjusted his wife's headrest so she could see and hear us better. Then he gave a nod. Our voices rose and warbled through "Hark, the Herald Angels Sing." Had our voices been given extra grace and beauty for this occasion? Perhaps they had—we sang rather well for such a motley, impromptu crew.

A smile flickered on the woman's gaunt, wrinkled, yet beautiful, face. Her eyes sparkled softly. Tears rolled down her cheeks. Her husband requested "Joy to the World" and "Silent Night," two of her favourites. As we finished our performance, her eyes closed. Now the man shed his own tears. Quietly, we turned to leave, closing the door softly on the housebound couple.

The winter moon and stars shone down upon us. It had become a silent night, a holy night, for we had been in the presence of love that was gentle and mild. All was calm; all was bright as we headed back to our residence. We had found, and maybe even given, the Christmas spirit.

Sharon Espeseth
Barrhead, Alberta

The Hero of Halifax Harbour

*A hundred times a day I remind myself that my
inner and outer lives are based on the labours of
other people, living and dead, and that I must
exert myself in order to give in the same measure
as I have received and am still receiving.*

Albert Einstein

There was a thin coat of snow on the slopes of Halifax
Harbour on December 6, 1917. Vincent Cole was a warm-
hearted family man who arrived at his office in Richmond
Station that day in the booming wartime port. He placed
his lunch pail on a shelf and began his day as a railway
dispatcher.

The Great War had brought prosperity to Halifax. The
quaint maritime harbour bustled with convoys of men
and materials bound for Europe. On this particular morning, a French munitions ship called the *Mont Blanc* was
moving slowly out into the narrows of Halifax Harbour,
on the Dartmouth side, at a lazy four knots. Her captain
was taking his ship to join a flotilla of supply vessels
bound for war-torn Europe.

Captain Le Medec was taking no chances. Four days earlier, his ship had been loaded to the hilt with 2,000 tonnes of picric acid, 180 tonnes of TNT, live rounds, gun cotton, and 32 tonnes of benzol. The *Mont Blanc* was now literally a floating bomb, but because it was wartime, she was not flying the mandatory explosives flag to warn others.

Coming in the other direction, destined for New York, was the *Imo*, a neutral Norwegian vessel running relief missions to Belgium. It should have been on the Halifax side, but for some reason, the *Imo* was running right down the *Mont Blanc's* channel.

When the two ships sighted each other, a volley of whistle blasts followed in an agonised attempt to persuade one or the other to move. At the last moment, the pilot of the *Mont Blanc* cried out an order to his helmsman to cut hard left. But it was too late. Seconds later the *Imo* sliced almost noiselessly through the starboard side of the *Mont Blanc's* hull, sending out a shower of sparks. By the time the two ships pulled apart, the *Mont Blanc* was in flames.

Well aware of the devastating explosion soon to follow, the captain and crew of the *Mont Blanc* wasted no time in taking to their lifeboats. They abandoned their burning ship, which drifted toward one of the Halifax piers.

As black smoke and flames rose from the *Mont Blanc*, crowds of people began gathering on the pier to watch the excitement, rushing to find the best vantage points. On every ship nearby, sailors and stevedores forgot their work and watched, unaware of the impending disaster. As soon as they were alerted of the crash, the Halifax fire department dispatched its new engine and two boat parties to fight what they thought was a simple fire.

Directly above Pier 9 lay Richmond Station and the freight yards of the Canadian Government Railway—where Vincent Coleman worked. Vincent and chief clerk William Lovett were sitting in the dispatch centre discussing the fire when suddenly a desperate looking sailor burst in yelling, "Commander says the burning ship is loaded with explosives! Get out quick!"

For a second, neither man moved. Then William leapt for the telephone and called the railway office on Cornwallis Street to warn others of the deadly explosion they now realized was imminent.

With that handled, William and Vincent made for the door in desperation. They had left the office and were fairly leaping across the tracks when Vincent suddenly stopped, a horror-stricken look on his face. He had suddenly remembered that just moments from now, several passenger trains carrying hundreds of people were scheduled to arrive and stop right in the centre of the danger zone. With all of those lives at stake, and an overwhelming feeling of responsibility, Vincent fell behind.

In amazement, William stopped and yelled back at him: "What do you think you're doing? We only have a minute or two left! You're a married man with a family to think of!" But by now Vincent could only think about the passenger trains filled with hundreds of innocent people, speeding toward the threatened harbour. His one and only purpose was to stop them.

As the others ran on, Vincent returned to his office and solemnly tapped out one last message: "Munitions ship on fire. Making for Pier 6. Good-bye." For a brief moment his thoughts turned to his loving wife and children.

At 9:05 A.M., a giant explosion shook Halifax and a pillar of white smoke rose eight kilometres into the sky. A tidal wave swept the shore and windows were broken miles away. The *Mont Blanc* was blown apart, and the *Imo* ran aground. The force of the blast was strong enough to hurl a clock out of a tower at Truro, 100 kilometres away. The shock was even felt in Sydney, on Cape Breton Island, more than 270 kilometres away.

Close to two thousand people perished in the inferno that day, including Vincent Coleman. But Vincent's final desperate message had been heard, and the trains managed to grind to a stop just in time to save the lives of the hundreds of people onboard.

Today, the half-ton shank of the *Mont Blanc's* anchor still lies where it landed, three kilometres from the explosion. A clock on the Halifax City Hall will rest forever at 9:05 A.M. The North Halifax Memorial Library stands as a monument to the events of December 6, 1917, and the incredibly selfless act of Vincent Coleman—and other heroes like him.

Darlene Montgomery
Toronto, Ontario

The Canadian Shepherds of Korenica

*The service we render to others is really the rent
we pay for our room on this earth.*

Sir Wilfred Grenfell

In 1993, Corporal Mike Floyd and Constable Roger
Morrow of the Royal Canadian Mounted Police (RCMP)
volunteered to serve on a peacekeeping mission as police
officers for the United Nations Civilian Police (UNCIVPOL)
in the former Yugoslavia. They were posted in Korenica, a
small village in Croatia held by the Serbs. Mike is a gre-
garious fellow with a big heart and liquid eyes that convey
compassion and respect for every living thing that crossed
his path. His partner, Roger Morrow, who had previously
been stationed in Red Deer, Alberta, was proud of the uniform he wore and took his role as a peacekeeper very
seriously.

With their pockets always filled with candies for the
children they met during their long and perilous patrols,
these Canadian peacekeepers became well-known and
respected by both sides in that sad war.

On the outskirts of Korenica, nestled in the forested

hills, was a small hamlet where an elderly Croatian farmer lived with his wife and sister-in-law. The old man had spent his whole life tending his farm and caring for his sheep. One quiet morning, the farmer and his family were visited by Serb rebels who forced him to watch as they violated and then killed his wife and sister-in-law. That morning the old man lost not only his family but also what was left of his faith in God and human nature.

When the rebels took the old man out to the fields to finish him off, he somehow managed to escape, hiding in the woods until he ran into a patrol of Czech peacekeepers. The local police were called in to investigate but, as is often the case in war, very little energy was put into attempting to bring the criminals to justice.

When our two Canadian Mounties heard of the incident, they drove out to the farm and met with the old man. Mike and Roger listened with compassion as the elderly farmer recounted the senseless loss of his soul mate and her sister. Worried that the thugs would be back to finish the job, Corporal Floyd and Constable Morrow tried to convince him to flee to safety on the other side of the border, where he had relatives. With his voice cracking in sorrow and desperation, the widower explained that not only did he not have the money and connections to make it across the border safely, but that he could not, even with his life in danger, abandon his sheep. They counted on him and under no circumstances could he leave them to fend for themselves.

When the two Mounties returned to Korenica, they convinced their United Nations (UN) colleagues to donate money to help the aged farmer reach what was left of his family across the border. Within a short period, they collected several hundred dollars.

With their pockets holding cash as well as candies, Mike and Roger drove their white vehicle with the black UN letters on the hood back toward the farmhouse. When they arrived, they found the old shepherd tending to his flock.

The farmer slowly made his way toward the two Canadians he had learned to trust. Corporal Floyd looked into the weather-beaten face of the old man. He explained to him again that he must leave his farm and go live with his relatives across the border. The farmer patiently listened to the young Canadian with the blue beret. He lowered his head and reiterated that he didn't have any money to make his way across the border.

At that point, Corporal Floyd handed him the money and told him they would arrange with the Red Cross to ensure his safe passage. The farmer shook his head and returned the bills to the peacekeepers. Though he had lost just about everything that was dear to him, he still had his pride. "I can't accept your money," he quietly said. "And besides, I have to think of the sheep."

Roger and Mike looked at each other. Mike had an idea. "What about this," he offered. "With this money, we'll buy your sheep from you. Then you'll have the money to go to your relatives."

"But who will take care of them?" asked the shepherd.

"Mike will," replied Roger with a grin. The old man stared long and hard at the Canadian Mounties—foreign police officers to him. With his voice cracking and his faith restored in his fellowman, he slowly answered, *"Hvallah,"* or, "Thank you."

With the Mounties' help and the money they had collected, the old man made it safely across the border. The peacekeepers took care of the flock as promised, until word was received that the old man had died. Working with a representative of the village, Mike and Roger then dispersed the old man's beloved sheep to those local area residents who most needed them. Soon after, our heroes' tours of duty were over, and they quietly returned to their law enforcement duties in a major Canadian city—where sheep are scarce and shepherds more so.

Who says there are no real heroes in Canada? Few Canadians know that in a small hamlet in a distant land, these two RCMP officers are remembered as "the Canadian shepherds of Korenica."

Wayne Watson
Orleans, Ontario

Thanks for Being Here

We are each of us angels with one wing, and can only fly embracing one another.

Luciano de Crescenzo

I had a bit of a fairy-tale upbringing, especially with regards to my music. My parents both came from very musical families. Mom taught me to step dance when I was five, and I started fiddling at age nine when a grand-uncle by the name of Charlie MacMaster sent me a fiddle from Boston. He said if I wanted to play it, I could keep it. It was a three-quarter size fiddle, which I had never tried before. Dad had lots of full-size fiddles in the house, but they were so big I couldn't stick them under my chin. So this was a tinier fiddle and it fit me perfectly.

The Cape Breton community that I grew up in was very into traditional music, and I'd already been in a few con-certs step dancing. So I'd had a good introduction to the stage by the time I played my first concert at age ten. Then I decided that I should take some lessons, so for the next three years I worked with my teacher, Stan Chapman.

It's very easy to get gigs when you're a fiddler in Cape

Breton, because no matter how long you've been playing, news travels fast, and all the little communities rely on local talent. I loved playing, and very soon I was performing at a lot of local concerts!

Now, of course, I travel everywhere, and my touring schedule is very full. In 1999, along with Amy Sky, I wrote a song called "In My Hands," which was a tribute to my fiddle and the great musical heritage it brings with it. For the next year I performed that song at all my concerts.

After a show, I usually sign autographs and CDs. People will often come up and say, "I really enjoyed your show, it was just tremendous," and their words make me feel so good.

I've also received many beautiful cards and letters from people, saying things like, "I was having a bad day and your music really picked me up," or simply, "You really brought a lot of joy to my heart." Comments like that not only make me feel good, they make me feel like I'm serving a purpose. And when I read them, I don't take it to heart as me bringing the joy, I take it as coming from the gift that God gave me. I feel so privileged to be able to deliver that to people.

A few months ago, a very special letter arrived that really touched me. It was a from a man named William who wrote:

> *Dear Natalie:*
>
> *Every morning when I wake up, I thank God for you because you changed my life. In June, I was very depressed because I had lost a job. One night, I began to think about the best way to kill myself. I said to myself, "My wife will have to make the trip to Canada by herself." Immediately I realized if I was dead, she would not go by herself. So then I said, "I'll wait until we get back from Canada."*

We had been planning to attend the tall ships event in Halifax, and when I saw your name on the program, I knew for sure I had to go. I had bought one of your CDs when we were in Canada the year before, but I had no idea how popular you are.

We got to the concert about an hour and a half early, but already there were no chairs left.

While we stood there waiting, I thought about my life. I have been fighting depression for a long time. When my son was very ill about ten years ago, I made a vow to stick around until he was grown. Last year he got married and moved out. Before he got sick, I had played the flute. But for ten years there had been no music in my heart, and I had not played my flute for a very long time.

When you did "In My Hands" I heard a voice say, "Go home and play." I realized then I had an instrument at home that belonged in my hands, every day.

The day after we got home I found a flute teacher and started lessons that week. I keep your picture on my music stand. You had signed it for me, "Thanks for being here." Of course, you were referring to the concert.

Now, "Thanks for being here" is my morning prayer every day. I get up at 4:00 A.M. in order to find practice time before I go to work. I have already mastered a Bach sonata, and have started on a Mozart one.

It was your music that taught my heart to sing again, and taught my feet to dance again. You are my angel who gave me the message from God that delivered me from death to life.

So every morning, for the rest of my life, I will wake up and thank God for you, and for the fact that I am still here on this earth.

With deepest affection,
William

When I received William's letter and read that he saw me as an angel who gave him a message from God, I was moved to tears. To me it's just incredible the contact we can have with other people without even knowing. For me, my schedule's crazy, and I'm going left, right and centre all the time, and sometimes I'm so busy that I don't slow down long enough to think about things. And William's letter really made me think for a moment about the impact that every one of us can have on each other as human beings.

And then there's the effect that he had on me. He spoke about how grateful he is for my presence in his life through my music. But with his heartfelt letter, he's given me something equally important. Which is just knowing that as I go about my life, doing the work that I love, that I can help make a difference.

Natalie MacMaster
Troy, Cape Breton Island,
Nova Scotia

In Flanders Fields

. . . lest we forget.

Canadian Major John McCrae sat on the back of an ambulance, parked just a few hundred yards north of Ypres, in France. Although he had been a member of Montreal's McGill faculty since 1900, and had served in the South African war, he was finding it impossible to get used to what he was experiencing. It was May of 1915, and the Great War raged around him.

As a Canadian surgeon attached to the 1st Field Artillery Brigade, his experience here in the Ypres Salient was an ordeal that he had hardly thought possible. In the last seventeen days he had seen and heard enough in his dressing station to last him a lifetime.

He had been particularly affected by the death of his young friend and former student, Alexis Helmer, from Ottawa. Alex had been killed the day before by a shell burst and had been buried later that day in the little cemetery nearby. In the absence of a chaplain, Major McCrae had personally performed the funeral ceremony for his friend.

His heart was heavy as he gazed at the scenes around him. In the nearby cemetery, he could see the wild poppies that sprang up quickly in the freshly turned earth in that part of Europe. And then, as he sat there on the back of the ambulance, the words began to flow into his mind. He grabbed a pen and paper and quickly wrote them down.

Cyril Allinson, a twenty-two-year-old sergeant major was delivering mail that day and approached Major McCrae as he wrote. He looked up, and then went on writing while the young soldier waited quietly. When he finished five minutes later, the major took his mail from Allinson and without a word, handed him the finished poem to read. What Cyril Allinson read astounded him.

In Flanders Fields the poppies blow
Between the crosses, row on row,
That mark our place; and in the sky
The larks still bravely singing, fly
Scarce heard amid the guns below.
We are the dead. Short days ago
We lived, felt dawn, saw sunset glow,
Loved, and were loved, and now we lie
In Flanders Fields.

Take up our quarrel with the foe:
To you from failing hand we throw
The torch; be yours to hold it high.
If ye break faith with us who die
We shall not sleep, though poppies grow
In Flanders Fields.

Allinson looked around and realized that the poem was almost an exact description of the scene before them.

Unhappy with it, Major McCrae tossed the poem away, but a fellow officer retrieved it and sent it to the newspapers in England, where shortly after that it was published by *Punch Magazine*. The effects of the poem washed across England like a giant wave. All of Britain was moved and encouraged by the words, and it quickly spread throughout the allied nations.

Soon, the poppy became a symbol of life and resurrection. Each part of the flower represented some part of this war experience. Life and freedom became represented, all in this tiny red flower.

In 1918, Colonel John McCrae was seriously wounded and taken to a hospital on the coast of France. He was placed in a room where he might look out the window toward the Dover cliffs across the channel. Before he died three nights later, his final words were reported to be: "Tell them this, if ye break faith with us who die, we shall not sleep."

Canadian Colonel John McCrae was buried in the cemetery of Wimereux, and his poem, "In Flanders Fields," remains to this day one of the most memorable war poems ever written. It is a lasting legacy of the brave men who fought for freedom in the Great War, and in the one that followed. Every year on November 11, Canadians from Cape Breton Island to Victoria wear their poppies in respect, and when McRae's poem "In Flanders Fields" is read in the Remembrance Day ceremonies, we stand in silence and we remember.

Colonel John McCrae
story adapted from Welcome to Flanders Fields,
by Daniel G. Dancocks

O Canada!

O Canada! Terre de nos aïeux,
Ton front est ceint de fleurons glorieux.
Car ton bras sait porter l'épée,
Il sait porter la croix.
Ton histoire est une épopée,
Des plus brillants exploits.
Et ta valeur, de foi trempée,
Protégera nos foyers et nos droits.
Protégera nos foyers et nos droits.

O Canada! Our home and native land!
True patriot love in all thy sons command.
With glowing hearts we see thee rise,
The True North strong and free!
From far and wide, O Canada,
We stand on guard for thee.
God keep our land glorious and free!
O Canada, we stand on guard for thee.
O Canada, we stand on guard for thee.

More Chicken Soup?

Many of the stories and poems you have read in this book were submitted by readers like you who had read earlier *Chicken Soup for the Soul* books. We publish at least five or six *Chicken Soup for the Soul* books every year. We invite you to contribute a story to one of these future volumes.

Stories may be up to twelve hundred words and must uplift or inspire. You may submit an original piece, something you have read or your favorite quotation on your refrigerator door.

To obtain a copy of our submission guidelines and a listing of upcoming *Chicken Soup for the Soul* books, please write, fax or check one of our Web sites.

Please send your submissions to:

Chicken Soup for the Soul
P.O. Box 30880, Santa Barbara, CA 93130
fax: 805-563-2945
Web sites: *www.chickensoup.com*
www.clubchickensoup.com

We will be sure that both you and the author are credited for your submission.

For information about speaking engagements, other books, audiotapes, workshops and training programs, please contact any of our authors directly.

In the Spirit of Giving

In the spirit of supporting children, the publisher and coauthors of *Chicken Soup for the Canadian Soul* will donate a portion of the proceeds from this book to:

The Tim Horton's Children's Foundation, Inc.
R.R. # 2, 264 Glen Morris Road East,
St. George, Ontario N0E 1N0
Phone: (519) 448-1248
Fax: 519-448-1415
www.timhortons.com

The Tim Horton Children's Foundation is a nonprofit, charitable organization committed to providing a fun-filled and memorable camp environment for children from economically disadvantaged homes. This foundation was established by Ron Joyce, cofounder of Tim Hortons in honour of his friend and National League Hockey star Tim Horton, to recognize his love for children and his desire to help those less fortunate.

Each year, local children are selected from each of the communities in which a Tim Horton's store operates. This gives thousands of children the opportunity to attend one of the six camps, five across Canada and one in the United States, each offering unique opportunities. The foundation covers all expenses for the child, including transportation, food and lodging. Highly trained staff, excellent facilities and programs provide all the fun that is consistent with a first-class children's camp. The camp experience is designed to give children confidence in their abilities, pride in their accomplishments and the chance to gain a positive view of this world and their future.

Information concerning Tim Horton's Children's Foundation, Inc. may be obtained from the Web site or by writing to the address above. To make a donation, please call 519-448-1248.

Who Is Jack Canfield?

Jack Canfield is one of North America's leading experts in the development of human potential and personal effectiveness. He is both a dynamic, entertaining speaker and a highly sought-after trainer. Jack has a wonderful ability to inform and inspire audiences toward increased levels of self-esteem and peak performance.

He is the author and narrator of several bestselling audio and videocassette programs, including *Self-Esteem and Peak Performance, How to Build High Self-Esteem, Self-Esteem in the Classroom* and *Chicken Soup for the Soul—Live.* He is regularly seen on television shows such as *Good Morning America, 20/20* and *NBC Nightly News.* Jack has co-authored numerous books, including the *Chicken Soup for the Soul* series, *Dare to Win* and *The Aladdin Factor* (all with Mark Victor Hansen), *100 Ways to Build Self-Concept in the Classroom* (with Harold C. Wells), *Heart at Work* (with Jacqueline Miller) and *The Power of Focus* (with Les Hewitt and Mark Victor Hansen).

Jack is a regularly featured speaker for professional associations, school districts, government agencies, churches, hospitals, sales organizations and corporations. His clients have included Achiever's Canada, the American Dental Association, the American Management Association, AT&T, Bob Proctor's seminars, Campbell's Soup, Clairol, Domino's Pizza, GE, ITT, Hartford Insurance, Johnson & Johnson, the Millionaire's Club, the Million Dollar Roundtable, NCR, New England Telephone, Re/Max, Scott Paper, Simon Fraser University, TRW and Virgin Records.

Jack conducts an annual eight-day Training of Trainers program in the areas of self-esteem and peak performance. It attracts educators, counselors, parenting trainers, corporate trainers, professional speakers, ministers and others interested in developing their speaking and seminar-leading skills.

For further information about Jack's books, tapes and training programs, or to schedule him for a speech or seminar, please contact:

Self-Esteem Seminars
P.O. Box 30880
Santa Barbara, CA USA 93130
Phone: 805-563-2935 • Fax: 805-563-2945
Web site: *www.chickensoup.com*

364 WHO IS MARK VICTOR HANSEN?

Who Is Mark Victor Hansen?

Mark Victor Hansen is a professional speaker who in the last twenty years has made over 4,000 presentations to more than 2 million people in thirty-two countries. His presentations cover sales excellence and strategies; personal empowerment and development; and how to triple your income and double your time off.

Mark has spent a lifetime dedicated to his mission of making a profound and positive difference in people's lives. Throughout his career, he has inspired hundreds of thousands of people to create a more powerful and purposeful future for themselves while stimulating the sale of billions of dollars worth of goods and services.

Mark is a prolific writer and has authored *Future Diary, How to Achieve Total Prosperity* and *The Miracle of Tithing.* He is coauthor of the *Chicken Soup for the Soul* series, *Dare to Win* and *The Aladdin Factor* (all with Jack Canfield), and *The Master Motivator* (with Joe Batten).

Mark has also produced a complete library of personal-empowerment audio and videocassette programs that have enabled his listeners to recognize and use their innate abilities in their business and personal lives. His message has made him a popular television and radio personality, with appearances on ABC, NBC, CBS, HBO, PBS and CNN. He has also appeared on the cover of numerous magazines, including *Success, Entrepreneur* and *Changes.*

Mark is a big man with a heart and spirit to match—an inspiration to all who seek to better themselves.

For further information about Mark, write:

MVH & Associates
P.O. Box 7665
Newport Beach, CA USA 92658
Phone: 949-759-9304 or 800-433-2314
Fax: 949-722-6912
Web site: *www.chickensoup.com*

Who Is Janet Matthews?

Janet Matthews (née Patterson) is a Canadian freelance writer and editor. After having spent the first twenty years of her professional life in Toronto's fast-paced fashion photography and advertising industry, Janet was asked in 1997 by Raymond Aaron to help produce and edit *Chicken Soup for the Parent's Soul*. When she was invited to coauthor *Chicken Soup for the Canadian Soul*, she jumped at the opportunity to use her unique skills and talents to help create this very special Canadian book. Janet says, "I'm so grateful for the opportunity both to speak to so many Canadians from all across the country and to help them tell their stories. I've been touched and inspired and moved to tears so many times."

In addition to writing, editing and collecting *Chicken Soup* stories, Janet is working with Daniel Keenan to produce a book-sized version of "The Navy's Baby," a wonderfully inspiring story that appears in *Chicken Soup for the Parent's Soul*. She is also compiling stories for a book on true spiritual experiences, life-changing awarenesses and miracles to be published in 2004. It will be a collection of stories to inspire and uplift spiritual seekers of all backgrounds.

After having read thousands of stories from parents all over the world for *Parent's Soul*, and then thousands more from Canadians for *Canadian Soul*, Janet now teaches a workshop on how to write a great story from the heart. While seeking stories for *Chicken Soup for the Canadian Soul*, she has been a guest on numerous radio talk shows across Canada, and she is available for guest spots and interviews. You can contact Janet at:

Chicken Soup for the Canadian Soul
2-9225 Leslie Street
Richmond Hill, ON Canada L4B 3H6
905-881-8995, Ext. 28
janet@canadiansoul.com

Who Is Raymond Aaron?

Raymond is a professional speaker and business coach, and co-author of *Chicken Soup for the Parent's Soul*. Since 1983, he has mentored thousands of Canadians to achieve brilliant new heights of entrepreneurial and investment success using his special proven principles.

Raymond offers his wisdom in The Monthly Mentor, a unique coaching service presented in Toronto, Calgary, Edmonton and Vancouver. In it, Raymond will teach you how to double your income doing what you love. Following his guidance, his Monthly Mentor members have dramatically increased their net worth and income, most in a surprisingly short time.

Raymond has appeared on almost every major Canadian radio and TV talk show explaining how mentoring can improve your wealth. He has delivered over 4,000 seminars, inspiring and educating his audiences using his patented techniques for achieving outrageous success "automagically."

Raymond's speeches are powerful, enjoyable, educational, contrarian and lots of fun. His commanding and entertaining style offers practical insights and unique business tools not available anywhere else.

His most popular audiotape program is "Double Your Income Doing What You Love," a double-cassette package selling for $199. One unique benefit of this tape set is you will learn how to eliminate all messes from your life. You can listen to it free at *www.Monthly Mentor.com*, or, as a special bonus, simply e-mail your credit card number and expiration date, and for $10.00 shipping, Raymond will mail it to you free of charge.

Raymond's favorite motto is: "Bite off more than you can chew, then chew like crazy!"

To be mentored by Raymond, engage him as a speaker or obtain his audiotapes, please contact:

The Monthly Mentor
2-9225 Leslie Street
Richmond Hill, ON Canada L4B 3H6
1-888-50goals
wealth@MonthlyMentor.com

Contributors

Several of the stories in this book were taken from previously published sources, such as books, magazines and newspapers. These sources are acknowledged in the permissions section. If you would like to contact any of the contributors for information about their writing, or would like to invite them to speak in your community, look for their contact information included in their biography.

The remainder of the stories were submitted by readers of our previous *Chicken Soup for the Soul* books who responded to our requests for stories. We have also included information about them.

Jann Arden was born and raised in Calgary, Alberta, and has become one of Canada's most precious resources. Admired worldwide for her singing and songwriting, Jann is equally respected for her comedic and motivational speaking talents. With five hit CDs, a collection of awards and years of charity work—see for yourself. *www.jannarden.com, www.worldvision.ca.*

Sally Armstrong is a journalist and human-rights activist. Editor-in-chief of *Homemaker's Magazine* from 1988 to 1999, she is presently editor-at-large for *Chatelaine Magazine* as well as a contributing editor at Maclean's. She has been honoured by the National Magazine Awards Foundation for her writing, the YWCA's Women of Distinction Award for communications, and in 1998 was made a member of the Order of Canada. In May 2002, Penguin books released her long-awaited book entitled *Veiled Threat: The Hidden Power of Women of Afghanistan.*

Jennifer Bailey was enrolled in a writing course when she was encouraged by her tutor to submit her story to *Chicken Soup for the Soul.* She enjoys reading as well as writing children's stories and skits that are based on Biblical truths.

Paul Banks has been a journalist since 1995. Now living in Gander, Newfoundland, he is currently the manager/editor of *Gander's Beacon* newspaper. A former editor of the *Flamborough Review* in Southern Ontario, he can be reached at *pbanks@nf.sympatico.ca.*

Karin Bjerke-Lisle and husband Doug live on the West Coast of Canada. Along with their four children, Forrest, Brontë, Paige and newborn Hunter, they take great delight in the ocean and the mountains. Forrest made a full recovery and is a truly wonderful big brother. The family hopes to welcome a new Great Dane into their lives soon.

Maree Benoit received her early childhood education diploma from Cariboo College in 1978. Maree taught preschool in Williams Lake for many years until her retirement. She and her husband, Leo, travelled all over the world before settling in McLeese Lake. Her main interest is providing good child care for all children. She can be reached at 250-297-6309.

Kurt Browning earned four World Figure Skating Championships and four Canadian Championships as an amateur skater. One of the best entertainers the sport has ever seen, when he turned professional in 1994 he won three consecutive World Professional and Canadian Professional Championships. Kurt has also released his own home video, "JUMP" and starred in three television specials. "You Must Remember This" won five Gemini Awards.

Linda Chamberlayne works as a special educator in Kelowna, British Columbia. She has also worked for Canadian publisher Wood Lake Books, writing church school curriculum and music for primary-aged children. Her book of songs and activities for church school, *Joyful Noise,* is available upon request at *bc_lc@silk.net.*

Katherine Cornell earned a B.A. in history from the University of Guelph and a M.A. in dance from York University. She cowrote one book and contributes to several magazines and anthologies. Katherine also teaches in the Learning Through the Arts Program. Please reach her at *kate_cornell@sympatico.ca.*

Faye Dance received her B.A. in applied arts from Ryerson University in Toronto in 1969. She has hosted many television shows and acted in commercials and movies. She and her husband, John Radford, have two sons, Jason, 20, and Mitchell, 14. She loves to read, work out, Rollerblade and spend time at the family cottage. Contact her through Sherrida Personal Management at 416-928-2323, or at *fayeradford@hotmail.com.*

Nancy Lee Doige lives in Aurora, Ontario, where she developed a national education program on transplantation and organ donation for grade five through eight students. The Classroom Connections "Gift of Life" Education Program is currently in 7,500 schools across Canada. Nancy draws on her education in family studies at Ryerson University, her work with children in elementary schools and her deeply moving experience when her son Ryan died. Visit her at *www.classroom-connections.com* or *www.ryanshope.net.*

Alex Domokos was born in 1921 in Szabadka, which was then in Hungary. He and his wife immigrated to Canada after the Hungarian Revolution. In the 1990s he returned to Hungary where five of his manuscripts were published. More recently, in Canada, two of his manuscripts were published by Crossroad Publisher as e-books. He now lives a modest and content life as a free man.

Peter Elliott is a Renaissance man with a strong passion for Canadian history and wilderness canoeing. He freelances as a video editor and cameraman in Toronto, but produces his own documentaries for television. Peter has worked as a living history animator, voyageur canoe guide and canoe ranger. He never stops. Contact him at *islandfalls@hotmail.com.*

Manuel Erickson received his B.A. from the University of Waterloo in 1974. Now retired, he owns a 1956 Cessna 172, writes, plays piano and surfs the Internet. His greatest love is for his life partner, Martha, to whom he has been married for over twenty years. Please contact him at *pilot@radiant.net*.

Sharon Espeseth lives in Barrhead, Alberta, with her husband, Hank, and is the proud mother of three young adults—Michael, Christie and Jenny. After numerous years teaching and later developing courses for distance education, she is retiring. Sharon plans to enjoy her family, travel with her husband and further her career as a freelance writer. She may be reached at 4504 56th Avenue, Barrhead, Alberta T7N 1K2.

Trent Evans lives in Sherwood Park, Alberta, with his wife, Laurel, and their sons Justin and Jarret. He supervises the ice-making team at Northlands Park's Skyreach Center. With all the continued attention around the loonie, Trent is currently working on an exciting new project. Stay tuned! You can reach Trent at *jevans2@telusplanet.net*

Vince Fantauzzi was born in the small town of Sora, near Rome, Italy. At age fifteen he moved to Toronto, Ontario. Vince works as a letter carrier for Canada Post. In his free time he enjoys painting, reading, and writing short stories, and he is currently working on a full-length novel. He can be contacted at *robbi4@home.com*.

Penny Fedorczenko lives in Oshawa, Ontario. She has a B.A. in sociology and presently teaches public school. She is also the mother of two adult children. Penny enjoys travelling, writing, theatre, music and sports. She can be reached at *pfed@infinity.net*.

Gregory Fouts is professor of psychology at the University of Calgary. His areas of expertise include how we become "attuned" with others and how we develop resilient personalities when faced with life's challenges. Dr. Fouts is the recipient of awards for exceptional teaching and community service. He can be reached at *gfouts@ucalgary.ca*.

Pat Fowler is a "people person." Her pleasant, outgoing and assuring presence entices people of all ages to open up to her and share their experiences in life, both happy and sad. Check out her web site at *http://www.geocities.com/cdnheroes/*, or contact her at *patfowler@interbaun.com* or at 780-464-7595.

Linda Gabris is a writer whose inspirational stories, articles and poetry have appeared in publications across North America and in England. She has been running creative and business writing workshops for over sixteen years and has a home-based writing consultant business. She can be reached by e-mail at *inkserv@attcanada.ca*.

Chief Dan George (1899–1981) was one of the most prominent First Nation Canadians. He dedicated his life to fostering awareness, understanding and friendship between the First Nations and white Canadian settlers. To all Vancouverites, Chief Dan George was known particularly for his moving and dramatically delivered soliloquies. Logger, musician, star of stage, screen and television, philosopher and advocate of the Indian cause—a very special kind of man! His book, *My Spirit Soars*, was published by Hancock House Publishing (1431 Harrison Avenue, Blaine, WA 98230-5005).

Lorrie Goldstein is the editor of *The Toronto Sun*. Veronika's mother Julie Hanning, who delivered the toast at Leah and Veronika's bat mitzvah, works as a professional model in Toronto.

Bill Gorman. Growing up in a small community on the edge of the Don Valley in Toronto, Bill Gorman and his friends spent many exciting days exploring the valley and looking for adventure. He now teaches elementary school in Toronto and shares his stories with his students.

Senator Jerry S. Grafstein, B.A., J.D., graduated from the University of Toronto Law School in 1958. Called to the Bar in 1960, he was made Queen's Counsel in 1972. In 1984, Prime Minister Trudeau appointed him to the Senate. As Senator from Metro Toronto, he continued to act as counsel to Minden, Gross, Grafstein & Greenstein in Toronto. Currently he co-chairs the Canada/U.S. Inter-Parliamentary Group, composed of Canadian Parliamentarians and Members of the U.S. Congress. You can reach him at *jgrafstein@mggg.com*.

Rick Hansen, C.C., O.B.C., lives with wife, Amanda, and three daughters in Vancouver, BC. He's president and CEO of the Rick Hansen Institute and Foundation, which has generated more than $137 million for spinal cord injury programs, and works to accelerate the discovery of a cure for spinal cord injury. In demand as a speaker, he has coauthored two books, and chairs the Fraser River Sturgeon Conservation Society and the Pacific Salmon Endowment Fund Society. For more info, or to make a donation, please contact him at 604-822-4433 or via e-mail at *www.rickhansen.org*.

Jayne Harvey works as a mother, wife and registered nurse. Her passion for caring for seniors and writing about those experiences has launched a career as a motivational speaker for care providers, volunteers and chaplain groups. She plans to continue her writing and speaking endeavours. Please reach her at *jayneharv@home.com* or at 157 Cedar Street, Keswick, Ontario, L4P 2J4, or by telephone at 905-476-1590.

Paul Henderson played in the NHL, first for the Detroit Red Wings and later for the Toronto Maple Leafs, from 1963 to 1974. He retired in 1979. He is now executive director of Leadership Ministries, a division of Campus Crusade for Christ, working with the businessmen and professional community developing Christian leadership skills. He can be reached at *paul@leadershipministries.com*.

Carl Hiebert wears several hats as an author, aviator, photographer and motivational speaker. He has published four bestselling photography books and specializes in low-level aerial photographs with his ultralight aircraft. His current work includes photographing for charities in Africa. He can be reached at *giftofwings@look.ca*.

Ruth Hilton-Hatfield was legally blind. She was an avid writer, typing by "feel," and published a book of short stories at age eighty-eight. She was born in Carleton, Nova Scotia, and graduated in 1928 from Acadia University in Wolfville, Nova Scotia. She died in 1998 at the age of ninety.

Allan Hirsh, M.A., is a psychotherapist, trainer and cartoonist. He uses gentle humour with his clients and in his stress management seminars. His latest book is *Relax for the Fun of It: A Cartoon & Audio Guide to Releasing Stress*, published by 2002 Caramal Publishing. Contact him by e-mail at *relax@hirsh.ca*, or at 705-476-2219, or at 348 Fraser, North Bay, Ontario P1B 3W7. His official Web site is *www.hirsh.ca*.

Michael Hogan wanted to travel the world but, because of his excessive weight, was having trouble walking three blocks. If you'd like to know how he learned to manage obstructive sleep apnea, lose eighty-five pounds and have some fun getting fit, contact him at *http://www.weight4life.com* or at *michael.hogan@shaw.ca*.

Susan Hreljac received her B.S.S. with honours from the University of Ottawa in 1982. Susan and Mark Hreljac run the Ryan's Well Foundation with the help of a small board and other dedicated volunteers. Visit the Ryan's Well Foundation web site at *www.ryanswell.ca*. E-mail Susan at *susan@ryanswell.ca*.

Wanda James has been both a class "A" automobile technician and a graphic designer. After becoming disabled with rheumatoid arthritis, she turned to writing as a source of interest and comfort. Her book, *Getting Up Is Hard to Do: Life with Rheumatoid Arthritis*, is available from Little Bear Publishing, P.O. Box 45, Morewood, Ontario, K0A 2R0 or from *wjames@igs.net*.

Jo-Ann Hartford Jaques, teacher and writer, has a specialist degree in English literature from the University of Toronto, and a B.E. in special education. A board-of-directors member of the Down Syndrome Association of Toronto, she is a regular contributor to its international newsletter and founded Camp Talkalot, a speech and language program for children with Down syndrome. Contact her at *jhartfordjaques@hotmail.com*.

Lynn Johnston has been sharing the amusing, moving lives of the Patterson family with millions of readers since 1979 in her award-winning comic strip *For Better or For Worse*. In 1992 Johnston was awarded the Order of Canada. Please reach her at *www.fborfw.com*.

Peter Jordan is host of the hardest working show on television, "It's a Living." Every week on CBC TV, he tries people's jobs for a day. Today he's trying to be a writer. He also contributes humorous stories for CBC's Olympic coverage on "Peter Jordan's Olympic Living."

Kahlee Keane, Root Woman, is an educator and eco-herbalist. Her books, courses and medicine walks stress the sustainable use of medicinal plants and teach others to make and use the medicines that are their birthright. The founder of Save Our Species, she has a memoir in progress to be published in 2004. She can be reached at *www.connect.to/rootwoman*, or *rootwoman@sk.*

sympatico.ca or at Box #27, 2001–8th Street, East, Saskatoon, Saskatchewan S7H OT8.

Craig Kielburger is the author of *Free the Children* (McClelland & Stewart) and coauthor of *Take Action: A Guide to Active Citizenship for Youth* (Gage Educational Publishing). For more information on how you can get involved in FTC's school building campaign or volunteer overseas, please visit: *www.freethe children.com* and *www.leaderstoday.com*. Or, contact by mail: 50 High Oak Trail, Richmond Hill, Ontario L4E 3L9.

W. P. Kinsella has published over thirty books and novels. *Shoeless Joe* (the most honoured novel in Canadian history) was turned into the Academy-Award-nominated movie *Field of Dreams*. He has been distinguished alumni lecturer at the University of Iowa. He is a winner of the Stephen Leacock Medal for Humour for his book *The Fencepost Chronicles*. Kinsella has three grown daughters and four grandsons. He lives in Chilliwack, British Columbia, in an 1891 Victorian Gothic home, which he and his wife, graphic artist Barbara Turner, are refurbishing. Contact him at *hm@buzzard2_99@yahoo.com*.

Ernest Kowalchuk was born in Rivers, Manitoba, in 1945, moved to Toronto in 1950, and taught there from 1966 to 1970. He attended the University of Western Ontario, graduating with a degree in geology. He moved to London in 1970, teaching there until retirement in 1998. Outside interests lie in antiques, gardening, fishing, hunting and family.

Gary Lautens (1928–1992) *The Toronto Star* newspaper columns of Gary Lautens, Canada's well-loved humorist and columnist, were syndicated throughout Canada, and briefly in the United States, during his thirty-year career at the *Star*. His columns have been compiled into several books, mostly on family themes. More information can be found at the Web site of his son, Stephen Lautens—*www.lautens.com*.

Mark Leiren-Young is a playwright, screenwriter, journalist, performer and Canucks fan. His plays, *Shylock* and *Articles of Faith*, are published by Anvil Press, and he created two CDs with his comedy troupe, Local Anxiety—*Greenpieces* and *Forgive Us, We're Canadian*. Contact him through *www.leiren-young.ca* or *mark@leiren-young.ca*.

Jeanette Lynes is a teacher, poet and novelist living in Antigonish, Nova Scotia. She is also an associate editor at *The Antigonish Review*, a journal of creative writing. She can be reached c/o *www.antigonishreview.com* or by e-mail at *jlynes@stfx.ca*.

Natalie MacMaster was born and raised in Cape Breton and started fiddling at age nine. She possesses a teaching degree, but has opted to pursue her music career, taking it to the international stage. Her accolades include a Grammy nomination, several East Coast Music Awards, Juno Awards and a Gemini Award. Catch the latest news on Natalie along with tour dates and locations at *www.nataliemacmaster.com*.

Steve Magee received his B.S., with Honours, and is vice principal of Erin District High School in Erin, Ontario. Steve anticipates "touching the face of nature" while canoeing and hiking over North America. Founder of the Harbourfront Canoe and Kayak Centre, you can contact him at *smagee@paddle-toronto.com.*

Ted Mahovlich is a schoolteacher and author. His last book, *The Big M: The Frank Mahovlich Story,* was a number-one national bestseller in Canada. Ted is currently writing the biography of hockey great Marcel Dionne. A music enthusiast, Ted loves spending time in New Orleans.

Brenda Mallory is a legally blind artist, author, motivational speaker, journalist and comic. She taught grade one for many years in British Columbia. She lives on a five-acre bird sanctuary where she pursues her many careers. Please reach her at 250-846-5095, or at Box 550, Telkwa, British Columbia V0J 2X0.

George Mapson received his grade nine education. He would have continued school, but to help his mother meet expenses he went to a logging camp to work when he was fourteen years old. He has been happily married for fifty-three years and has been blessed with six children and eleven grandchildren. His hobbies are fishing, hunting and bird-carving.

Paul Martini skated with partner Barbara Underhill for twenty-one years. Before retiring in 1998, they were five-time Canadian Pair Champions, 1984 World Pair Champions, two-time Olympians, and won seven professional titles. In 1988 they were inducted into the Canadian Sports Hall of Fame. Paul has provided colour commentary for skating events on CBC TV since 1991, including three Olympic Games. He and wife Elizabeth have two children, Robert and Kate. In addition to working with the CBC, Paul is the president of iskater, a company with a Web site dedicated to the sport of figure skating, *www.iskater.com.*

Shelly McEwan lives in Sarnia, Ontario, with her husband Gord and their sons Joshua, Adam and Noah. She is an Early Childhood Educator at Lambton College. "Letters of Hope" was written for Gord's grandparents, William and Martha Lindsay, who are now together in heaven, never again to be parted.

Darlene Montgomery is an internationally respected authority on dreams, spiritual perspectives and ideas. Author, speaker and clergywoman, she speaks to groups and organizations on uplifting subjects. Her book, *Dream Yourself Awake,* chronicles her personal journey to discover her own divine mission. To learn more about Darlene Montgomery's keynotes and seminars visit *www.lifedreams.org,* call 416-696-1684, or e-mail her at *lifedreams@idirect.com.*

Marc André Morel is one of Canada's most sought-after speakers on business and personal success. He delivers powerful keynotes to Fortune 500 corporations, associations and organizations around the world. Past president of the Montreal Chapter of the Canadian Association for Professional Speakers, he is also the founder of the Morel Centre of Leadership for Youth and of the Winners Circle of Montreal. He has been interviewed and featured in

Canadian business journals. *www.marcandremorel.com*

Mary Lee Moynan is an optimist, a Christian, a passionate wife, and a compassionate mother and grandmother. Her inspirational book, *Get off Your Knees*, is available through her publisher at *www.publishamerica.com*, or by calling PublishAmerica, Inc. directly at 1-877-333-7422.

Elizabeth Munsterhjelm earned her M.B.A. and M.A. from the University of Western Ontario, which included a year at the University of Madrid, Spain. During her teaching career, Elizabeth took a year's leave to travel extensively around Latin America. She currently owns two import boutiques and can be reached at *lizjudy@kelcom.igs.net.*

Vern Murphy served almost twenty years in the Royal Canadian Navy and eighteen years as director of public relations with Veterans Affairs Canada in Ottawa, Ontario. As a writer he has produced various recollections of his experiences. He and his wife Pat reside in Charlotetown, Prince Edward Island, and can be reached at *vmurphy@pei.eastlink.ca.*

Diane C. Nicholson is a freelance writter and award-winning photographer living in British Columbia. She and her family own Twin Heart Photo Productions and sell photo art prints and Limited Edition Prints, specializing in horses and companion animals through their Web site at *www.twinheart photo.com*. She can be contacted at 250-375-2525 or at *mail@twinheartphoto.com.*

Tim O'Driscoll is a Burlington, Ontario lawyer. His general practise focuses on wills, estates and real estate. Tim is Karen's happy husband and Liam's proud father. For legal services, please contact Tim at 905-634-5581. For speech-writing (weddings, eulogies, etc.) or other writing assignments, please reach Tim at *timothy@cleavercrawford.ca.*

Susan Owen is a Kingston, Ontario writer. Her main focus is short story and memoir writing, but truth be told, procrastination is her specialty.

Bob Proctor is the bestselling author of *You Were Born Rich*. Author, business consultant, Fortune 500 trainer—these are just some of the many hats Bob Proctor wears. His phenomenal track record for helping individuals improve their results has won him global acclaim. Bob lives in Toronto with his wife, Linda, and their two dogs. Reach him at *www.bobproctor.com.*

Alan Ralston is a farmer, plays the trumpet, runs a business, and he and wife, Shirley have three very active children. Alan and Shirley were with Carl Hiebert at his accident, and Carl lived with them afterwards. On the day they smuggled Carl out of the hospital, tied him into the ultralight and launched him—leaving his wheelchair behind—Alan was happy to comply with Carl's request to capture it on film.

Chris Robertson is a past president of CAPS, founder of the Canadian Speaking Hall of Fame and has been voted Best Canadian Keynote Speaker. Chris is the author of the bestselling book, *To The Top Canada* and *Exceeding*

Expectations: The Strategy of Personal & Organizational Excellence. Chris can be contacted at 905-387-0721 or at *www.chrisrobertson.com.*

Ruth Robins-Jeffery, a former lounge pianist and credit manager in Southern Ontario, now operates Landfall, a small bed and breakfast on the south shore of Prince Edward Island. Her e-mail address is *rrobjeff@pei.sympatico.ca.*

Ariel Rogers has been involved in the entertainment industry since early childhood. A member of The Players Guild of Hamilton, she has won numerous dramatic and musical awards over the years. She manages Fogarty's Cove Music, the company founded by her late husband. Reach her at *www.stanrogers.net.*

Leslie Scrivener is faith and ethics reporter at *The Toronto Star* newspaper. She covered Terry Fox's Marathon of Hope for the *Star* and later was asked by Terry to write the story of his run, *Terry Fox: His Story,* published by McClelland & Stewart.

John Seagrave lives in Yellowknife, Northwest Territories, which is in the Arctic. He was one of the last generation of Canadian fur traders and witnessed the closing of an era of our history. He is presently writing a book chronicling his humorous adventures living amongst the Aboriginal people of Canada's far north. John can be contacted at 5009-57 Street, Yellowknife, NWT, Canada, X1A 1Y4, or by e-mail at *seagrave@canada.com.*

Doug Setter is completing a B.S. in nutrition at the University of Manitoba. A former soldier and welterweight kickboxing champion, Doug teaches fitness, kickboxing and self-defense. He is the author of *Stomach Flattening* and *Women's Kickboxing.* Doug can be reached at: *dougsetter@hotmail.com.*

Carol Sharpe is the mother of five children and a grandmother of nine. She has recently received her diploma in creative writing. A very busy lady who enjoys sports, she also plays competitive billiards.

Stella Shepard lives on an organic farm in Morell, Prince Edward Island (PEI), with her husband Reg Phelan and son, Joshua. In 2000, Stella graduated from Holland College in PEI with a degree in journalism. She enjoys writing and caring for her gardens and many pets. She and Reg love working the land together growing cole crops for market. She dedicates "The Red Sweater" to her mom, Florence Fougere Shepard, who died December 5, 1997. Contact Stella at *rphelan@pei.sympatico.ca.*

Neil Simpson became fascinated with Canadian history when he discovered that Canada actually had one. Born and raised in Brighton, Ontario, Neil moved to Peterborough in 1971 to attend Trent University, and he has since made it his home. Contact Neil at *goweezer@sympatico.ca.*

Mary Turner received her B.A. in English from the University of Manitoba. She is the mother of two grown sons and lives in Victoria, British Columbia. Mary has written for the *Winnipeg Free Press* and the *Victoria Times Colonist.* She also enjoys writing inspirational fiction and poetry.

Barbara Underhill skated with partner Paul Martini for twenty-one years. Before retiring in 1998, they were five-time Canadian Pair Champions, 1984 World Pair Champions, two-time Olympians, won seven Professional World titles, and in 1988 were inducted into Canadian Sports Hall of Fame. Barbara has done colour commentary for skating events with various TV networks since 1992, including three Olympic Games. She and husband, Rick Gaetz, have three children, Samantha, Matthew and Scott. After the sudden death of their daughter in 1993, Barbara and Rick founded The Stephanie Gaetz Keepsafe Foundation. Now in demand as a motivational speaker, Barbara shares her story with audiences everywhere. Contact her at *www.keepsafefoundation.com*.

Penny and Vicky Vilagos specialize in inspiring team excellence and are members of the Canadian Olympic Hall of Fame. As motivational speakers they translate "What it takes to succeed in sports" to "What it takes to succeed in business." To arrange a speaking engagement to inspire your team, in English or French, call 1-866-426-5122, or e-mail them at *info@VilagosInternational.com*. Web site: *www.VilagosInternational.com*.

Pamela Wallin is a respected broadcaster and journalist. She currently hosts and produces *Pamela Wallin's Talk TV* for the CTV Group through Pamela Wallin Productions, Inc. Her latest book, *Speaking of Success: Collected Wisdom, Insights and Reflections,* shares the perspectives of many of the celebrated people she has interviewed. In 1998, she published her bestselling memoir, *Since You Asked,* and in 2000, she hosted the Canadian edition of *Who Wants To Be a Millionaire.* She serves on many volunteer boards, supports many charities, holds four honourary degrees, and has been recognized both by Queen Elizabeth as an Outstanding Canadian Achiever and by the UN for outstanding contributions toward the advancement of women.

Gary Walsh lives in Toronto and owns Walsh & Walsh Court & Tribunal Agents, a paralegal and investigations firm specializing in inquest law and criminal injuries compensation applications. He is working on his first book, *Proud to Have Served,* detailing his experiences as a Toronto ambulance officer. His story, "Into The Night," is dedicated to legendary paramedic Anton Tyukodi, who was killed in 2001 while serving others.

Wayne Watson is a member of the Royal Canadian Mounted Police, working out of Ottawa, Ontario. He enjoys reading, writing, playing guitar and skiing. Wayne writes police management articles as well as short stories on family related subjects. He can be reached at *wwatson@cyberus.ca*.

Crystal Wood is a freelance writer living in Winnipeg. She has had several articles published in community newspapers and is working on her first novel. Ms. Wood has a B.A. in English from the University of Manitoba and is in her final year of study for a journalism degree. She enjoys reading, dance and interior design. Contact her at *angiew@mb.sympatico.ca*.

Frances Wright is president and CEO of the Famous 5 Foundation and a superb speaker. The magnificent *Women are Persons!* monuments in Olympic Plaza in Calgary and on Parliament Hill in Ottawa were funded ($1 million) by five remarkable women and their families: Ann McCaig and her daughters, Roxanne and Jane; Dr. Maria Eriksen and Ayala Manolson; Kiki Delaney; Senator Vivienne Poy and Heather Reisman. Thanks, also, to the fabulous volunteers, corporations and governments who have been our partners. Contact Frances at *www.famous5.org*

Sigrun Goodman Zatorsky has a lengthy association with libraries, both from having worked as a cataloguer for schools and lately as an advocate for libraries and literacy. He is an avid reader and has also attained some success in writing, especially with stories about his home province, city and his family. His e-mail address is *youngsnamb@sympatico.ca.*

The Legacy of Mary. Reprinted by permission of Maree M. Benoit. ©1995 Maree M. Benoit.

Love Is a Two-Way Street. Reprinted by permission of Carol Sharpe. ©1996 Carol Sharpe.

With a Little Help from Your Friends. Reprinted by permission of Sun Media Corporation. ©2000 Sun Media Corporation. As published in *The Toronto Sun* on January 16, 2000 by Lorrie Goldstein.

Four-Legged Guardian Angels. Reprinted by permission of Karin Bjerke-Lisle. ©2001 Karin Bjerke-Lisle.

Christmas Lights. Reprinted by permission of Michael Hogan. ©1999 Michael Hogan.

Ryan's Hope. Reprinted by permission of Nancy Lee Doige. ©1999 Nancy Lee Doige.

The Red Sweater. Reprinted by permission of Stella Shepard. ©1998 Stella Shepard.

Tommy's Tangerine Tree. Reprinted by permission of Margaret A. Hatfield-Herman. ©1987 Ruth Hilton-Hatfield.

The Littlest Angel. Reprinted by permission of Brenda Mallory. ©1992 Brenda Mallory.

Motherly Advice. Reprinted by permission of Kurt Browning. ©2002 Kurt Browning.

A Christmas to Remember. Reprinted by permission of Ruth Robins-Jeffrey. ©1998 Ruth Robins-Jeffrey.

A Change of Heart. Reprinted by permission of George Thomas Mapson. ©1994 George Thomas Mapson.

Monsieur Gaton. Reprinted by permission of Jayne Harvey. ©1998 Jayne Harvey.

Finding Your Own Medicine. Reprinted by permission of Kahlee Keane. ©1999 Kahlee Keane.

Three Words. Reprinted courtesy of Chatelaine Magazine, ©Rogers Publishing Ltd.

The Orange Tabletop. Reprinted by permission of William D. Gorman. ©1999 William D. Gorman.

Peacekeeper's Coffee. Reprinted by permission of Douglas Charles Setter. ©2000 Douglas Charles Setter.

Also Available

Chicken Soup for the Baseball Fan's Soul
Chicken Soup for the Canadian Soul
Chicken Soup for the Cat & Dog Lover's Soul
Chicken Soup for the Christian Family Soul
Chicken Soup for the Christian Soul
Chicken Soup for the Christian Woman's Soul
Chicken Soup for the College Soul
Chicken Soup for the Country Soul
Chicken Soup for the Couple's Soul
Chicken Soup for the Expectant Mother's Soul
Chicken Soup for the Father's Soul
Chicken Soup for the Gardener's Soul
Chicken Soup for the Golden Soul
Chicken Soup for the Golfer's Soul, Vol. I, II
Chicken Soup for the Grandparent's Soul
Chicken Soup for the Jewish Soul
Chicken Soup for the Kid's Soul
Chicken Soup for the Little Souls
Chicken Soup for the Mother's Soul, Vol. I, II
Chicken Soup for the Nurse's Soul
Chicken Soup for the Parent's Soul
Chicken Soup for the Pet Lover's Soul
Chicken Soup for the Preteen Soul
Chicken Soup for the Prisoner's Soul
Chicken Soup for the Single's Soul
Chicken Soup for the Sister's Soul
Chicken Soup for the Soul, Vol. I-VI
Chicken Soup for the Soul of America
Chicken Soup for the Soul at Work
Chicken Soup for the Soul Cookbook
Chicken Soup for the Soul Christmas Treasury, hardcover
Chicken Soup for the Soul Christmas Treasury for Kids, hardcover
Chicken Soup for the Soul Personal Journal
Chicken Soup for the Sports Fan's Soul
Chicken Soup for the Surviving Soul
Chicken Soup for the Teacher's Soul
Chicken Soup for the Teenage Soul, Vol. I, II, III
Chicken Soup for the Teenage Soul Journal
Chicken Soup for the Teenage Soul Letters
Chicken Soup for the Teenage Soul on Love & Friendship
Chicken Soup for the Teenage Soul on Tough Stuff
Chicken Soup for the Traveler's Soul
Chicken Soup for the Unsinkable Soul
Chicken Soup for the Veteran's Soul
Chicken Soup for the Volunteer's Soul
Chicken Soup for the Woman's Soul, Vol. I, II
Chicken Soup for the Writer's Soul
Condensed Chicken Soup for the Soul
Cup of Chicken Soup for the Soul

Selected titles available in Spanish, hardcover and audio format.